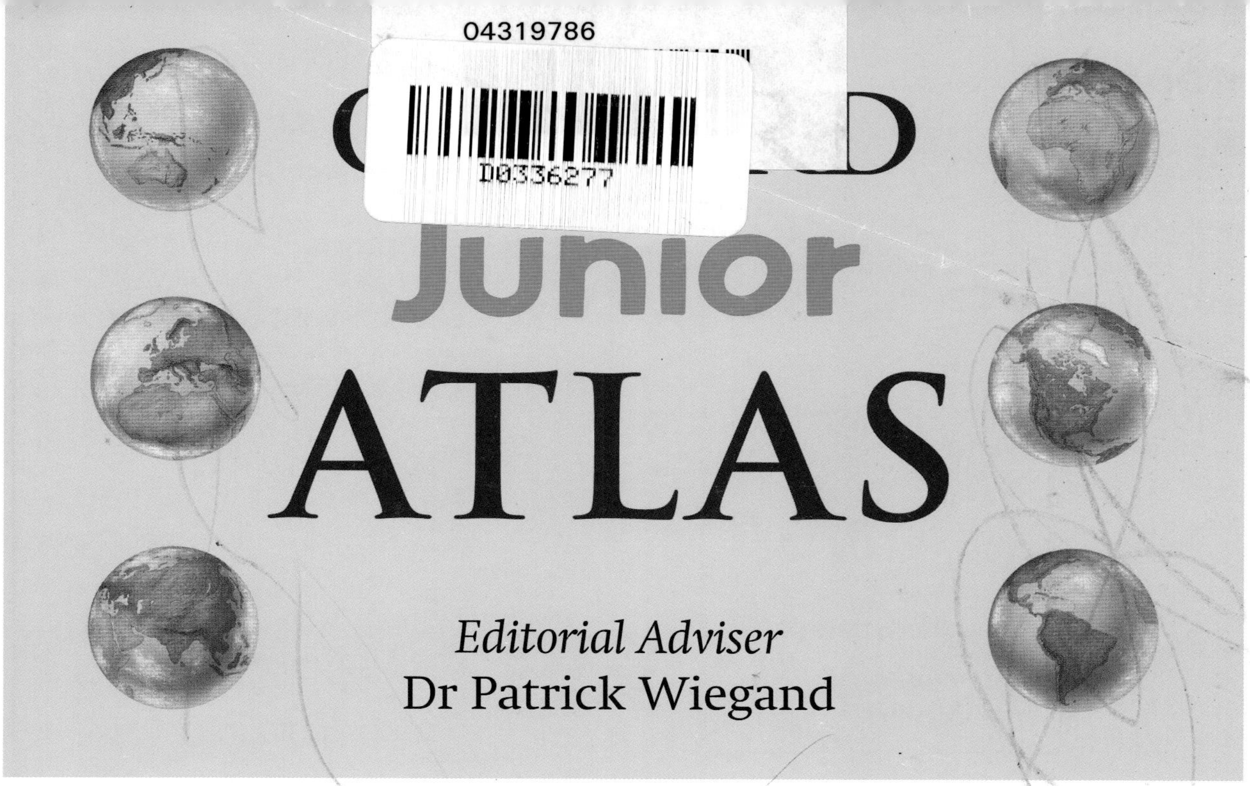

OXFORD
UNIVERSITY PRESS

Great Clarendon Street, Oxford OX2 6DP

Oxford University Press is a department of the University of Oxford. It furthers the University's objective of excellence in research, scholarship, and education by publishing worldwide in

Oxford New York

Auckland Cape Town Dar es Salaam Hong Kong Karachi Kuala Lumpur Madrid Melbourne Mexico City Nairobi New Delhi Shanghai Taipei Toronto

With offices in

Argentina Austria Brazil Chile Czech Republic France Greece Guatemala Hungary Italy Japan Poland Portugal Singapore South Korea Switzerland Thailand Turkey Ukraine Vietnam

Oxford is a registered trade mark of Oxford University Press in the UK and in certain other countries

First published 2005

Reprinted with corrections 2007

ISBN 978 0 19 832158 3 (hardback)
ISBN 978 0 19 832157 6 (paperback)

5 7 9 10 8 6

Printed in Singapore

Paper used in the production of this book is a natural, recyclable product made from wood grown in sustainable forests. The manufacturing process conforms to the environmental regulations of the country of origin.

Acknowledgements

The publishers would like to thank the following for permission to reproduce the following photographs:
Bryan & Cherry Alexander Photography: 58 middle, 61 middle; Austin Brown/Aviation Picture Library: 66 right; British Petroleum Shipping Ltd (Fotoflite): 67 right; Comstock Photo Library: 54, 58 bottom left, 59 middle, 60 bottom middle, 61 right; The Environmental Picture Library: 63 left; Greg Evans International: 58 bottom middle, 58 bottom right, 59 bottom left; FLPA: 60 bottom right; Robert Harding Picture Library Ltd: 33 top, 37 top right, 37 bottom left, 60 top right, 62 top; Jason Hawkes Aerial Photo Library: 7 top left, 7 top right, 7 middle; Holt Studios International: 31 all; The Hutchison Library: 33 bottom, 62 bottom; David Keith Jones/Images of Africa Photobank: 59 bottom right; Mark Mason: 4 top right, 5; National Remote Sensing Centre (Airphotogroup): 4 top left; Marilyn O'Brien: 37 bottom right; Christine Osborne Pictures: 60 bottom left; Port of Felixstowe: 67 left; The Photolibrary Wales: 7 bottom left, 7 bottom right, 33 middle, 37 top left; Rex Features: 62 middle; Science Photo Library: 14, 56 middle, 57, 60 top left, 66 left; Sealand Aerial Photography: 13, 30 all, 32 all, 34 left; Skyscan: 34 right; Still Pictures: 36, 56 bottom; The Telegraph Colour Library: 59 bottom middle, 60 top middle, 65; Tropix Photographic Library: 63 right; United States Atlantic Fleet Submarine Force: Public Affairs Office 55.

Cover image: Tom Van Sant / Geosphere Projection, Santa Monica, Science Photo Library.

The illustrations are by Chapman Bounford, Hardlines, Mike Harkins, and Gary Hinks.

The page design is by Adrian Smith.

Contents

Atlas information

Round Earth 4

Flat map 5

Scale 6

Settlements 7

Land height 8

Rivers 9

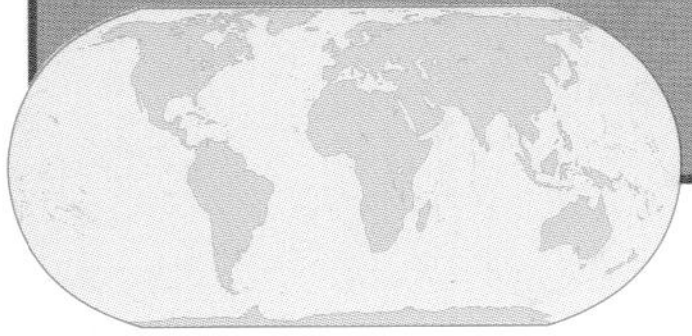

Countries of the World 10–11

The British Isles

Countries 12

Land height and rivers 13

Weather and climate 14–15

Topographic map 16

The United Kingdom

Topographic map 16

Orkney and Shetland Islands 17

Scottish Highlands and Islands 18–19

Northern Ireland 20

Southern Scotland 21

Northern England 22–23

Wales 24

English West Midlands 25

South East England 26–27

South West England 28–29

People and cities 30

Farms and forests 31

Factories and offices 32

Energy 33

Roads and railways 34

Ports and airports 35

Pollution 36

Conservation 37

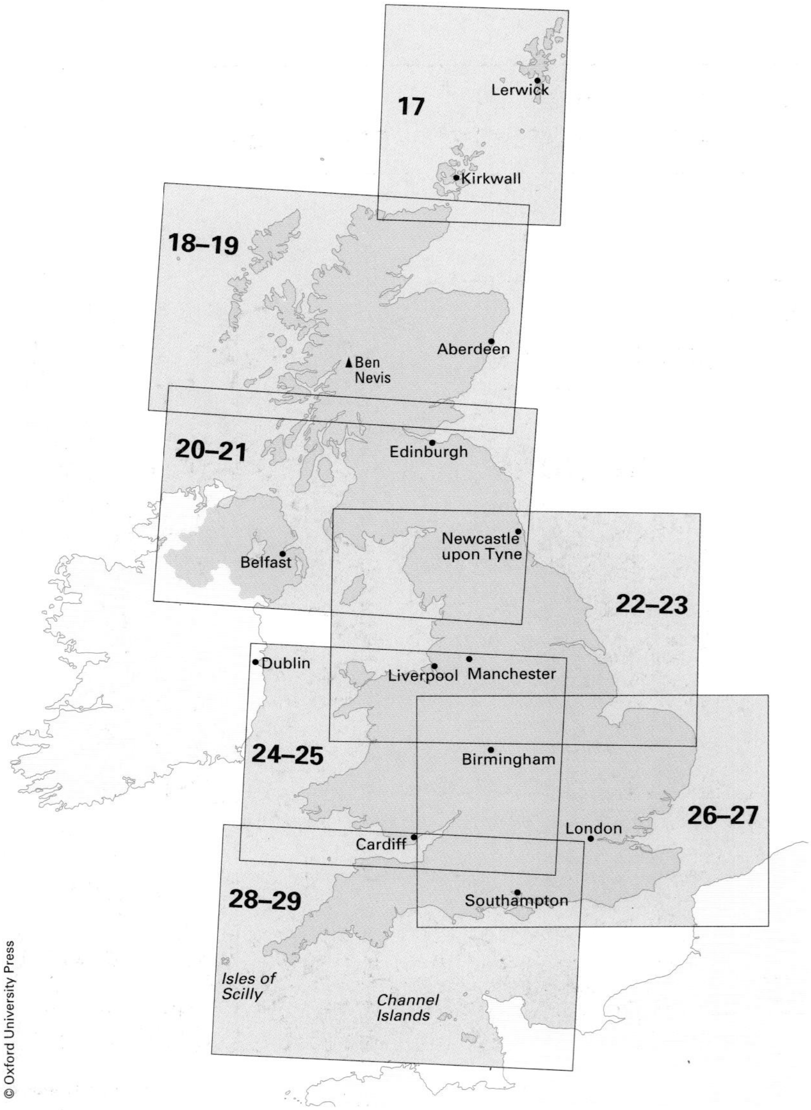

Contents

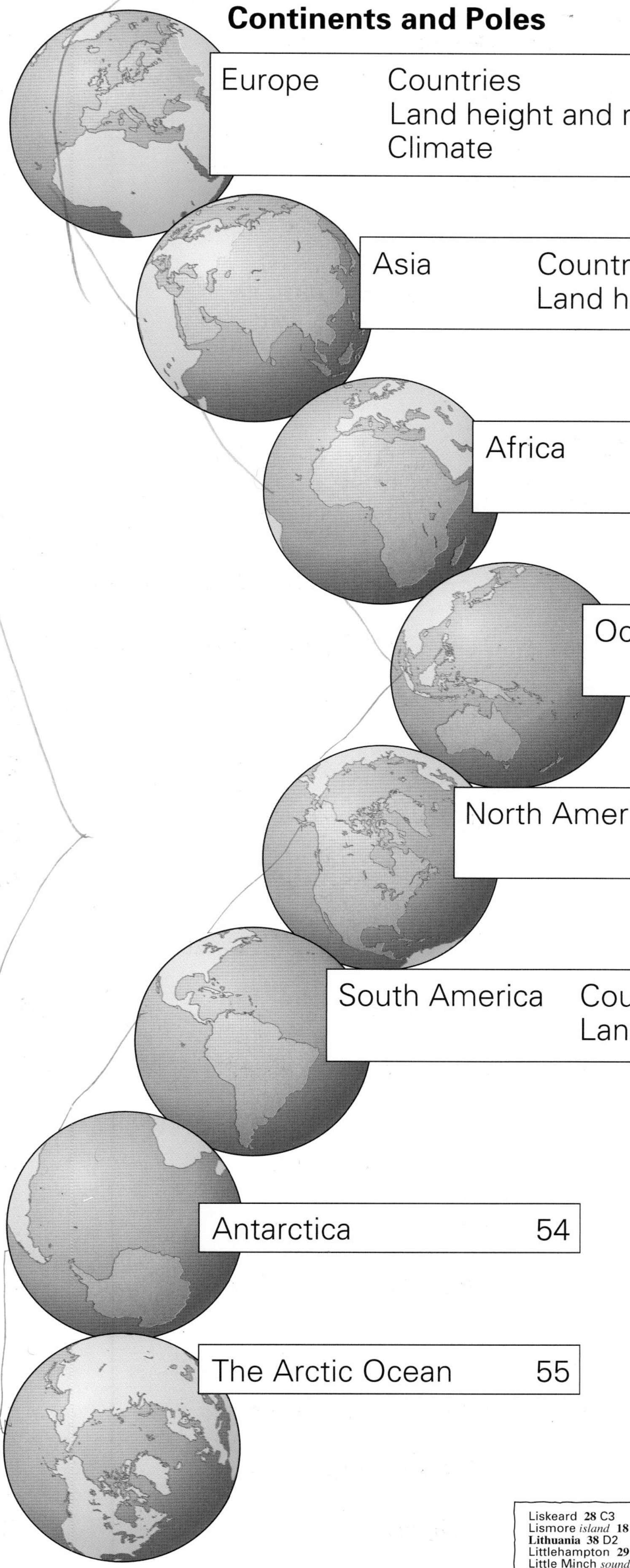

Continents and Poles

Europe	Countries	38–39
	Land height and rivers	40
	Climate	41
Asia	Countries	42–43
	Land height and rivers	44–45
Africa	Countries	46
	Land height and rivers	47
Oceania	Countries	48
	Land height and rivers	49
North America	Countries	50
	Land height and rivers	51
South America	Countries	52
	Land height and rivers	53
Antarctica		54
The Arctic Ocean		55

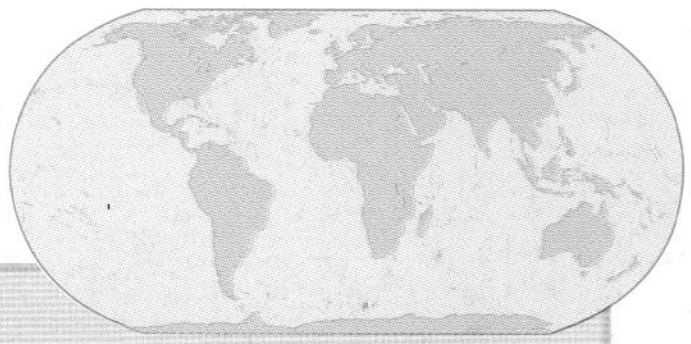

The World

Countries	10–11
Land height and rivers	56–57
Climate	58–59
Environments	60–61
Environmental problems	62–63
People and cities	64–65
Ports and airports	66–67

Liskeard **28** C3
Lismore *island* **18** D1
Lithuania 38 D2
Littlehampton **29** G3
Little Minch *sound* **18** C2
Little Ouse *river* **27** E3

Index

How to use the index	68
Alphabetical list of places	68–72

4 Round Earth

A globe shows the Earth as a sphere.

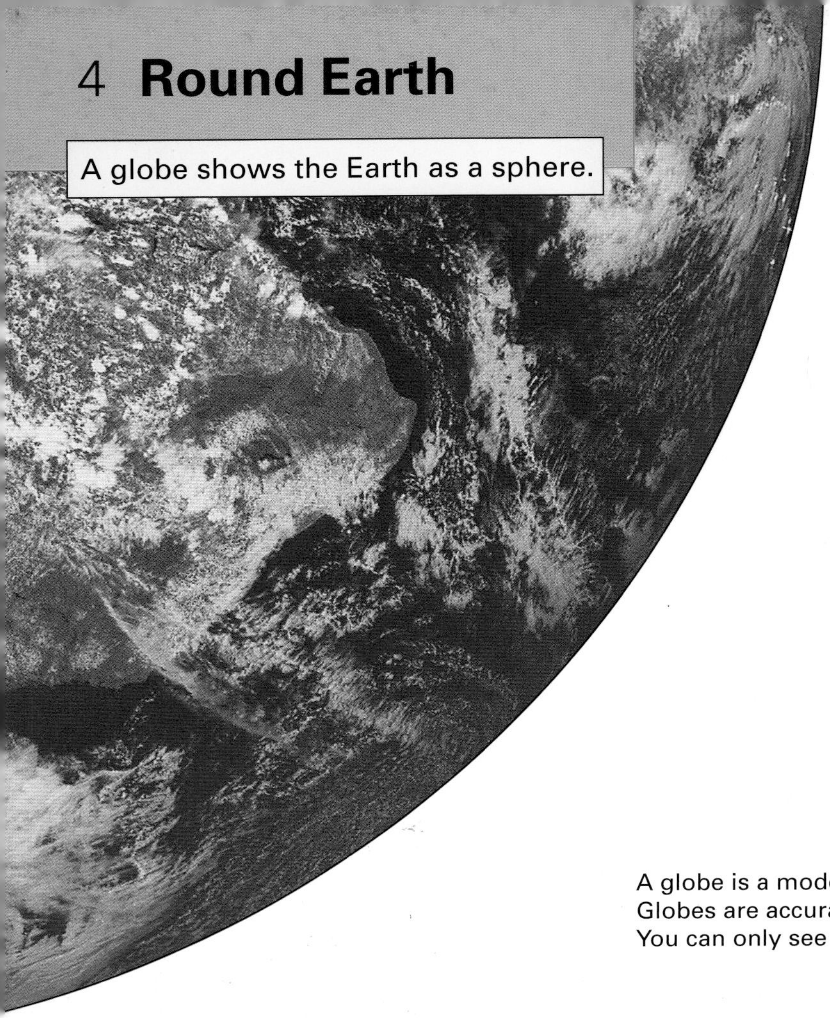

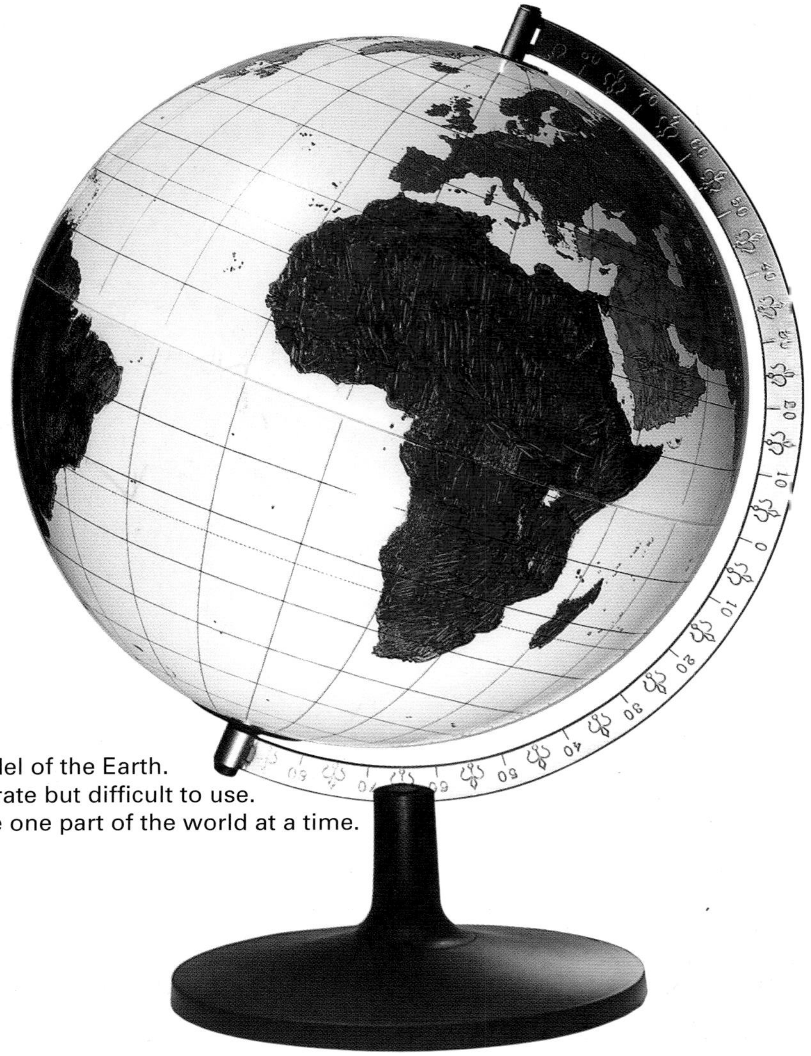

A globe is a model of the Earth.
Globes are accurate but difficult to use.
You can only see one part of the world at a time.

Globes have two sets of lines to help us describe where places are on the Earth.
All the lines are numbered and some have special names.

North Pole

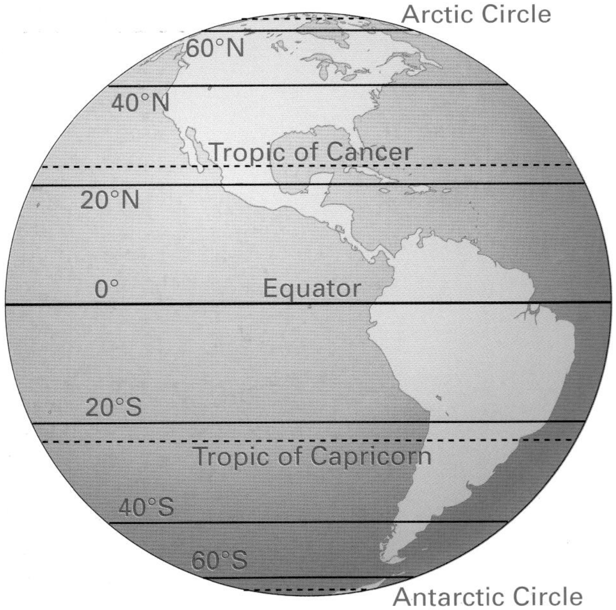

South Pole

These are lines of latitude.

North Pole

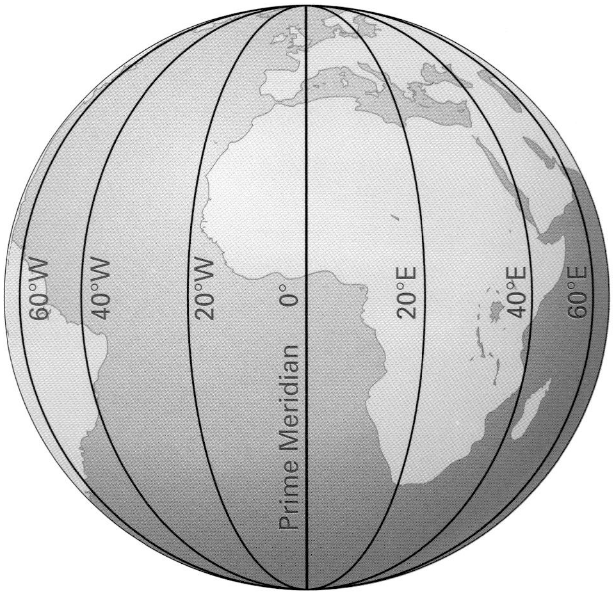

South Pole

These are lines of longitude.

A world map shows the Earth on a flat piece of paper.

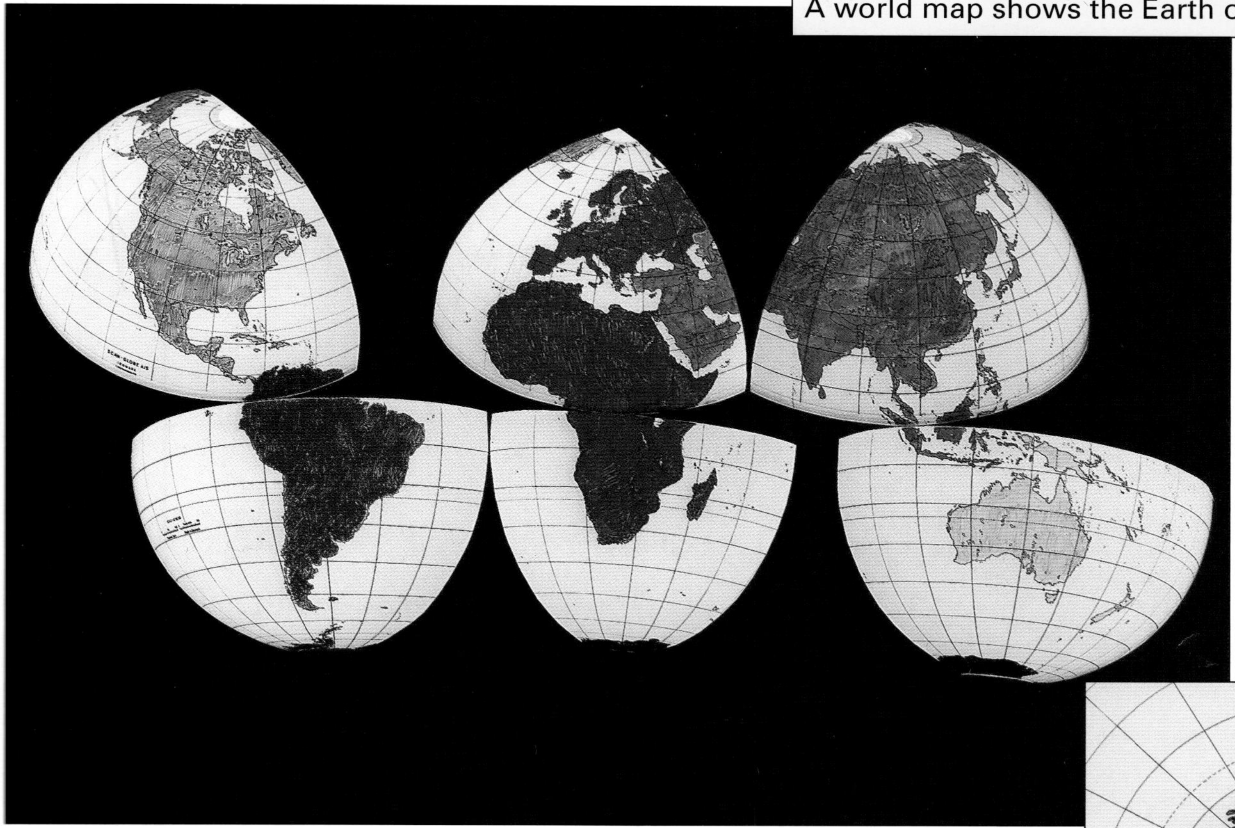

It is difficult to show shapes from a round Earth on a flat map.

Most world maps do not show Antarctica clearly.

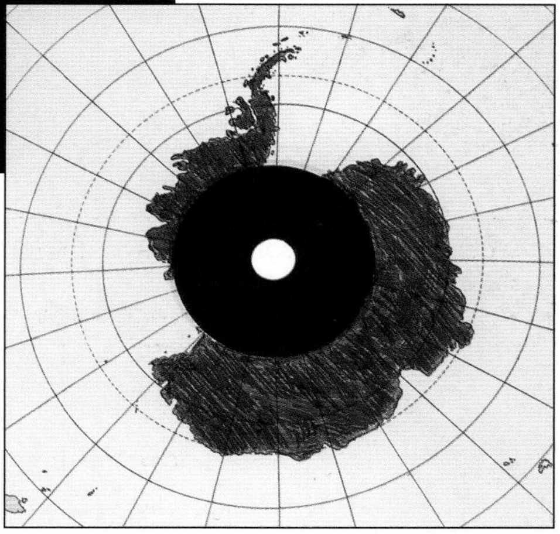

Not all world maps look the same.
There are differences in the shapes and sizes of the continents.
The patterns made by the lines of latitude and longitude are different.
Compare each world map with a globe.

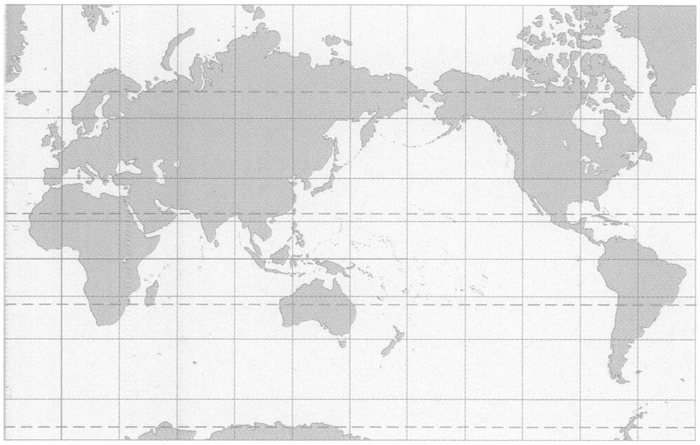

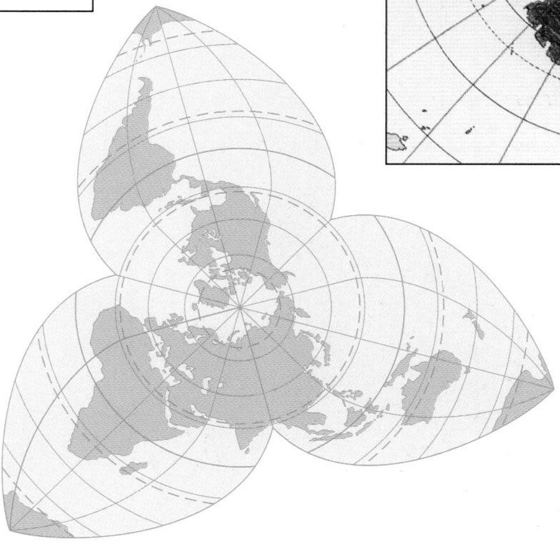

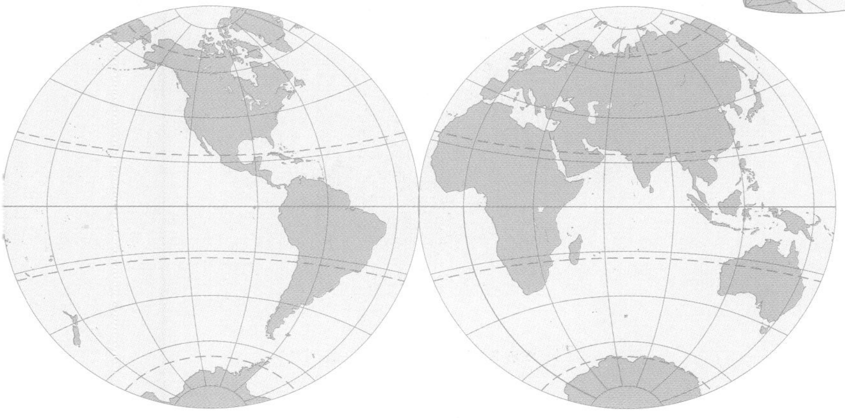

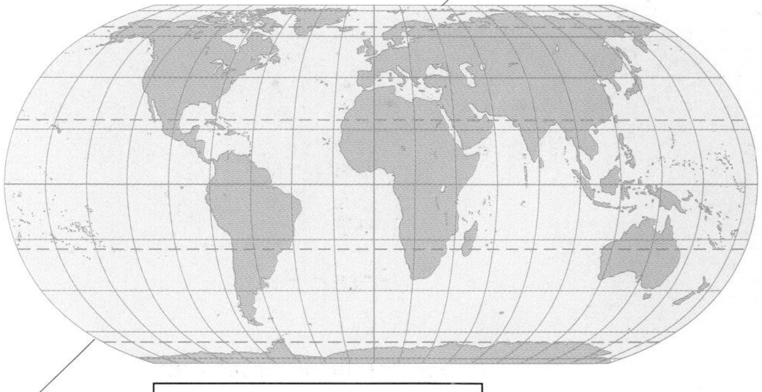

This is the world map used in this atlas.

6 Scale

Atlas maps have to be much, much smaller than the countries they show.

One centimetre on a map has to stand for many kilometres on the ground.

Every map in this atlas has a sign like this :

12 km
one cm

One centimetre on a map with *this* sign would stand for 12 kilometres on the ground.

You can see more detail on some maps than others. The amount of detail depends on the **scale** of the map. See how the British Isles become smaller as the scale changes on the maps below.

Scale

20 km
one cm

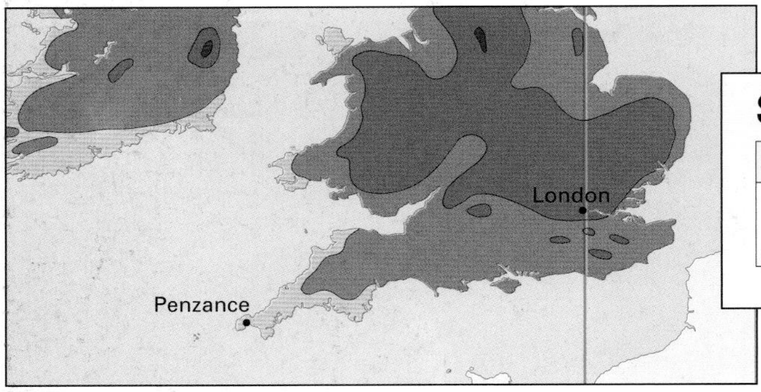

Scale

100 km
one cm

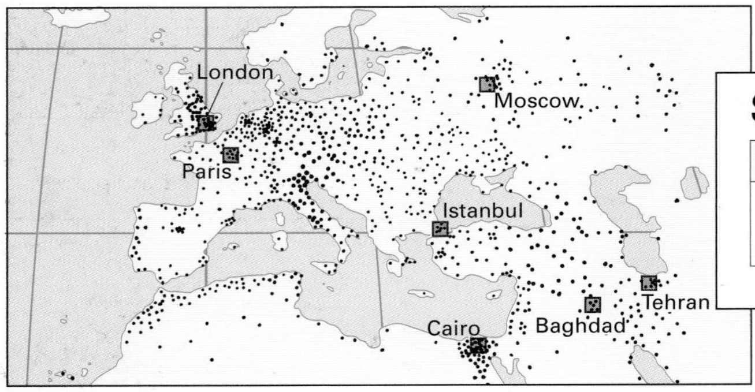

Scale

1000 km
one cm

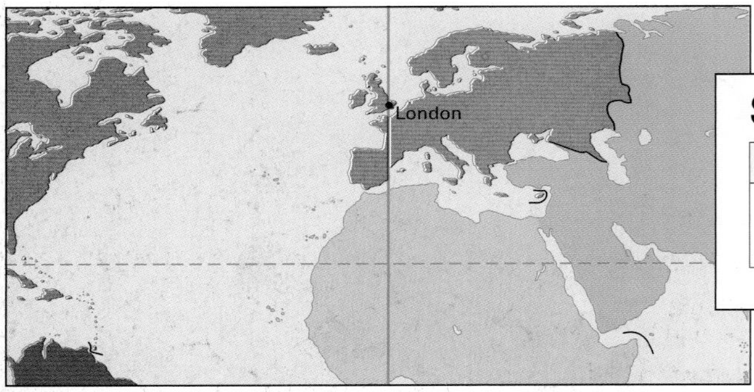

Scale

2000 km
one cm

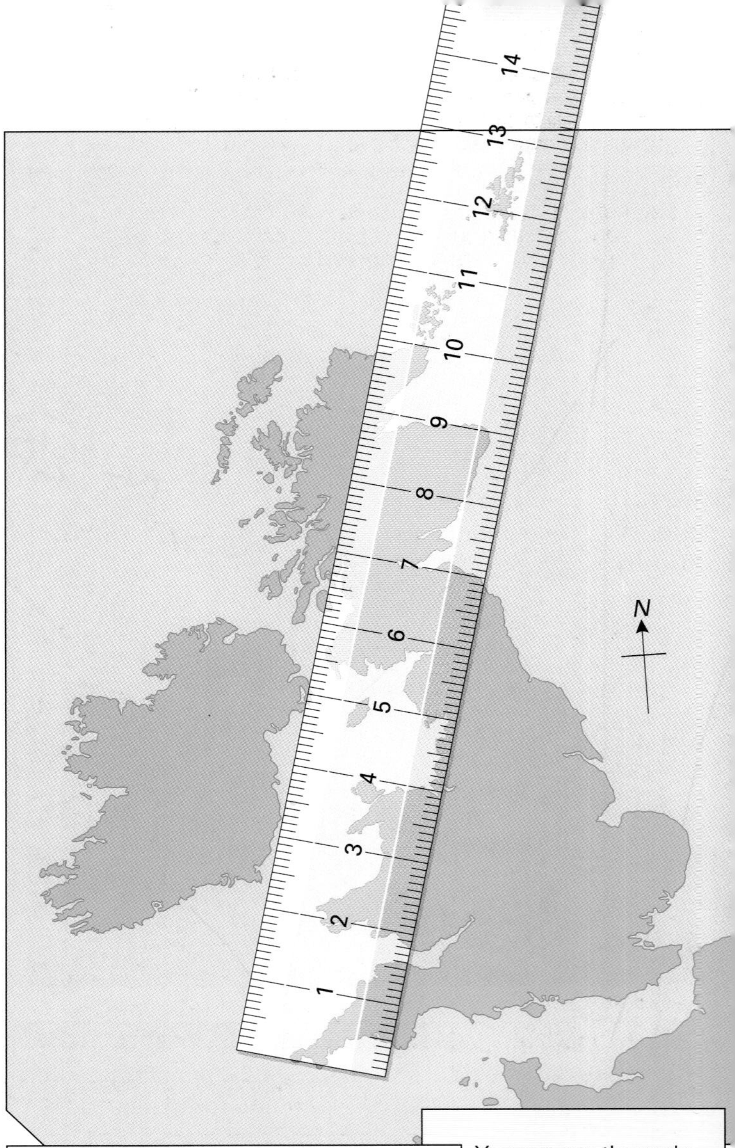

100 km
one cm

One centimetre on the map measures 100 kilometres on the ground.

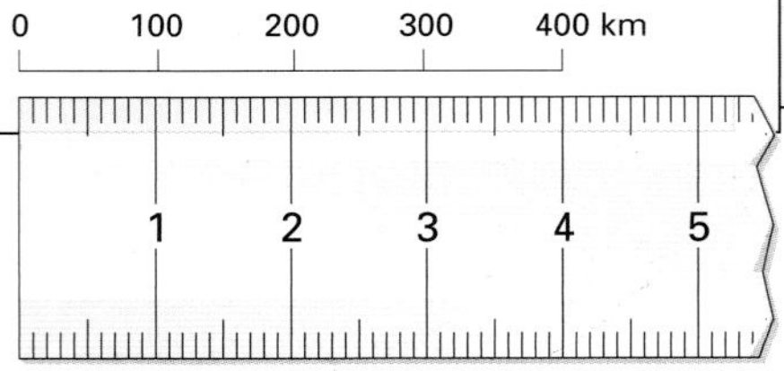

You can use the scale information to measure distances on maps.

Great Britain is approximately 1000 km from north to south.

Check it with your ruler.

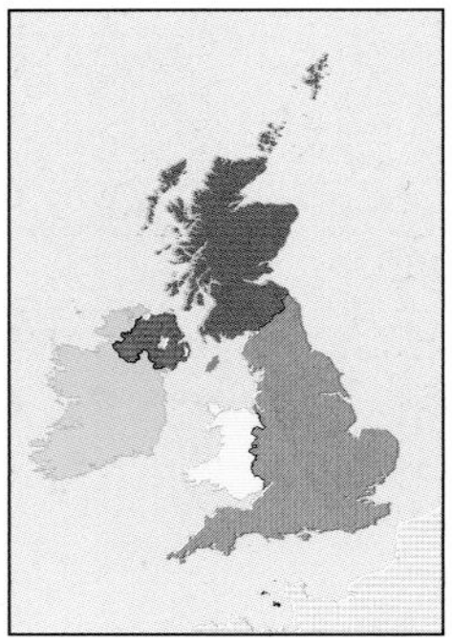

Small maps like this on some pages of the atlas help you to compare the size of other countries with the British Isles.

Most people in Britain live in towns. Some towns are large, others are small. In many parts of the country several towns have grown so large that they have joined to form one huge built-up area.

Each size of settlement has its own map symbol and style of lettering for the place name. Only the largest settlements are marked on atlas maps.

People live in settlements of different sizes.

Largest built-up areas
more than 1 million people

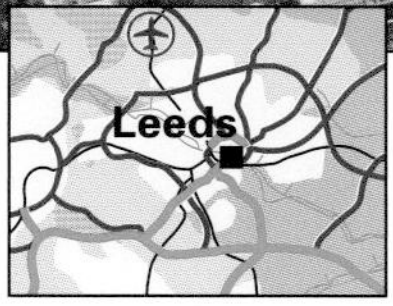

■ **Largest towns**
100 000 - 1 million people

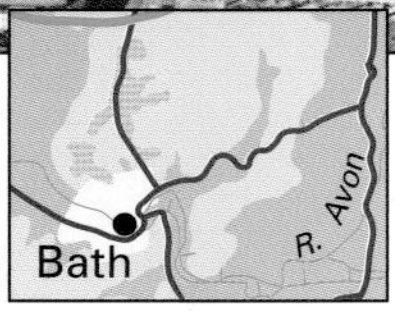

● **Large towns**
25 000 - 100 000 people

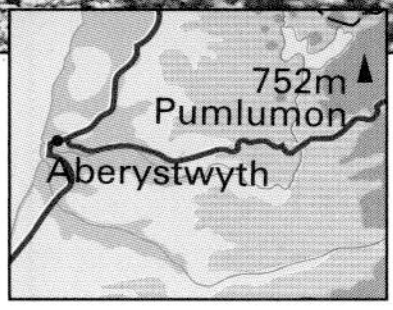

• **Small towns**
10 000 - 25 000 people

• **Small towns and villages**
fewer than 10 000 people

Many very small towns and villages are not shown on atlas maps.

8 Land Height

On atlas maps the height of the land above sea level is shown by colours.

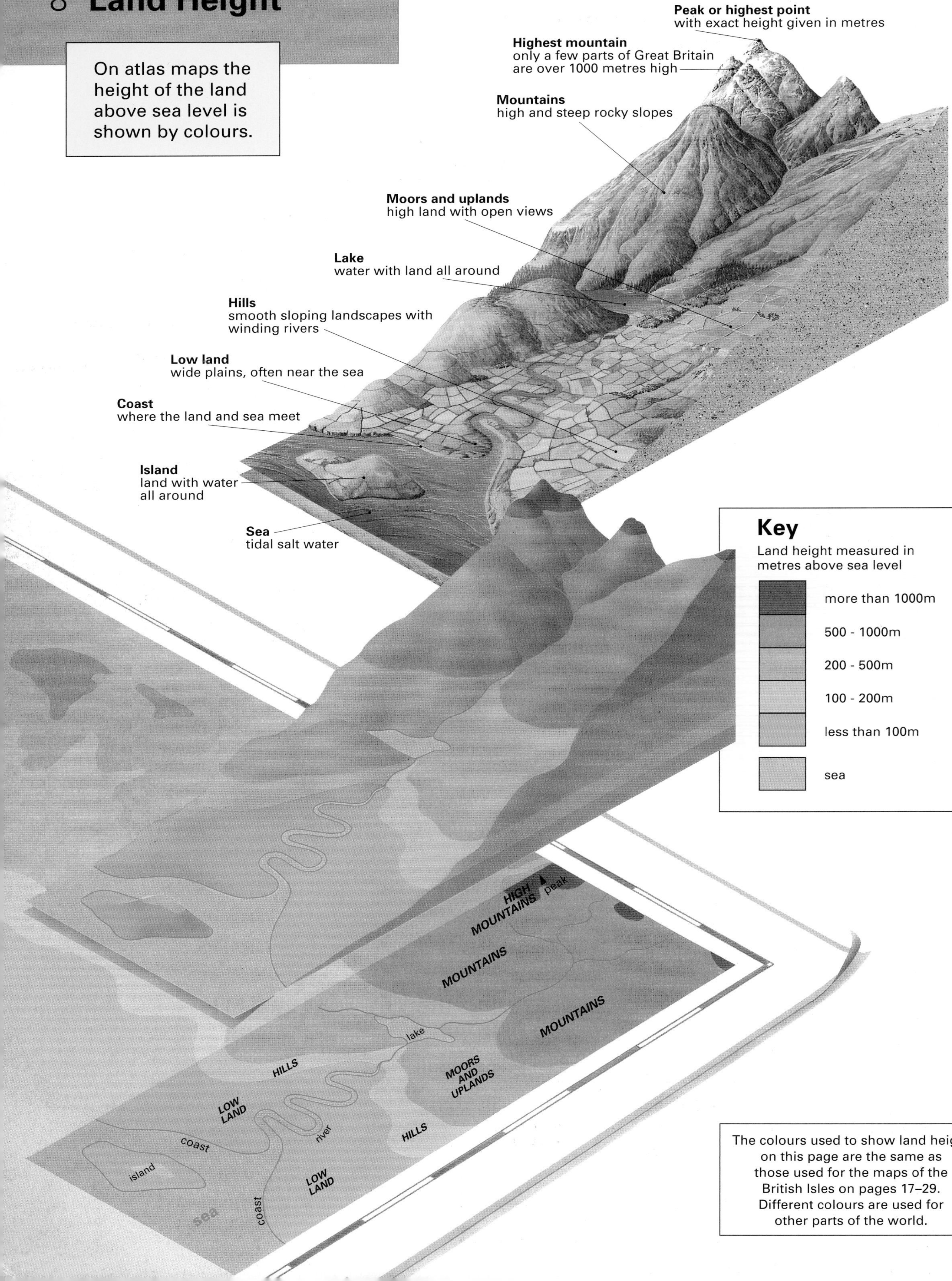

Key

Land height measured in metres above sea level

- more than 1000m
- 500 - 1000m
- 200 - 500m
- 100 - 200m
- less than 100m
- sea

The colours used to show land height on this page are the same as those used for the maps of the British Isles on pages 17–29. Different colours are used for other parts of the world.

Most landscapes in Great Britain have been shaped by rivers.

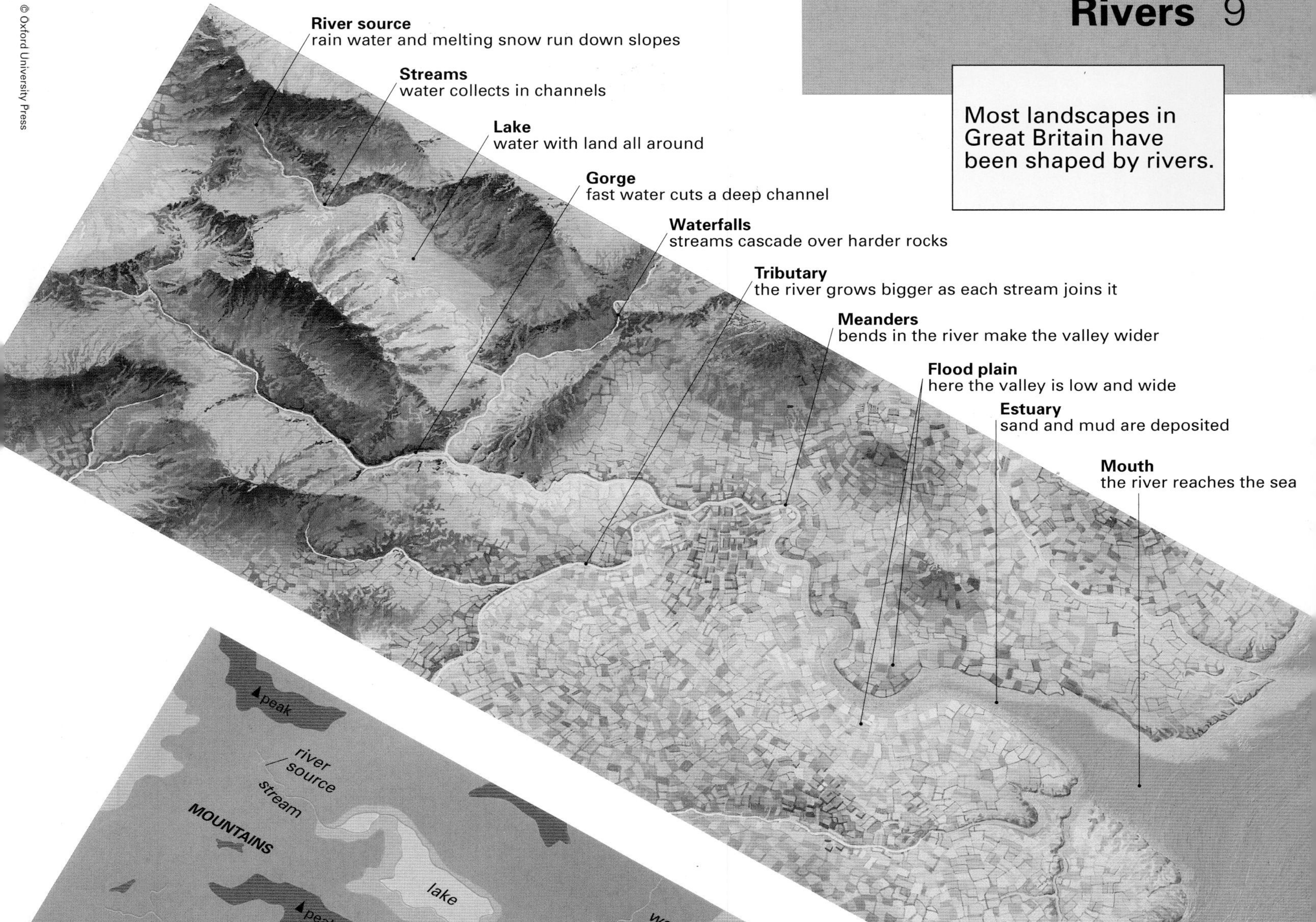

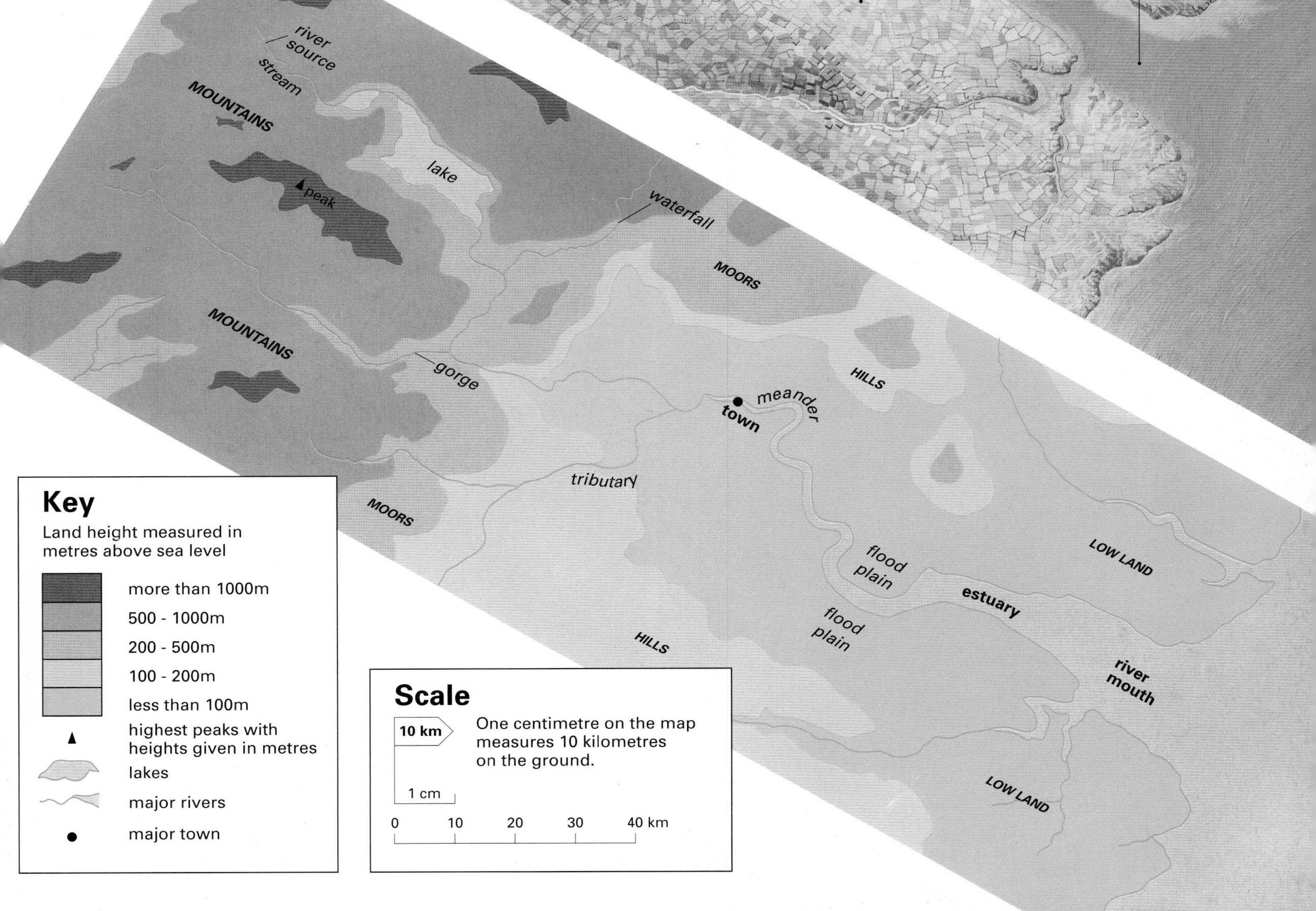

Countries of the World

A country is a land with its own people and its own government.

Scale

1050 km

One centimetre on the map measures 1050 kilometres on the ground at the Equator.

1 cm

0 1050 2100 3150 4200 km

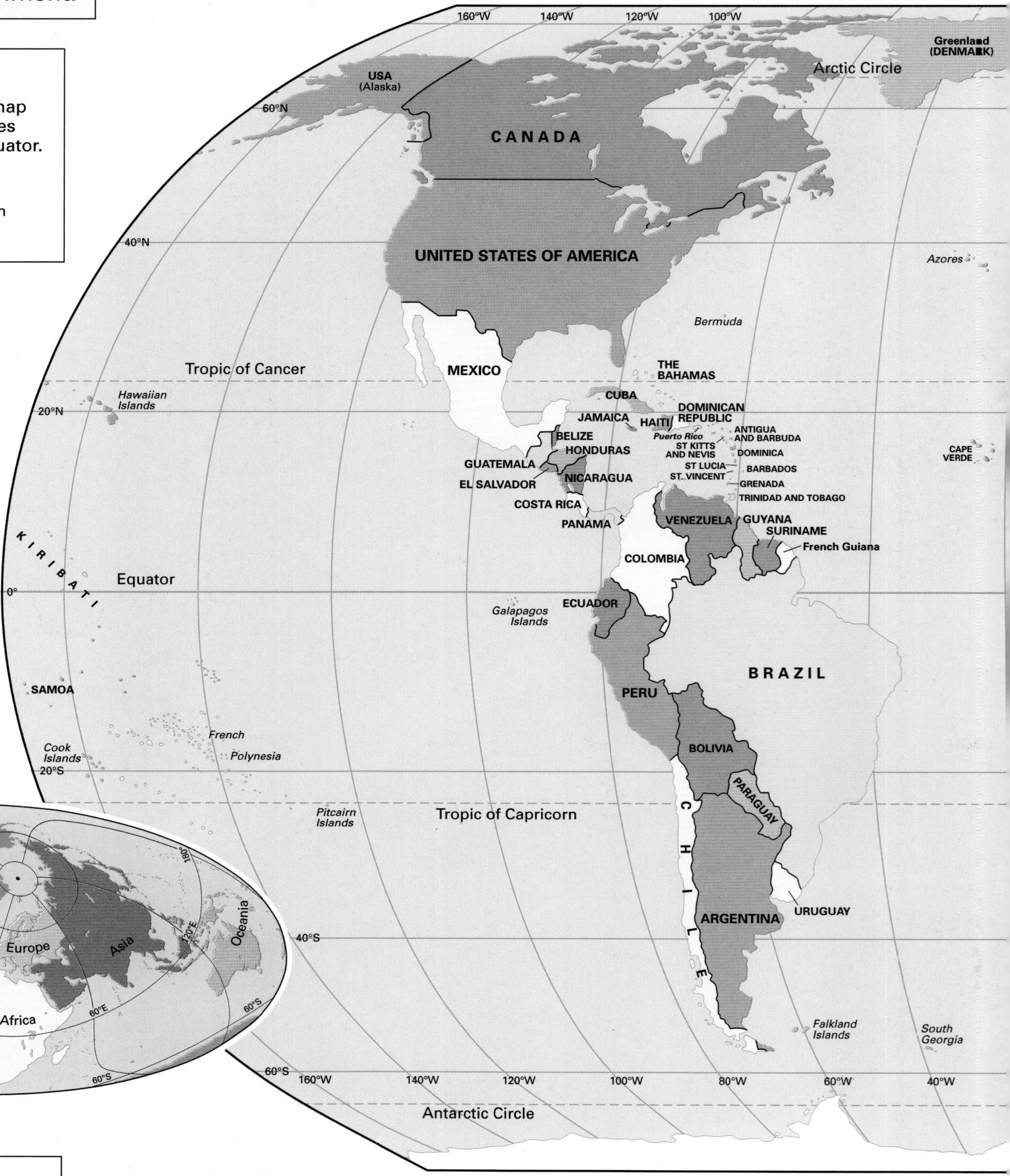

The Continents

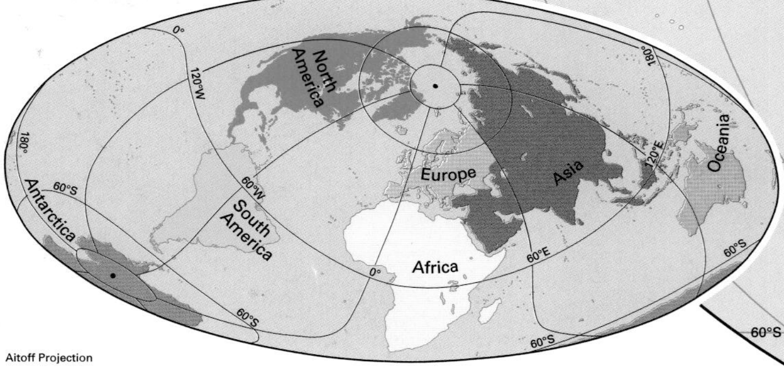

Aitoff Projection

Key

CANADA The names of countries are shown with this type of lettering.

Countries that are too small to be named on the map are shown by the first few letters of their name.

These colours are used to show where one country ends and another begins.

- A ALBANIA
- AR ARMENIA
- AU AUSTRIA
- AZ AZERBAIJAN
- B BELGIUM
- BE BENIN
- BH BOSNIA-HERZEGOVINA
- BR BRUNEI
- BU BURKINA
- C CROATIA
- CAR CENTRAL AFRICAN REPUBLIC
- CZ CZECH REPUBLIC
- G THE GAMBIA
- G-B GUINEA-BISSAU
- H HUNGARY
- IS ISRAEL
- L LEBANON
- LI LITHUANIA
- LU LUXEMBOURG
- M MACEDONIA (FORMER YUGOSLAV REPUBLIC)
- MT MONTENEGRO
- N NETHERLANDS
- Q QATAR
- R ROMANIA
- S SLOVAKIA
- SE SERBIA
- SL SLOVENIA
- SW SWITZERLAND
- T TAJIKISTAN
- TU TURKMENISTAN
- U UGANDA
- UAE UNITED ARAB EMIRATES
- ZIM ZIMBABWE

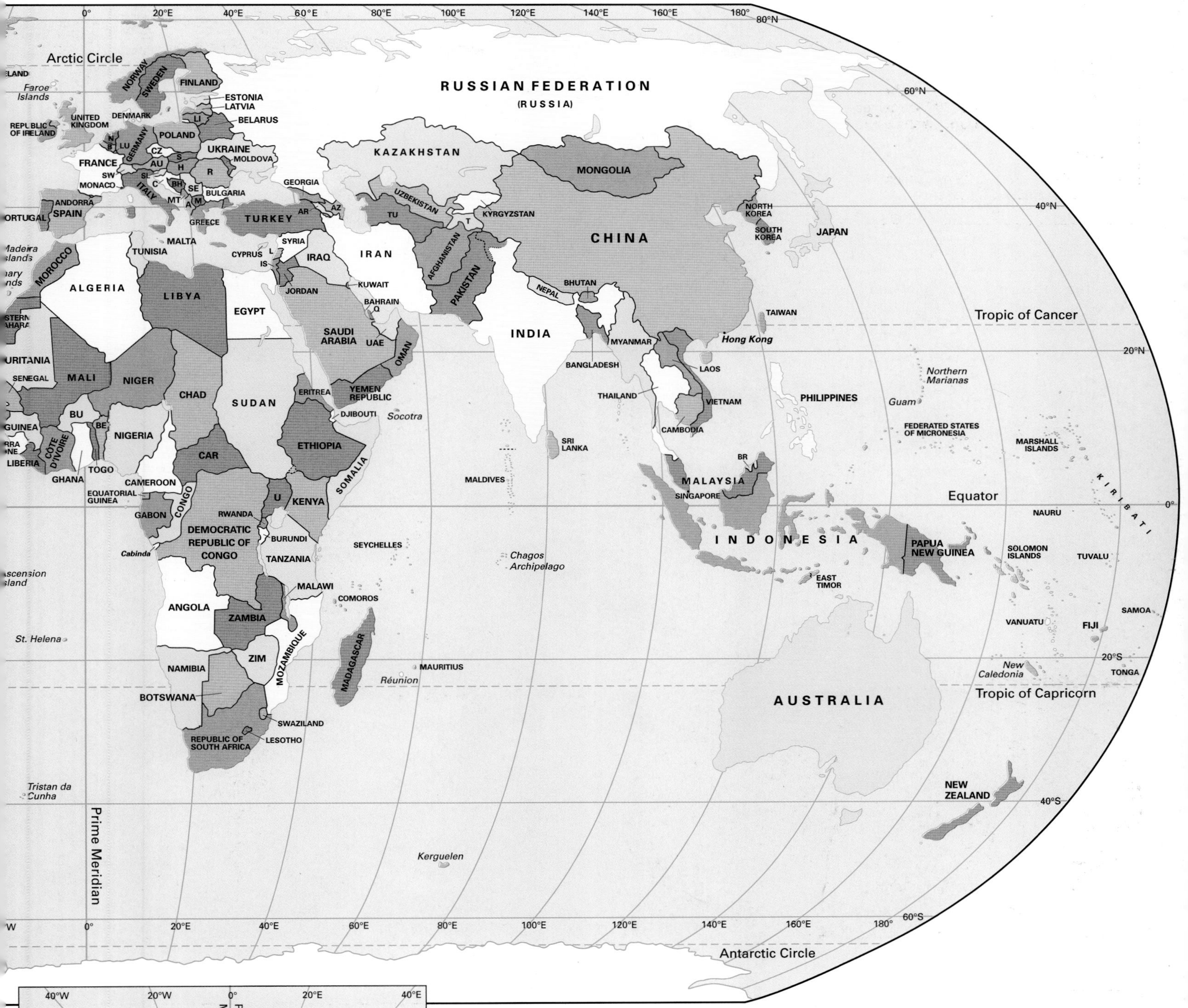

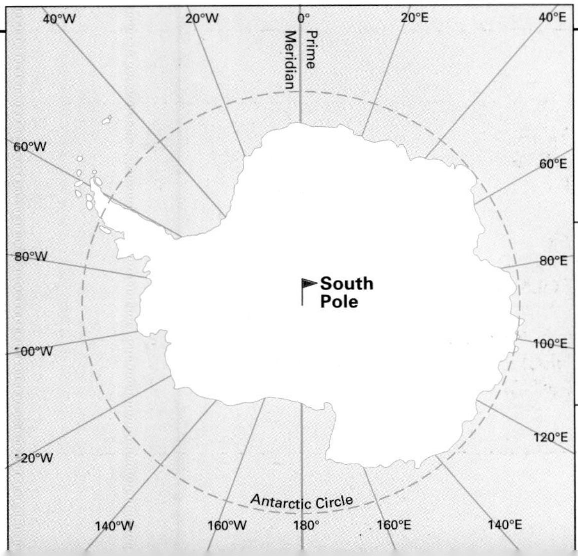

There are no countries in Antarctica. Scientists from all over the world live and work there in research stations.

There are more than 200 countries in the world. The exact number is always changing. Sometimes countries break up into separate states and others join up to make new countries.

Eckert IV Projection

The British Isles Countries

England, Scotland, and Wales, together with Northern Ireland, form the United Kingdom. The Republic of Ireland is a separate country.

Scale

45 km — 1 cm

One centimetre on the map measures 45 kilometres on the ground

0 45 90 135 180 km

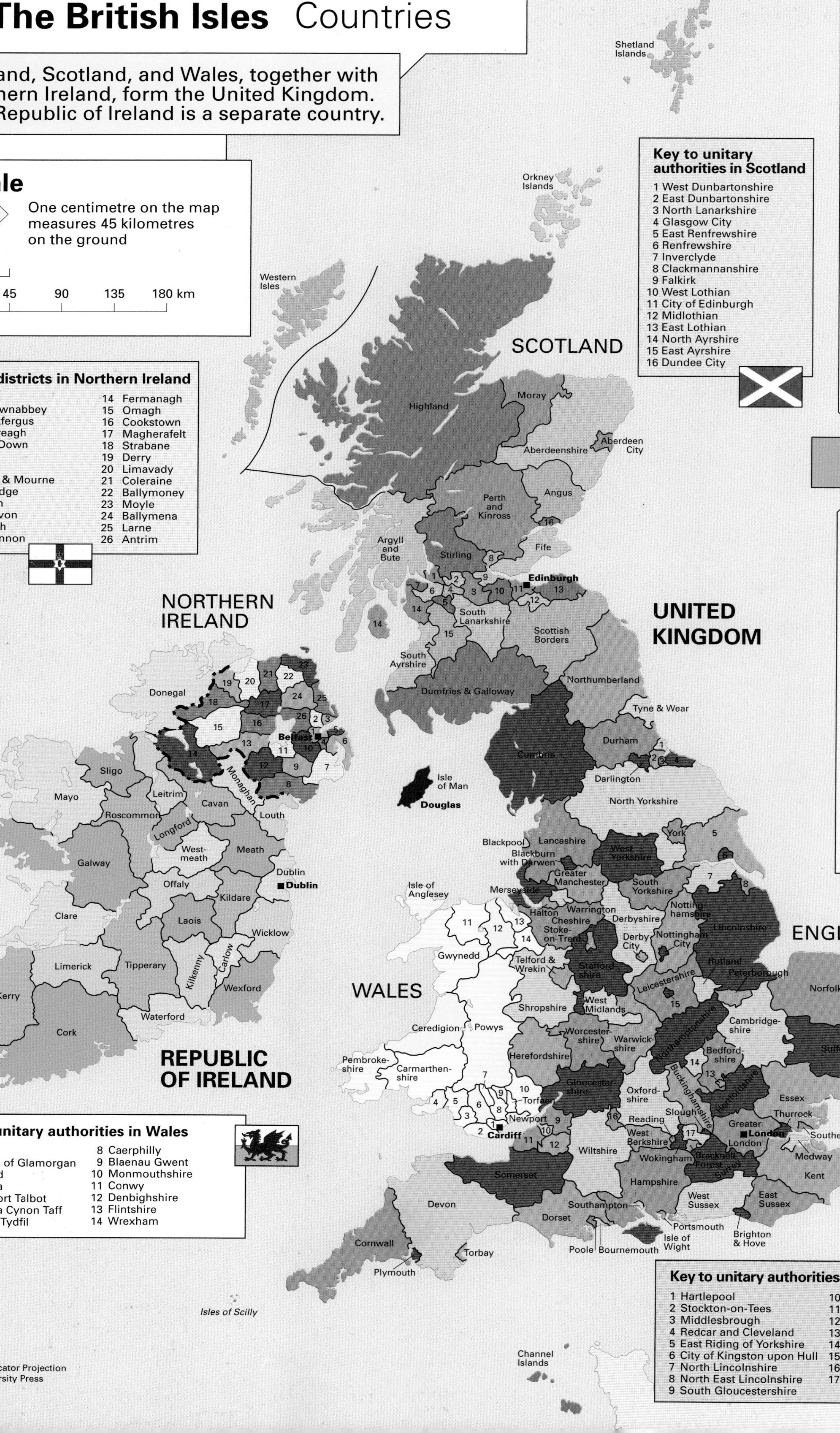

Key to unitary authorities in Scotland

1 West Dunbartonshire
2 East Dunbartonshire
3 North Lanarkshire
4 Glasgow City
5 East Renfrewshire
6 Renfrewshire
7 Inverclyde
8 Clackmannanshire
9 Falkirk
10 West Lothian
11 City of Edinburgh
12 Midlothian
13 East Lothian
14 North Ayrshire
15 East Ayrshire
16 Dundee City

Key to districts in Northern Ireland

1 Belfast
2 Newtownabbey
3 Carrickfergus
4 Castlereagh
5 North Down
6 Ards
7 Down
8 Newry & Mourne
9 Banbridge
10 Lisburn
11 Craigavon
12 Armagh
13 Dungannon
14 Fermanagh
15 Omagh
16 Cookstown
17 Magherafelt
18 Strabane
19 Derry
20 Limavady
21 Coleraine
22 Ballymoney
23 Moyle
24 Ballymena
25 Larne
26 Antrim

Key to unitary authorities in Wales

1 Cardiff
2 The Vale of Glamorgan
3 Bridgend
4 Swansea
5 Neath Port Talbot
6 Rhondda Cynon Taff
7 Merthyr Tydfil
8 Caerphilly
9 Blaenau Gwent
10 Monmouthshire
11 Conwy
12 Denbighshire
13 Flintshire
14 Wrexham

Key to unitary authorities in England

1 Hartlepool
2 Stockton-on-Tees
3 Middlesbrough
4 Redcar and Cleveland
5 East Riding of Yorkshire
6 City of Kingston upon Hull
7 North Lincolnshire
8 North East Lincolnshire
9 South Gloucestershire
10 Bristol
11 North Somerset
12 Bath and North East Somerset
13 Luton
14 Milton Keynes
15 Leicester City
16 Swindon
17 Windsor & Maidenhead

Transverse Mercator Projection

England is divided into counties and some new unitary authorities. Wales and Scotland are divided into unitary authorities. Northern Ireland is divided into districts.

The Republic of Ireland is divided into counties.

Republic of Ireland

United Kingdom

The British Isles consists of the two large islands of Great Britain and Ireland and a number of smaller islands.

The British Isles Land height and rivers

The highest parts of Great Britain are mostly in the north and west.

Key

Land height measured in metres above sea level

- more than 1000m
- 500 - 1000m
- 200 - 500m
- 100 - 200m
- less than 100m
- ▲ highest peaks with heights given in metres
- lakes
- major rivers

Scale

45 km — One centimetre on the map measures 45 kilometres on the ground.

1 cm

0 45 90 135 180 km

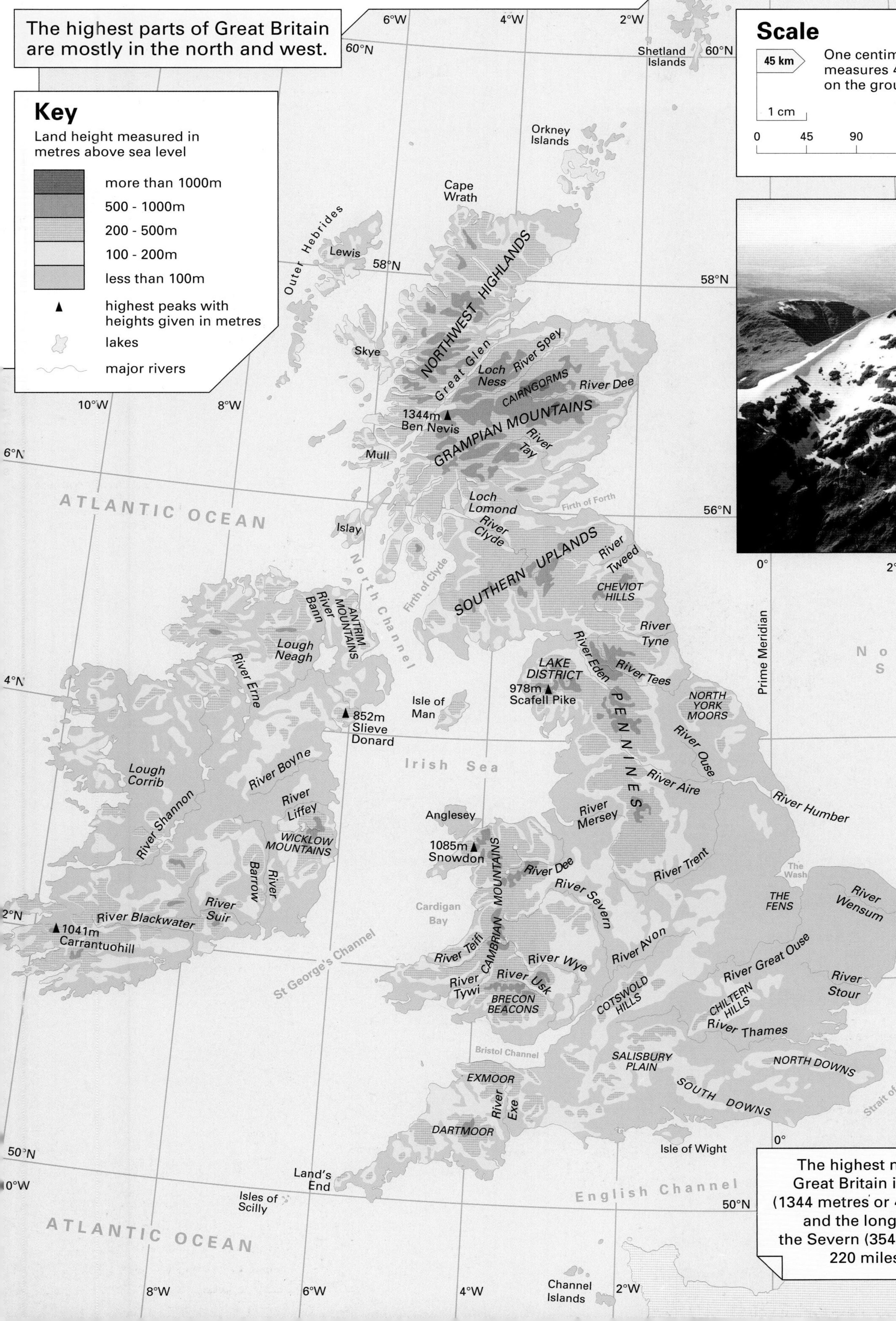

The highest mountain in Great Britain is Ben Nevis (1344 metres or 4406 feet high) and the longest river is the Severn (354 kilometres or 220 miles long).

Transverse Mercator Projection

Climate describes the average pattern of weather over a number of years.

During the year many wet weather fronts pass over the British Isles whilst southern Europe stays dry and warm. This is a satellite picture of the weather in western Europe on 6 August 1987.
Satellite pictures like this use colours that are different from the way the land looks to us.

Rainfall

The eastern parts of the British Isles are drier than the western parts. Mountains are wetter than lowlands.

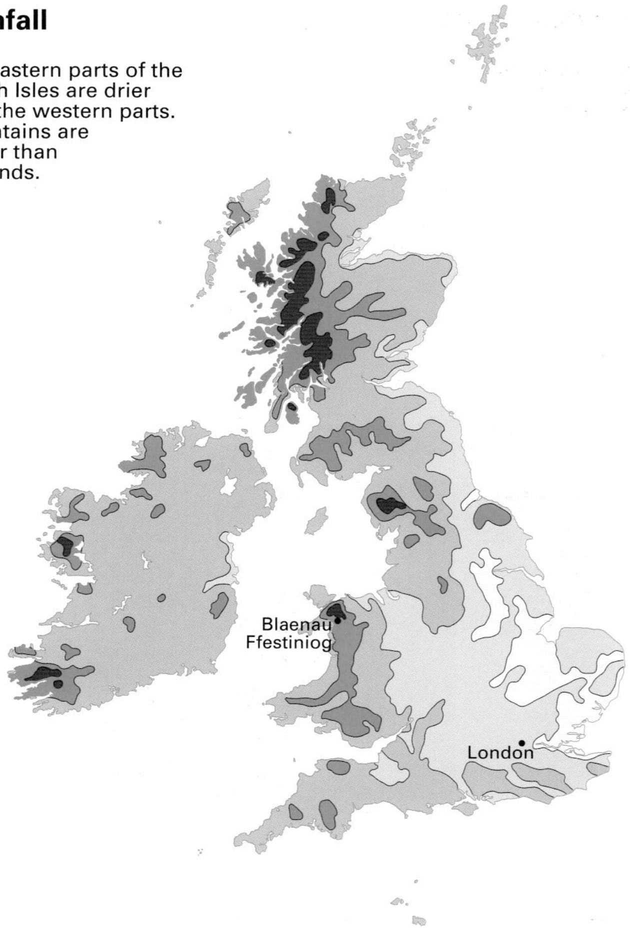

Average annual rainfall in millimetres

(darkest shade)	over 2400	very wet
	1500 - 2400	quite wet
	800 - 1500	wet
	600 - 800	quite dry
(white)	less than 600	very dry

Average annual rainfall

The graphs show the amount of rainfall in Blaenau Ffestiniog and London for one year.
Blaenau Ffestiniog is wetter in winter.
London has about the same amount of rainfall each month.

All the rain that falls in one year is the **annual rainfall**. Blaenau Ffestiniog has much more rain than London over the whole year.

Some years are wetter than others. The map shows the amount of rainfall you would expect in an average year.

Blaenau Ffestiniog

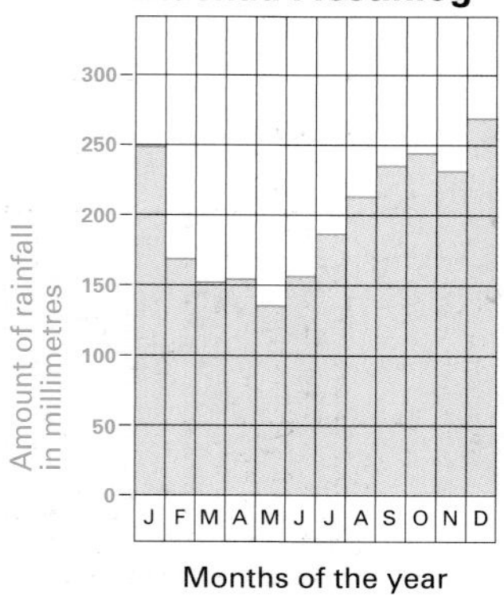

London

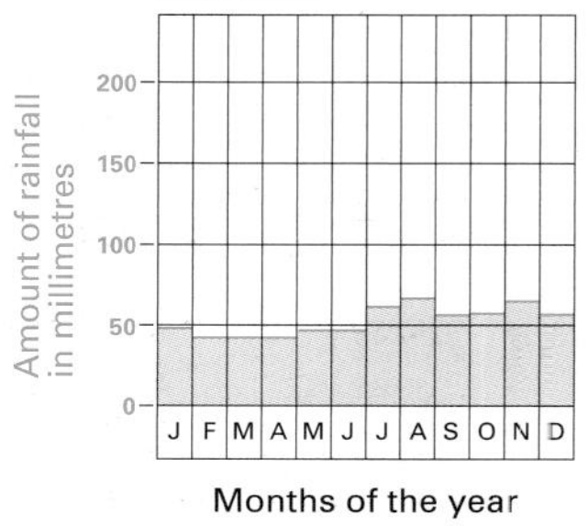

Transverse Mercator Projection

January temperatures

In winter the mountains of Scotland are the coldest parts of the British Isles.

July temperatures

In summer the coasts of southern England are the warmest parts of the British Isles.

Scale

100 km — One centimetre on the map measures 100 kilometres on the ground.

1 cm

0 100 200 300 400 km

In the British Isles it is usually colder in January than in July. However, some years might be very cold whilst others are quite warm. The maps show the temperatures you would expect in an average year.

Average temperatures in °Celsius

above 16	hot
14 - 16	very warm
12 - 14	warm
10 - 12	quite warm
8 - 10	quite cool
6 - 8	cool
4 - 6	quite cold
2 - 4	cold
0 - 2	very cold
below 0	freezing

Average temperatures in winter and summer

The graphs show the average temperatures each month for Stornoway, Braemar, London, and Valley. In all four places it is warmer in summer than in winter.

Summers in Stornoway and Braemar are much cooler than in London or Valley. Winter in Braemar is very cold.

Stornoway

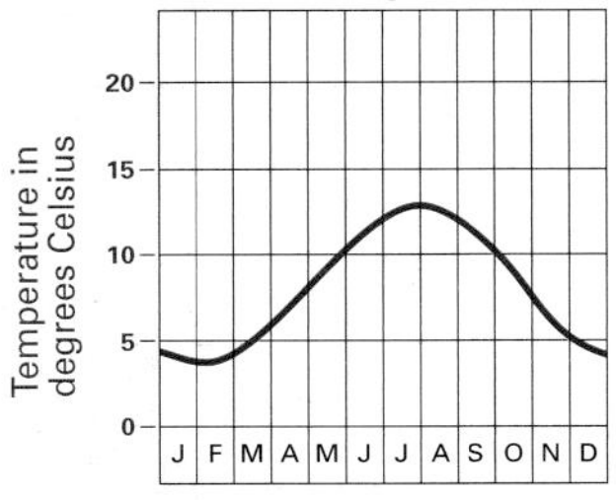

Braemar

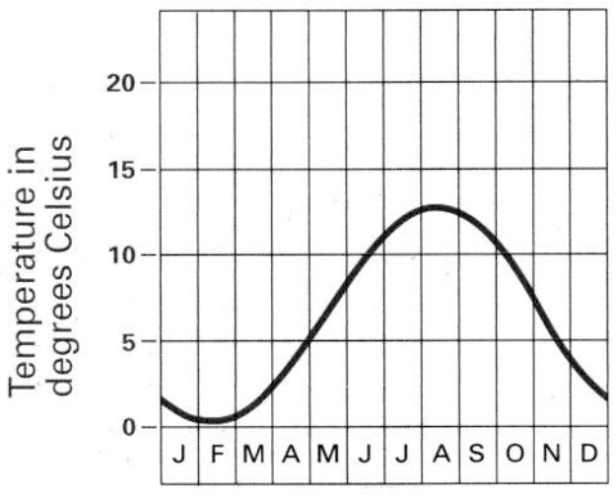

London

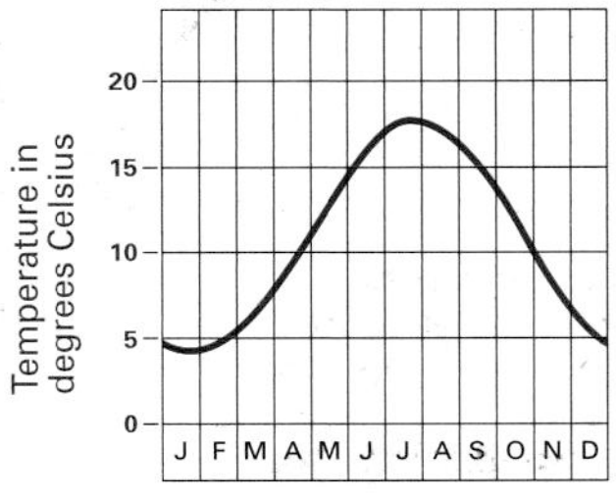

Valley

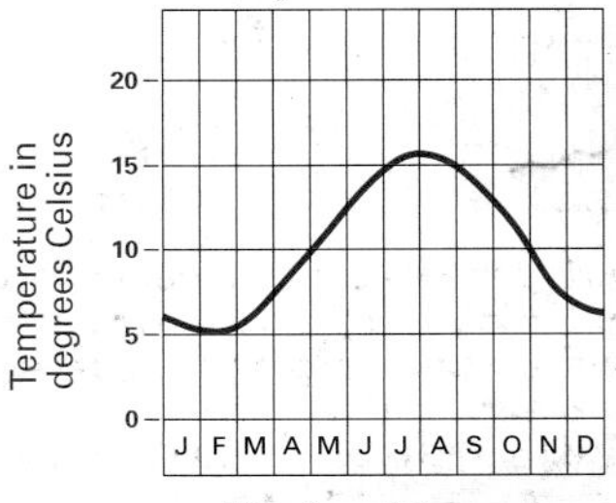

The British Isles Topographic map

Maps that show all the most important features of the landscape are called **topographic** maps.

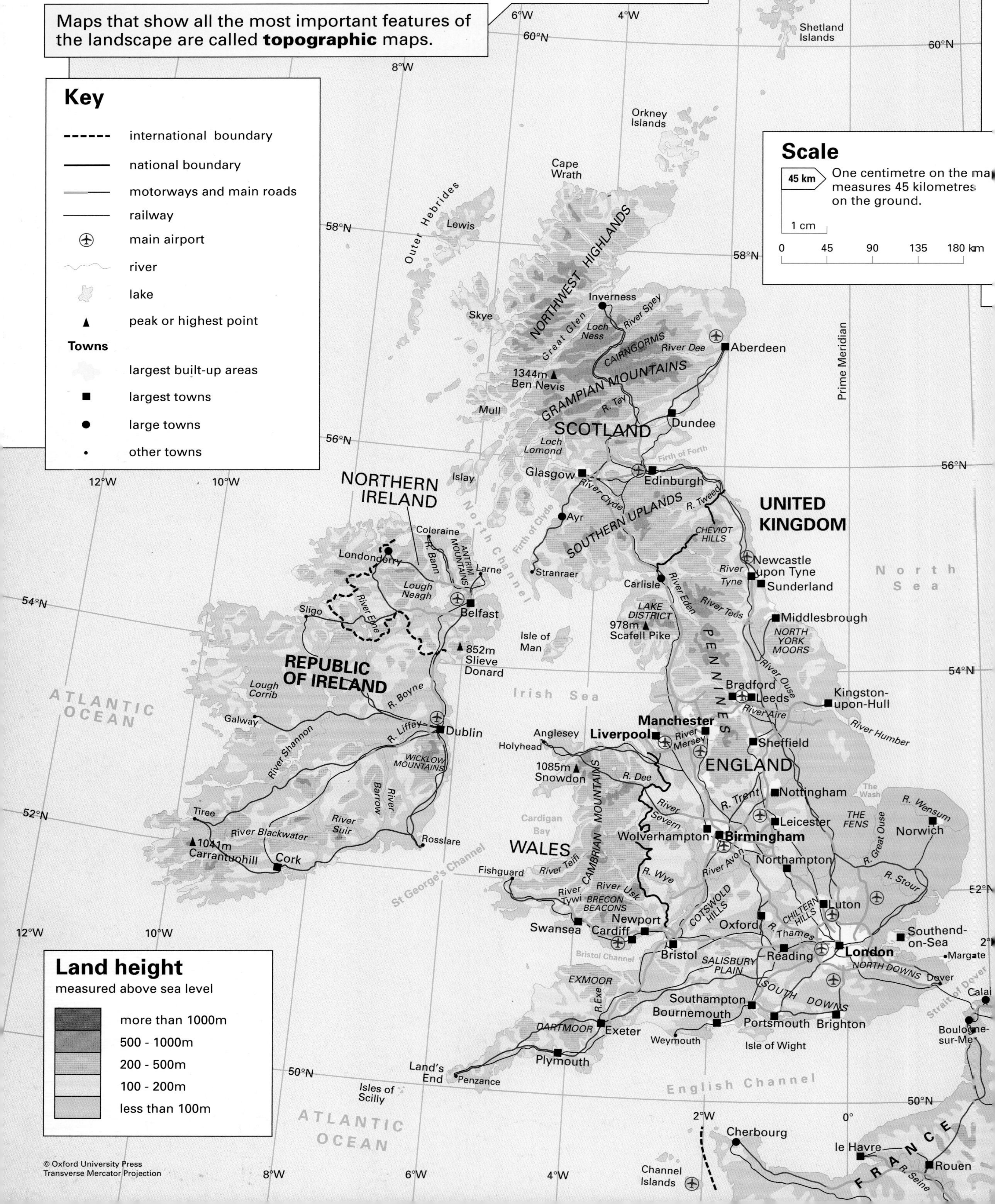

Scale

10 km

One centimetre on the map measures 10 kilometres on the ground.

1 cm

0 10 20 30 40 km

Key

- county or region boundary
- motorway and main roads
- railway
- main airport
- river
- lake
- peak or highest point
- towns

Land height

measured above sea level

- 200-500m
- 100-200m
- less than 100m

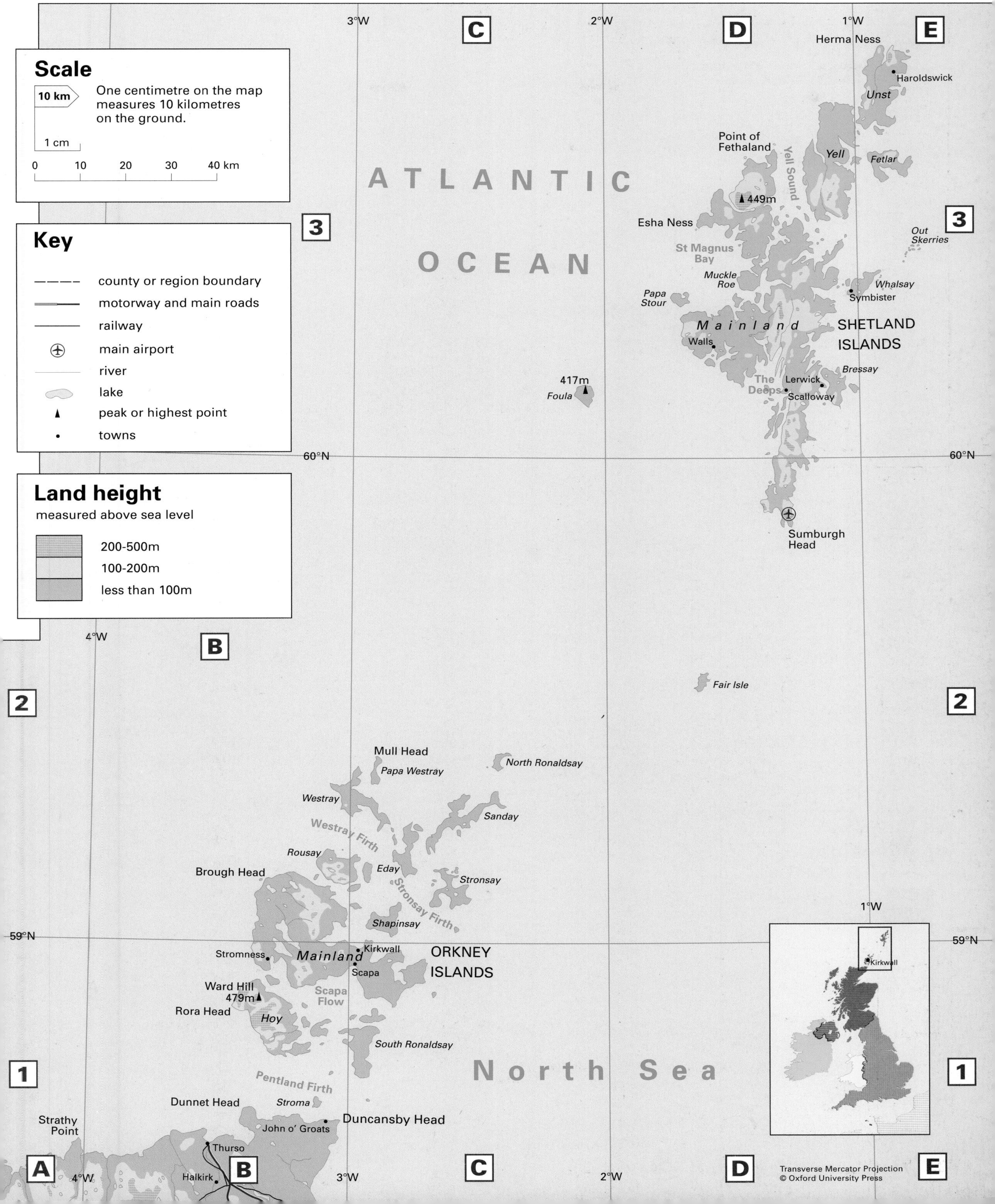

Transverse Mercator Projection

Scottish Highlands and Islands

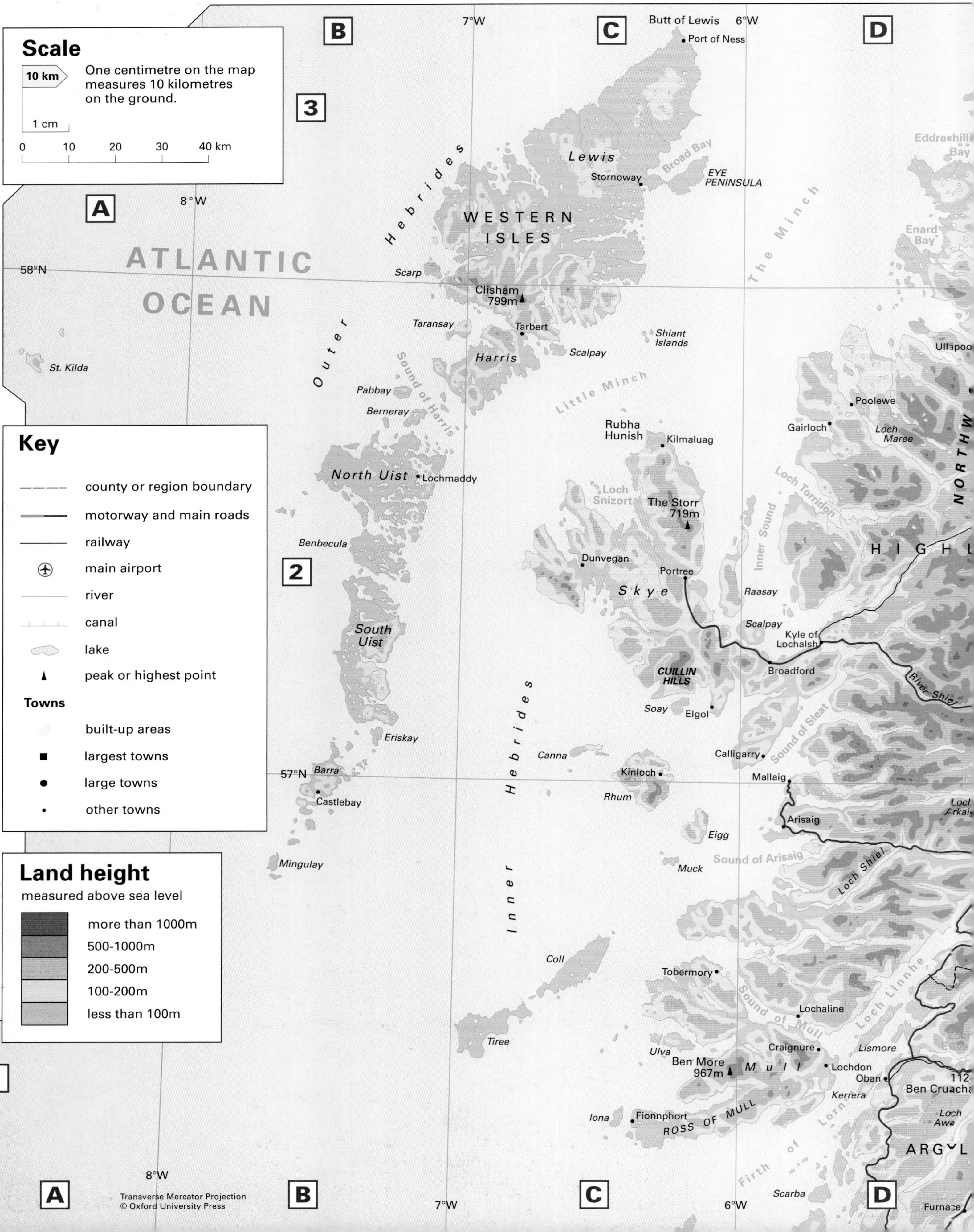

Scottish Highlands and Islands

Transverse Mercator Projection

Northern Ireland

Key

- international boundary
- national boundary
- county or region boundary
- motorway and main roads
- railway
- main airport
- river
- canal
- lake
- peak or highest point

Towns

- built-up areas
- largest towns
- large towns
- other towns

Land height

measured above sea level

- more than 1000m
- 500-1000m
- 200-500m
- 100-200m
- less than 100m

Scale
10 km
One centimetre on the map measures 10 kilometres on the ground.
1 cm
0 10 20 30 40 km
Transverse Mercator Projection
© Oxford University Press
E
F
G
H
4
3
2
1
4°W
3°W
2°W
56°N
55°N
54°N
1174m
Ben More
Loch Earn
Perth
Crieff
River Earn
Newburgh
St Andrews
Cupar
Auchterarder
OCHIL HILLS
Auchtermuchty
Crail
Loch Katrine
Callander
FIFE
Glenrothes
Anstruther
Ben Lomond
974m
STIRLING
Kinross
Dunblane
CLACKMANNAN-SHIRE
Loch Leven
Buckhaven
River Forth
Loch Lomond
Alloa
Stirling
M90
Kirkcaldy
Firth of Forth
North Berwick
Dunfermline
WEST DUNBARTONSHIRE
Grangemouth
Bo'ness
FALKIRK
Inverkeithing
CAMPSIE FELLS
Dunbar
North Sea
Alexandria
EAST DUNBARTONSHIRE
Falkirk
Edinburgh
Dumbarton
Cumbernauld
Linlithgow
EAST LOTHIAN
Port
Kirkintilloch
Bathgate
CITY OF EDINBURGH
Musselburgh
LAMMERMUIR HILLS
St Abb's Head
Bearsden
Eyemouth
Clydebank
Airdrie
Livingston
Coatbridge
M8
MIDLOTHIAN
Paisley
Glasgow
NORTH LANARKSHIRE
WEST LOTHIAN
GLASGOW CITY
Johnstone
Penicuik
PENTLAND HILLS
Duns
Whiteadder Water
Berwick-upon-Tweed
Hamilton
Motherwell
Wishaw
EAST RENFREWSHIRE
East Kilbride
Leader Water
M74
R. Clyde
Holy Island
River Tweed
Coldstream
Peebles
Lanark
Galashiels
Bamburgh
Kilmarnock
SOUTH LANARKSHIRE
Biggar
Innerleithen
Melrose
Darvel
Kelso
SOUTHERN UPLANDS
SCOTLAND
Selkirk
Wooler
Troon
EAST AYRSHIRE
River Tweed
Broad Law
840m
Yarrow Water
SCOTTISH BORDERS
Jedburgh
815m
The Cheviot
River Ayr
AYRSHIRE
St Mary's Loch
River Teviot
River Aln
Alnwick
Ayr
Cumnock
Hawick
New Cumnock
LOWTHER HILLS
Daer Reservoir
Amble
Maybole
River Doon
Sanquhar
Moffat
River Coquet
SOUTH AYRSHIRE
River Nith
602m
Peel Fell
River Rede
R. Annan
Thornhill
River Esk
CHEVIOT HILLS
Kielder Water
NORTHUMBERLAND
Ashington
River Stinchar
Loch Doon
River Wansbeck
Blyth
DUMFRIES AND GALLOWAY
Lockerbie
Langholm
Liddel Water
River Blyth
St John's Town of Dalry
Lochmaben
Cramlington
New Galloway
Dumfries
Whitley Bay
Loch Ken
River Annan
Newcastle upon Tyne
R. Cree
Annan
River Irthing
Haltwhistle
River Tyne
Newton Stewart
Castle Douglas
Hexham
Gateshead
Dalbeattie
Brampton
Washington
Kirkbean
Carlisle
Consett
Gatehouse of Fleet
River Dee
Solway Firth
River Derwent
Chester-le-Street
Wigtown
Kirkcudbright
Wigton
River Eden
Durham
Wigtown Bay
Cross Fell
893m
River Wear
A1(M)
Whithorn
M6
Spennymoor
Maryport
River Ellen
DURHAM
Bishop Auckland
R. Derwent
Cockermouth
Skiddaw
931m
Penrith
River Tees
Newton Aycliffe
Workington
PENNINES
790m
Mickle Fell
DARLINGTON
Irish Sea
Keswick
Derwent Water
CUMBRIA
Barnard Castle
Darlington
Whitehaven
Ullswater
Appleby-in-Westmorland
Brough
Helvellyn
950m
ENGLAND
St Bees Head
LAKE DISTRICT
Kirkby Stephen
River Swale
Scafell Pike
978m
Ambleside
Richmond
Point of Ayre
Seascale
Windermere
Windermere
Coniston Water
Leyburn
Kendal
River Ure
Snaefell
620m
Ramsey
NORTH YORKSHIRE
Kirk Michael
Whernside
737m
River Lune
Peel
ISLE OF MAN
River Greta
Ingleborough
723m
River Wharfe
South Barrule
483m
Douglas
693m
Pen-y-Ghent
704m
Great Whernside
Ripon
Dalton-in-Furness
R. Nidd
Barrow-in-Furness
Morecambe Bay
Carnforth
River Aire
Morecambe
Lancaster
Heysham
560m
Ward's Stone
Castletown
M6
Skipton

Northern England

Transverse Mercator Projection

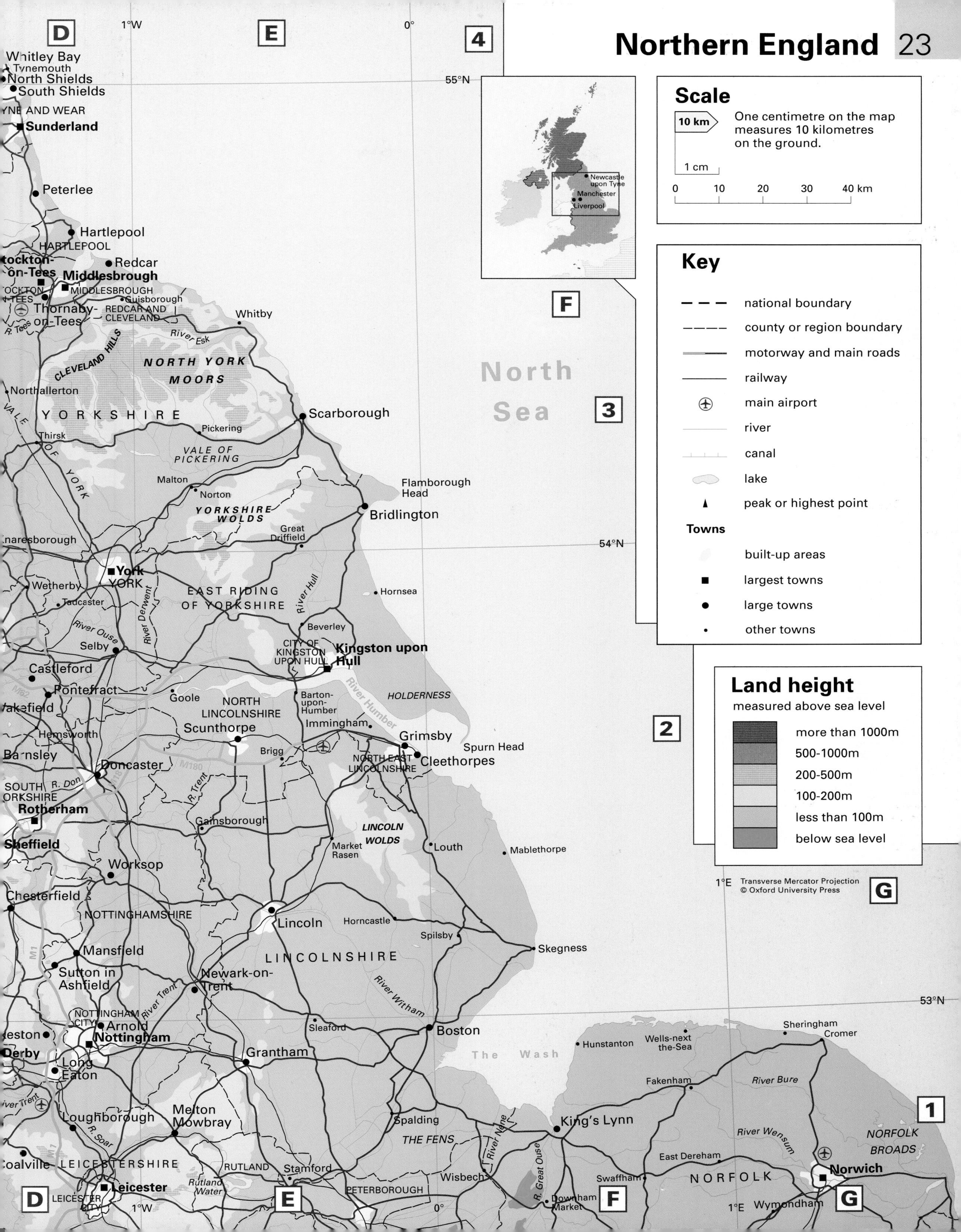

Scale
10 km
1 cm
One centimetre on the map measures 10 kilometres on the ground.
0 10 20 30 40 km
Newcastle upon Tyne
Manchester
Liverpool
Key
national boundary
county or region boundary
motorway and main roads
railway
main airport
river
canal
lake
peak or highest point
Towns
built-up areas
largest towns
large towns
other towns
Land height
measured above sea level
more than 1000m
500-1000m
200-500m
100-200m
less than 100m
below sea level
Transverse Mercator Projection
© Oxford University Press
D
E
F
G
1
2
3
4
1°W
0°
1°E
55°N
54°N
53°N
North Sea
Whitley Bay
Tynemouth
North Shields
South Shields
TYNE AND WEAR
Sunderland
Peterlee
Hartlepool
HARTLEPOOL
Stockton-on-Tees
Middlesbrough
MIDDLESBROUGH
Redcar
Guisborough
Thornaby-on-Tees
REDCAR AND CLEVELAND
R. Tees
Whitby
River Esk
CLEVELAND HILLS
NORTH YORK MOORS
Northallerton
VALE OF YORK
YORKSHIRE
Scarborough
Pickering
Thirsk
VALE OF PICKERING
Malton
Norton
Flamborough Head
YORKSHIRE WOLDS
Bridlington
Great Driffield
Knaresborough
York
YORK
Wetherby
Tadcaster
EAST RIDING OF YORKSHIRE
River Derwent
River Hull
Hornsea
Beverley
River Ouse
Selby
CITY OF KINGSTON UPON HULL
Kingston upon Hull
Castleford
M62
Pontefract
Goole
NORTH LINCOLNSHIRE
Barton-upon-Humber
River Humber
HOLDERNESS
Wakefield
Scunthorpe
Immingham
Hemsworth
Grimsby
Spurn Head
Brigg
Barnsley
Doncaster
M180
NORTH EAST LINCOLNSHIRE
Cleethorpes
SOUTH YORKSHIRE
R. Don
R. Trent
Rotherham
Gainsborough
LINCOLN WOLDS
Sheffield
Market Rasen
Louth
Mablethorpe
Worksop
Chesterfield
NOTTINGHAMSHIRE
Lincoln
Horncastle
Spilsby
M1
Mansfield
Skegness
LINCOLNSHIRE
Sutton in Ashfield
Newark-on-Trent
River Witham
River Trent
NOTTINGHAM CITY
Arnold
Ilkeston
Nottingham
Sleaford
Boston
Derby
Sheringham
Cromer
Hunstanton
Wells-next-the-Sea
Grantham
The Wash
Long Eaton
Fakenham
River Bure
River Trent
Loughborough
Melton Mowbray
Spalding
King's Lynn
River Wensum
NORFOLK BROADS
R. Soar
THE FENS
River Nene
Coalville
LEICESTERSHIRE
RUTLAND
Stamford
R. Great Ouse
East Dereham
Norwich
Wisbech
Swaffham
NORFOLK
Leicester
Rutland Water
LEICESTER CITY
PETERBOROUGH
Downham Market
Wymondham

A
B
C
D
6°W
5°W
4°W
3°W
3
2
1
53°N
52°N
Malahide
Howth
Dublin
Dún Laoghaire
Bray
Greystones
REPUBLIC OF IRELAND
Wicklow
Arklow
Irish Sea
Carmel Head
Amlwch
Holyhead
Holy Island
ISLE OF ANGLESEY
Llangefni
Bangor
Llandudno
Conwy
Colwyn Bay
Rhyl
Prestatyn
River Dee
Formby
MERSEYSIDE
Bootle
Wallasey
Liverpool
Birkenhead
FLINTSHIRE
Flint
Denbigh
River Clwyd
R. Conwy
Mold
Bethesda
Caernarfon
Caernarfon Bay
Snowdon 1085m
CONWY
DENBIGHSHIRE
Wrexham
Blaenau Ffestiniog
LLŶN PENINSULA
Porthmadog
Pwllheli
Harlech
River Dee
Llangollen
Bala
Bala Lake
Oswestry
GWYNEDD
905m
Aran Fawddwy
Lake Vyrnwy
R. Vyrnwy
Bardsey Island
Barmouth
Dolgellau
Cader Idris 892m
Welshpool
Cardigan Bay
R. Dyfi
Machynlleth
WALES
CAMBRIAN MOUNTAINS
R. Severn
Newtown
752m
Plynlimon
Llanidloes
Aberystwyth
Knighton
CEREDIGION
Rhayader
Aberaeron
New Quay
River Teifi
Llandrindod Wells
POWYS
Builth Wells
St George's Channel
Cemaes Head
Cardigan
River Teifi
Lampeter
MYNYDD EPPYNT
R. Wye
Hay-or-Wye
Strumble Head
Newcastle Emlyn
Llandovery
Fishguard
MYNYDD PRESELI
R. Tywi
River Usk
Brecon
811m
BLACK MOUNTAINS
St David's Head
St David's
PEMBROKESHIRE
CARMARTHENSHIRE
BRECON 886m BEACONS
Carmarthen
Llandeilo
Haverfordwest
St Brides Bay
R. Tywi
Ammanford
Abergavenny
Milford Haven
Merthyr Tydfil
Ebbw Vale
BLAENAU GWENT
Kidwelly
Burry Port
Pontardulais
Aberdare
MERTHYR TYDFIL
Abertillery
TORFAEN
Carmarthen Bay
SWANSEA
NEATH PORT TALBOT
RHONDDA
Pembroke
Tenby
Llanelli
Neath
CYNON
Pontypool
Cwmbran
Swansea
Rhondda
TAFF
CAERPHILLY
GOWER
Pontypridd
Port Talbot
Caerphilly
Newport
Worms Head
BRIDGEND
CARDIFF
NEWPORT
ATLANTIC
Bridgend
Cardiff
THE VALE OF GLAMORGAN
Barry
OCEAN
Bristol Channel
Weston-super-Mare
Bridgwater Bay
Lynton
Ilfracombe
Minehead
Dunkery Beacon 519m
Lundy
DEVON
EXMOOR
Transverse Mercator Projection
© Oxford University Press

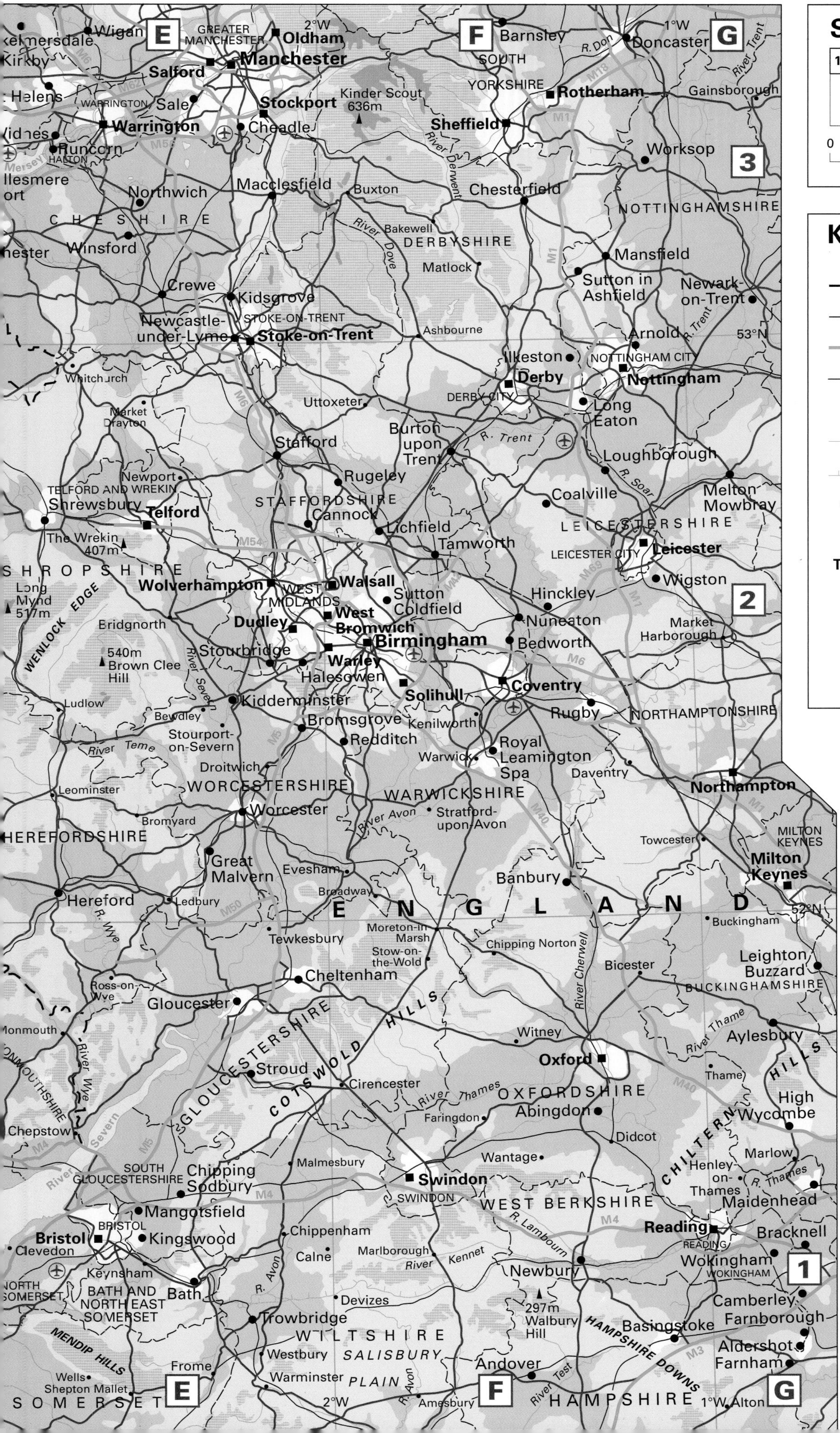

Scale

One centimetre on the map measures 10 kilometres on the ground.

10 km — 1 cm

0 10 20 30 40 km

Key

- national boundary
- county or region boundary
- motorway and main roads
- railway
- main airport
- river
- canal
- lake
- peak or highest point

Towns

- built-up areas
- largest towns
- large towns
- other towns

Land height

measured above sea level

- more than 1000m
- 500-1000m
- 200-500m
- 100-200m
- less than 100m

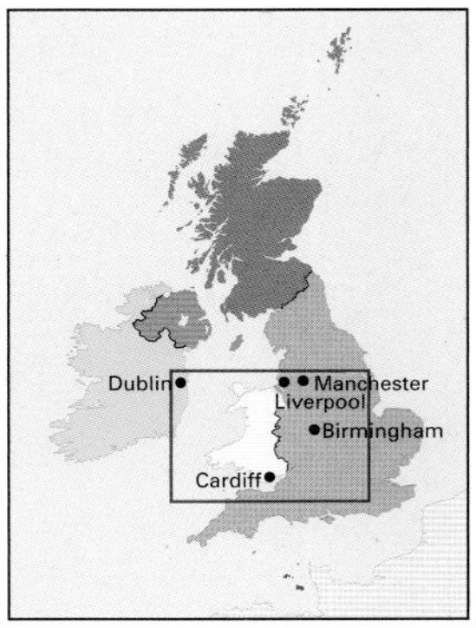

South East England

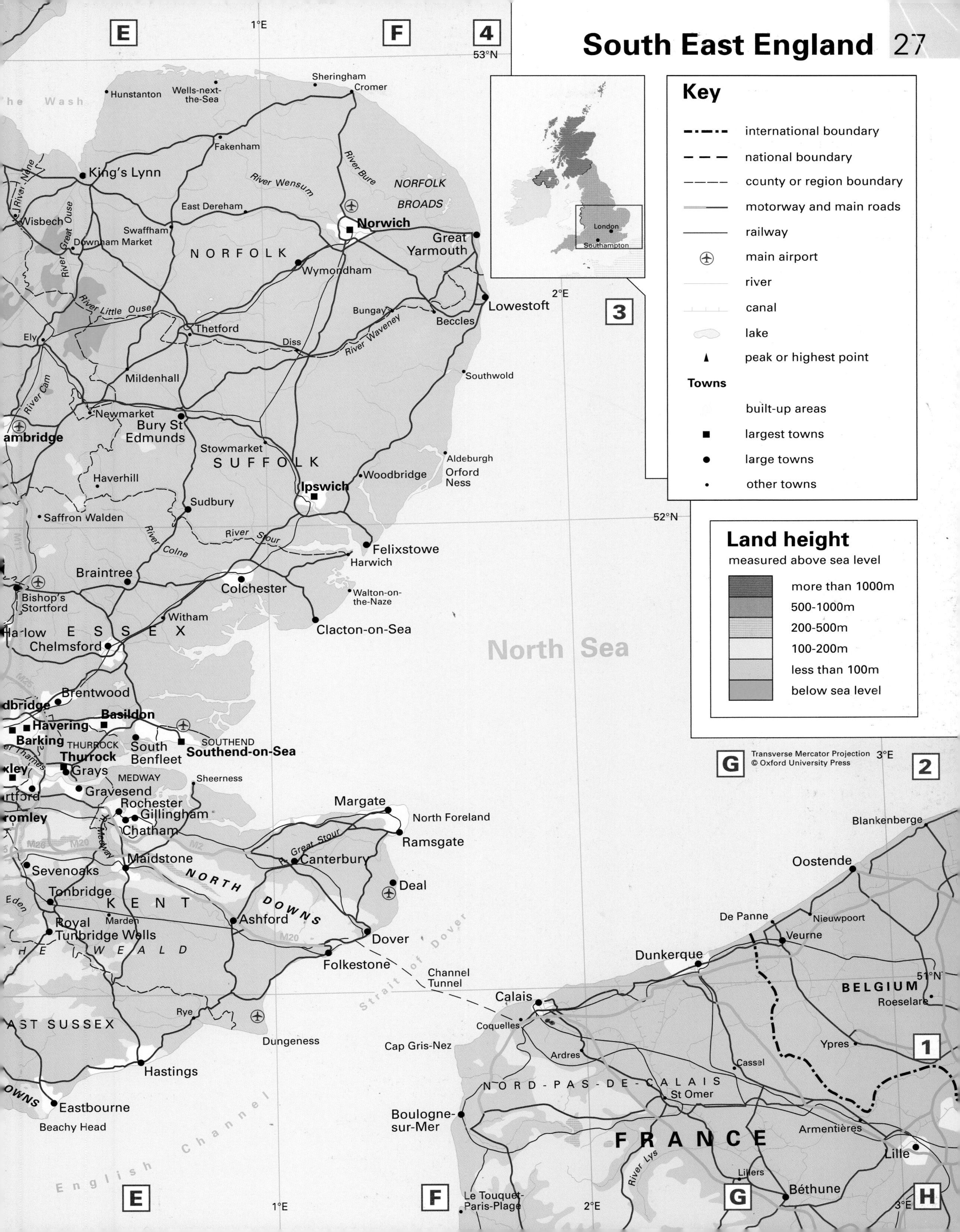
Key
international boundary
national boundary
county or region boundary
motorway and main roads
railway
main airport
river
canal
lake
peak or highest point
Towns
built-up areas
largest towns
large towns
other towns
Land height
measured above sea level
more than 1000m
500-1000m
200-500m
100-200m
less than 100m
below sea level
Transverse Mercator Projection
© Oxford University Press
London
Southampton
North Sea
NORFOLK
SUFFOLK
ESSEX
KENT
AST SUSSEX
NORFOLK BROADS
NORTH DOWNS
WEALD
Strait of Dover
English Channel
Channel Tunnel
he Wash
Hunstanton
Wells-next-the-Sea
Sheringham
Cromer
Fakenham
King's Lynn
River Wensum
River Bure
East Dereham
Norwich
Great Yarmouth
Wisbech
Swaffham
Downham Market
Great Ouse
Wymondham
River Little Ouse
Thetford
Bungay
Beccles
Lowestoft
River Waveney
Diss
Ely
Mildenhall
Southwold
River Cam
Newmarket
Bury St Edmunds
ambridge
Stowmarket
Haverhill
Aldeburgh
Orford Ness
Woodbridge
Ipswich
Sudbury
Saffron Walden
River Colne
River Stour
Felixstowe
Harwich
Braintree
Colchester
Bishop's Stortford
Walton-on-the-Naze
Witham
Clacton-on-Sea
Harlow
Chelmsford
Brentwood
dbridge
Havering
Basildon
Barking
THURROCK
Thurrock
South Benfleet
SOUTHEND
Southend-on-Sea
Grays
MEDWAY
Sheerness
Gravesend
Rochester
Gillingham
Chatham
rtford
romley
Margate
North Foreland
Ramsgate
Great Stour
Canterbury
Maidstone
Medway
Sevenoaks
Deal
Tonbridge
Eden
Marden
Ashford
Royal Tunbridge Wells
Dover
Folkestone
Rye
Dungeness
Hastings
Eastbourne
Beachy Head
OWNS
M25
M20
M26
M2
M11
Cap Gris-Nez
Coquelles
Calais
Ardres
Dunkerque
De Panne
Veurne
Nieuwpoort
Oostende
Blankenberge
BELGIUM
Roeselare
Ypres
Cassal
NORD-PAS-DE-CALAIS
St Omer
Boulogne-sur-Mer
FRANCE
River Lys
Armentières
Lille
Lillers
Béthune
Le Touquet-Paris-Plage
1°E
2°E
3°E
51°N
52°N
53°N
E
F
G
H
1
2
3
4

South West England

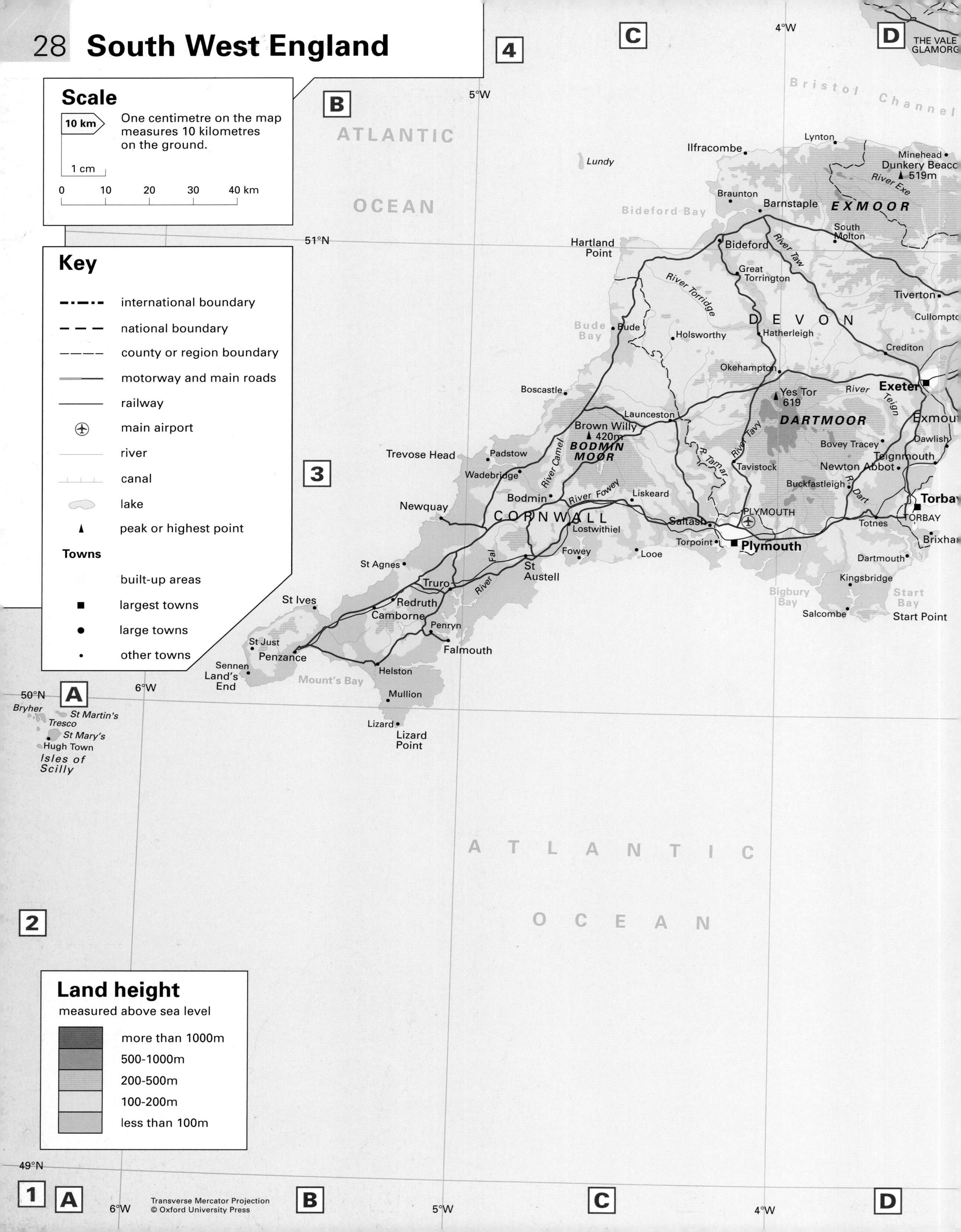

D
E
F
G
D
E
F
G
4
3
2
1
3°W
2°W
1°W
51°N
50°N
49°N
Cardiff
Barry
Clevedon
Bristol
BRISTOL
Kingswood
Keynsham
Chippenham
Calne
Bath
NORTH SOMERSET
BATH AND NORTH EAST SOMERSET
Weston-super-Mare
Bridgwater Bay
MENDIP HILLS
QUANTOCK HILLS
Devizes
Trowbridge
WILTSHIRE
Westbury
SALISBURY PLAIN
Frome
Warminster
Wells
Shepton Mallet
Glastonbury
Bridgwater
R. Parrett
SOMERSET
Taunton
Wellington
River Tone
Wincanton
Mere
Amesbury
Salisbury
Shaftesbury
River Yeo
Ilchester
Yeovil
Sherborne
Ilminster
Crewkerne
Chard
River Axe
Honiton
Axminster
DORSET
Blandford Forum
River Stour
Wimborne Minster
Ringwood
River Avon
Bridport
Lyme Regis
Seaton
Sidmouth
Lyme Bay
Dorchester
River Frome
Poole
POOLE
BOURNEMOUTH
Bournemouth
Christchurch
Wareham
Weymouth
Swanage
St Alban's Head
Portland Bill
297m Walbury Hill
Andover
River Test
Stockbridge
R. Itchen
Winchester
HAMPSHIRE
HAMPSHIRE DOWNS
Basingstoke
M3
Camberley
Farnborough
Aldershot
Farnham
Woking
Epsom
SURREY
Guildford
Dorking
NORTH DOWNS
Alton
Haslemere
R. Arun
Horsham
Petersfield
WEST SUSSEX
Romsey
Eastleigh
Totton
Southampton
SOUTHAMPTON
River Meon
Waterlooville
Havant
M27
SOUTH DOWNS
Arundel
Chichester
Worthing
Fareham
Gosport
Fawley
PORTSMOUTH
Portsmouth
Littlehampton
Bognor Regis
Selsey Bill
Lymington
The Solent
Cowes
Ryde
Newport
ISLE OF WIGHT
Sandown
Shanklin
The Needles
St Catherine's Point
English Channel
Cap de la Hague
Auderville
Alderney
Barfleur
Cherbourg
Baie de la Seine
Valognes
Guernsey
St Peter-Port
Sark
FRANCE
Carteret
CHANNEL ISLANDS
Carentan
Isigny-sur-Mer
Jersey
St Helier
Lessay
River Vire
St-Lô
Coutainville
Coutances
River Orne
Cardiff
Southampton
Isles of Scilly
Channel Islands
Transverse Mercator Projection
© Oxford University Press

The United Kingdom People and cities

Most people in the United Kingdom live in large towns or cities.

Total number of people, 2001

England	50 million
Scotland	5 million
Wales	3 million
N. Ireland	2 million
U.K.	**60 million**

one kilometre

one kilometre

More than 250 people live in this square kilometre.

one kilometre

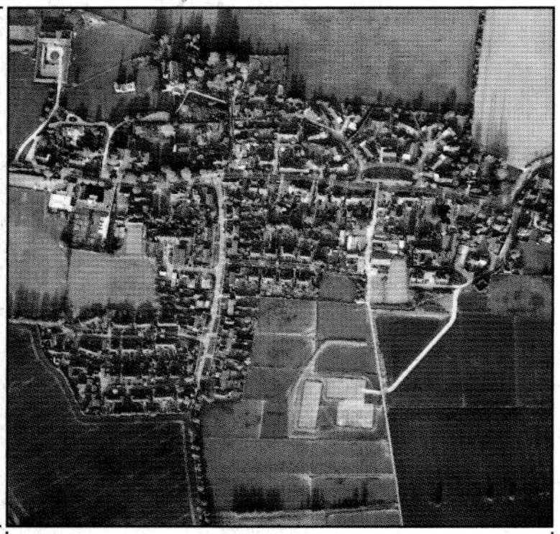

one kilometre

About 100 people live in this square kilometre.

one kilometre

one kilometre

Fewer than 50 people live in this square kilometre.

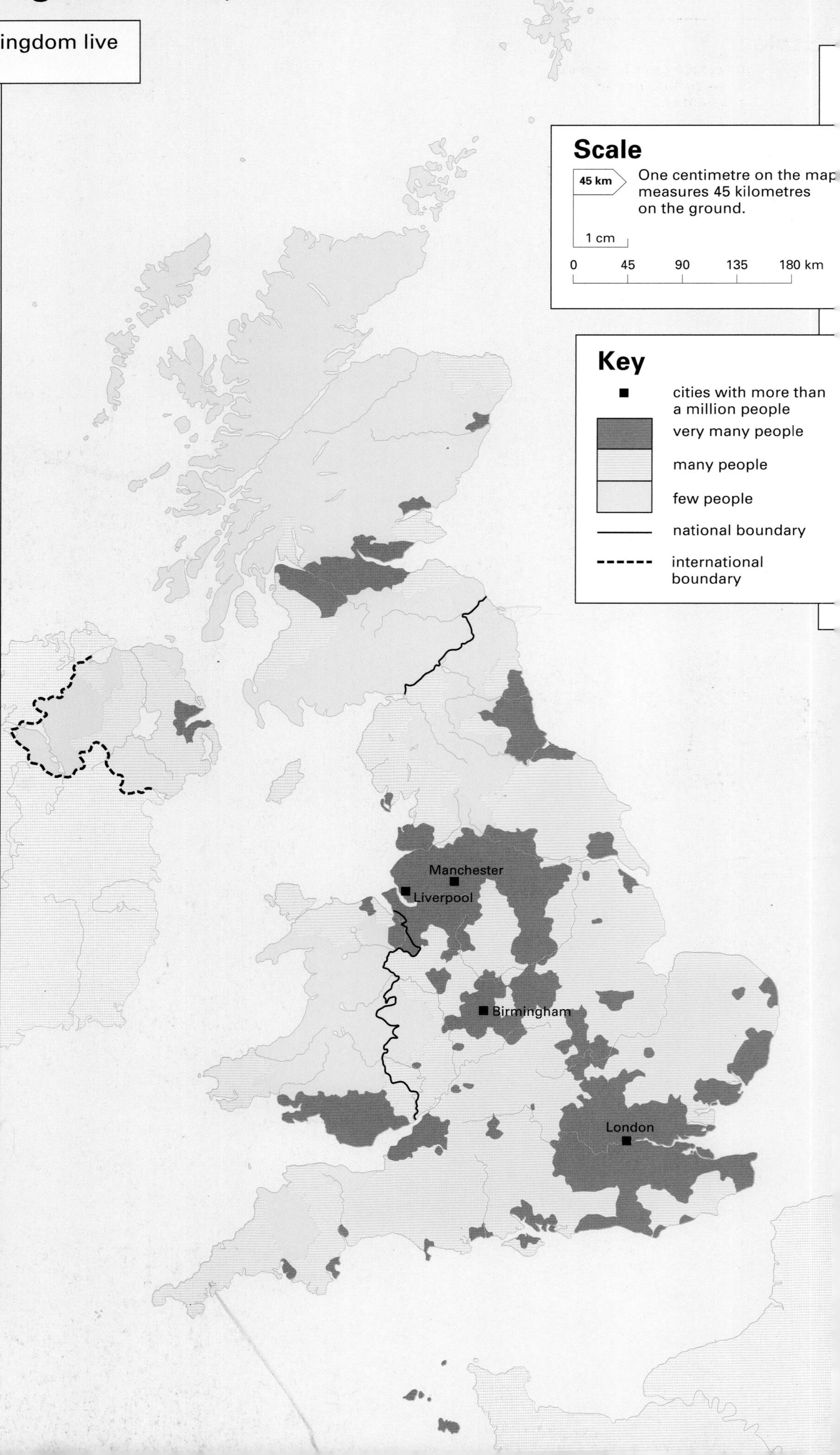

Transverse Mercator Projection

Farmers produce food by growing crops and keeping animals.

Key

	mostly livestock farms	cattle are kept for meat
	mostly hill farms	sheep are kept for meat and wool
	mostly dairy farms	cows are kept for milk
	mostly arable farms	crops are grown

Many farms in Britain are mixed farms. Farmers grow crops *and* keep animals.

	forestry	trees are planted for wood
	market gardening	fruit and vegetables are grown
	no farming	built-up areas

Transverse Mercator Projection

The United Kingdom Factories and offices

More people work in offices than in factories in the United Kingdom.

Scale

45 km — One centimetre on the map measures 45 kilometres on the ground.

1 cm

0 45 90 135 180 km

Key

- major industrial area
- office and business centre
- national boundary
- international boundary

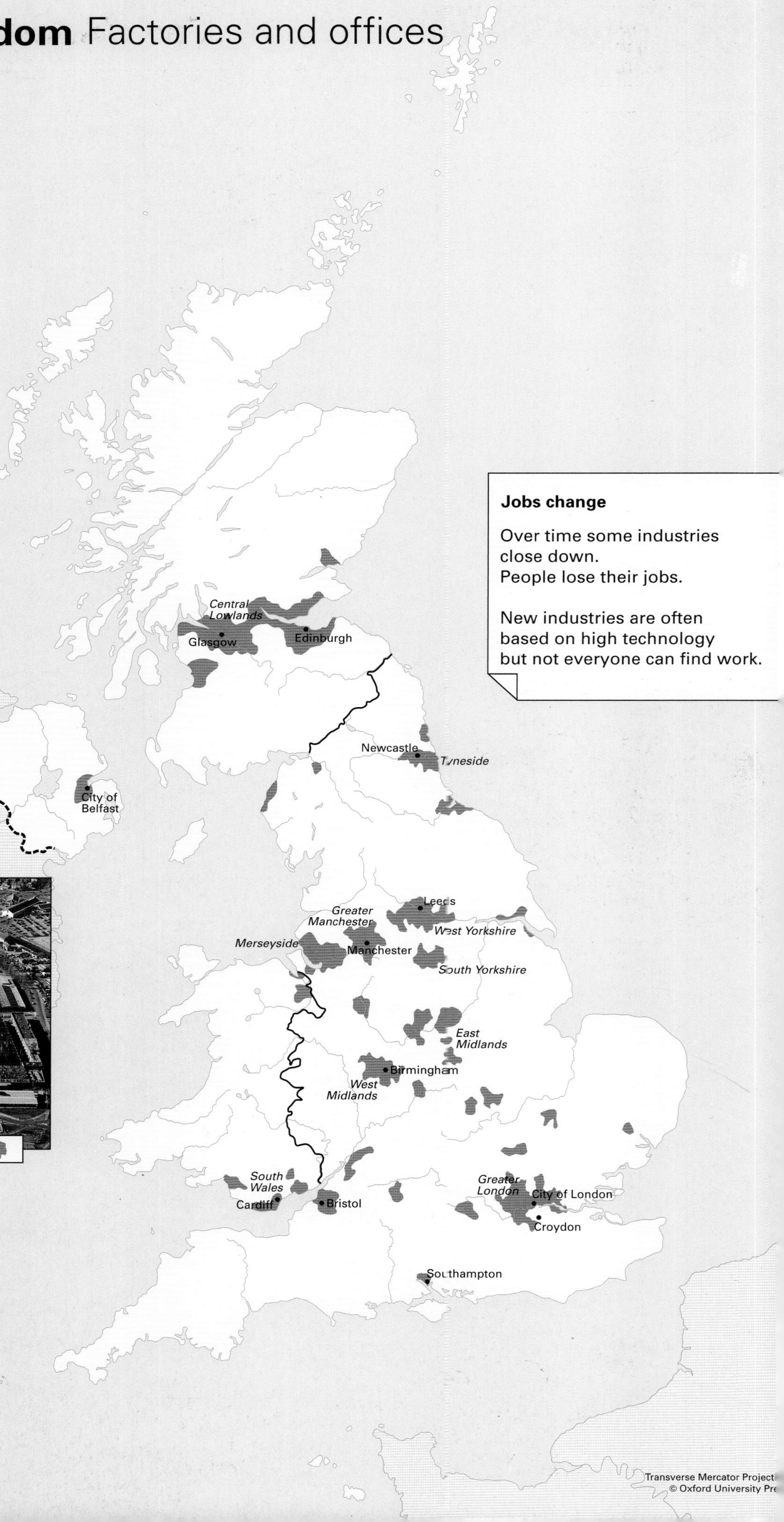

Jobs change

Over time some industries close down.
People lose their jobs.

New industries are often based on high technology but not everyone can find work.

Transverse Mercator Projection

Coal, oil, and natural gas hold energy which originally came from the sun.

Scale

60 km — One centimetre on the map measures 60 kilometres on the ground.

1 cm

0 60 120 180 240 km

oil field
Claymore Platform, North Sea

Key

- ● largest coal mines
- gas field and pipeline
- oil field and pipeline

Largest power stations

- ▲ burning coal, oil or gas
- ▲ using water power
- ▲ using nuclear power
- △ using wind power

△ **wind generator**
Blackmill Windfarm, near Bridgend

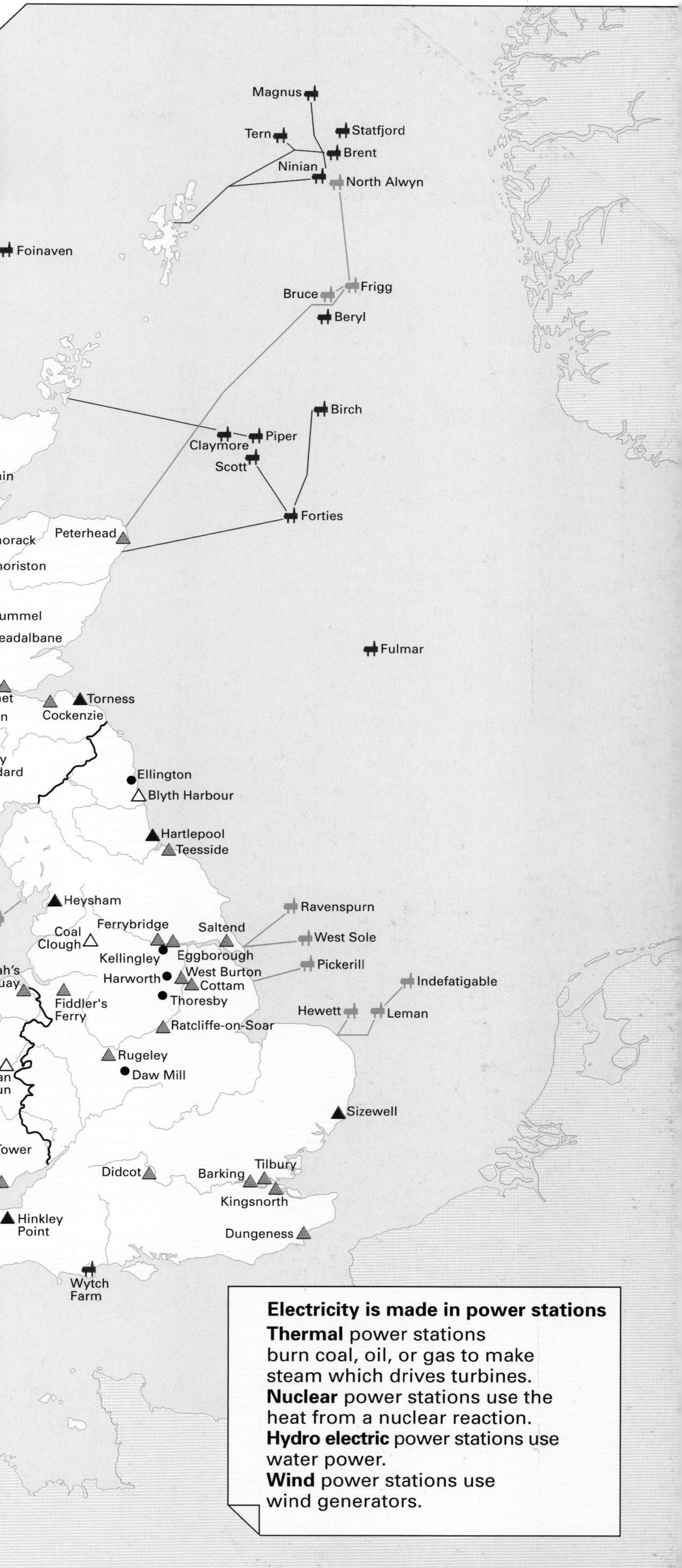

▲ **power station burning coal**
Didcot Power Station, Oxfordshire

Electricity is made in power stations

Thermal power stations burn coal, oil, or gas to make steam which drives turbines.
Nuclear power stations use the heat from a nuclear reaction.
Hydro electric power stations use water power.
Wind power stations use wind generators.

Transverse Mercator Projection

The United Kingdom Roads and railways

Roads and railways do not always take the shortest route between places.

Scale

45 km — One centimetre on the map measures 45 kilometres on the ground.

1 cm

0 45 90 135 180 km

Key

- major road
- motorway
- main railway
- road or rail terminal
- built-up areas
- land over 200 metres
- land below 200 metres
- national boundary

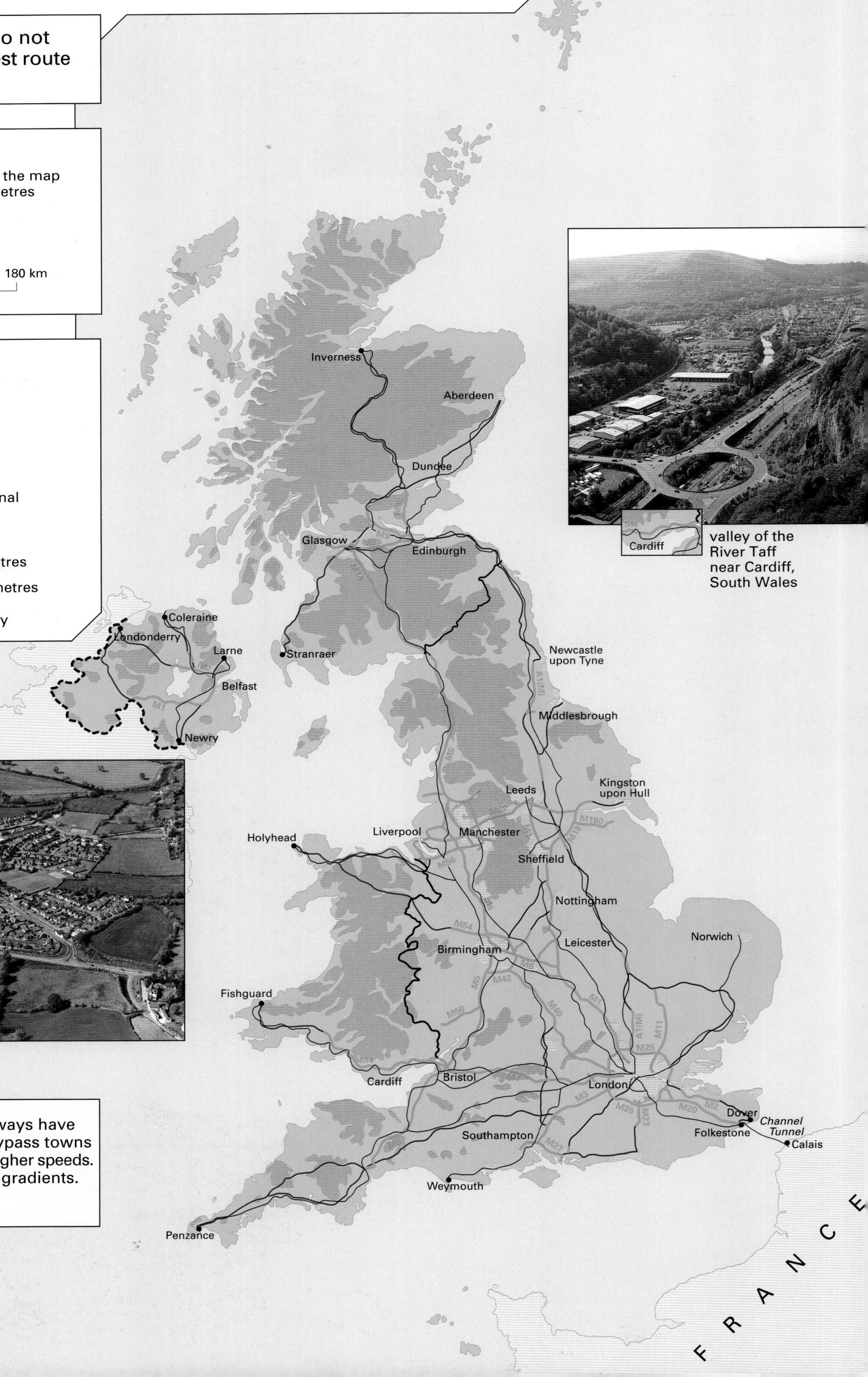

valley of the River Taff near Cardiff, South Wales

bypass

Modern roads and motorways have gentle curves and often bypass towns to allow traffic to move at higher speeds. Rail networks avoid steep gradients.

Transverse Mercator Projection

Key

- country boundary
- main United Kingdom airways
- other airways
- major United Kingdom airport
- other major airport
- car ferry route
- major car ferry port
- major United Kingdom sea port
- built-up areas

Scale

90 km — One centimetre on the map measures 90 kilometres on the ground.

1 cm

0 — 90 — 180 — 270 — 360 km

Ports and airports link the United Kingdom with the rest of the world.

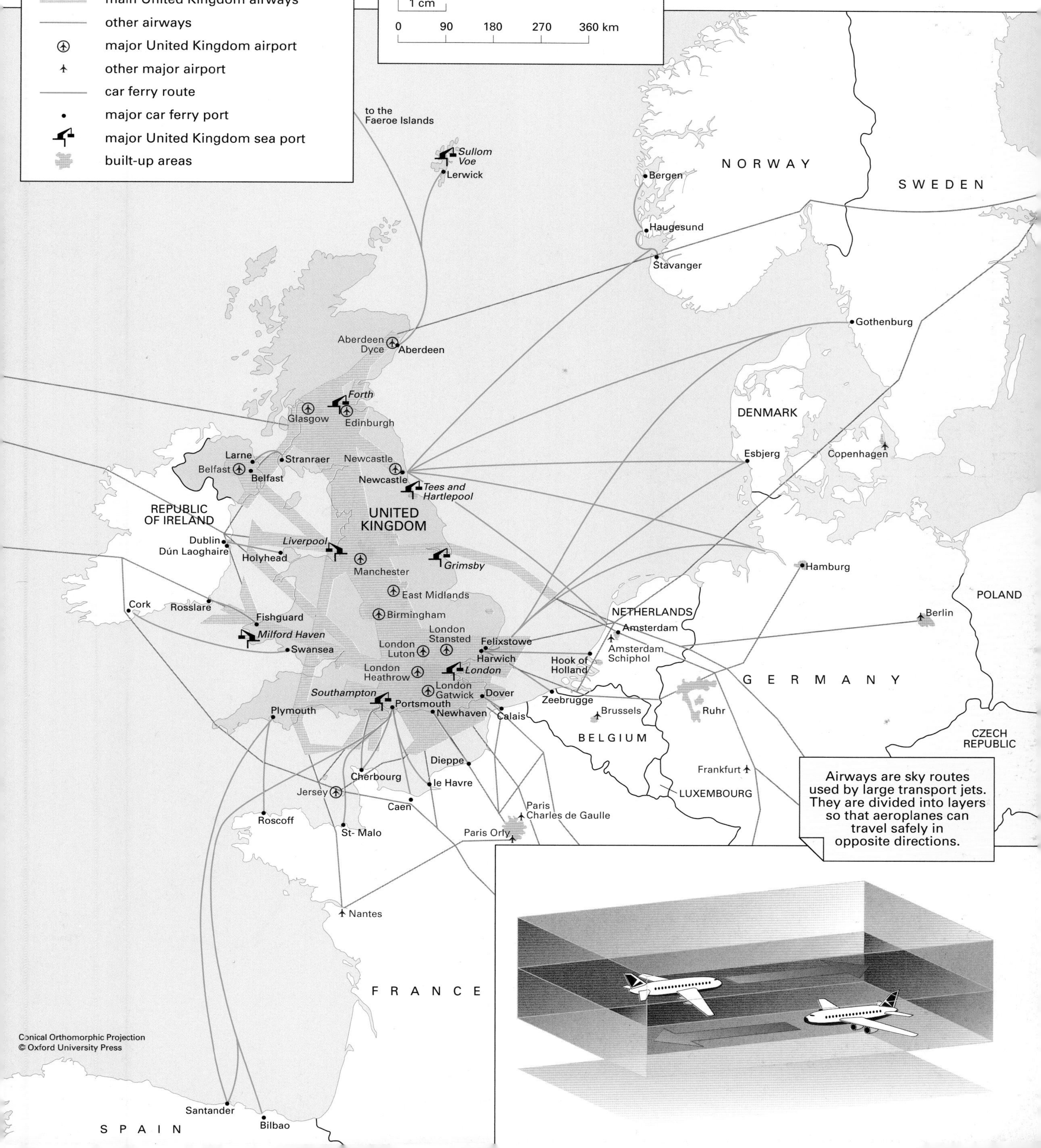

Airways are sky routes used by large transport jets. They are divided into layers so that aeroplanes can travel safely in opposite directions.

The United Kingdom Pollution

Damage to our land, sea, and air is called pollution.

Scale

45 km — One centimetre on the map measures 45 kilometres on the ground.

1 cm

0 45 90 135 180 km

Key

- built-up areas
- most polluted rivers and estuaries
- most polluted coasts and beaches

Areas affected by acid rain

- heavy pollution
- moderate pollution
- light pollution

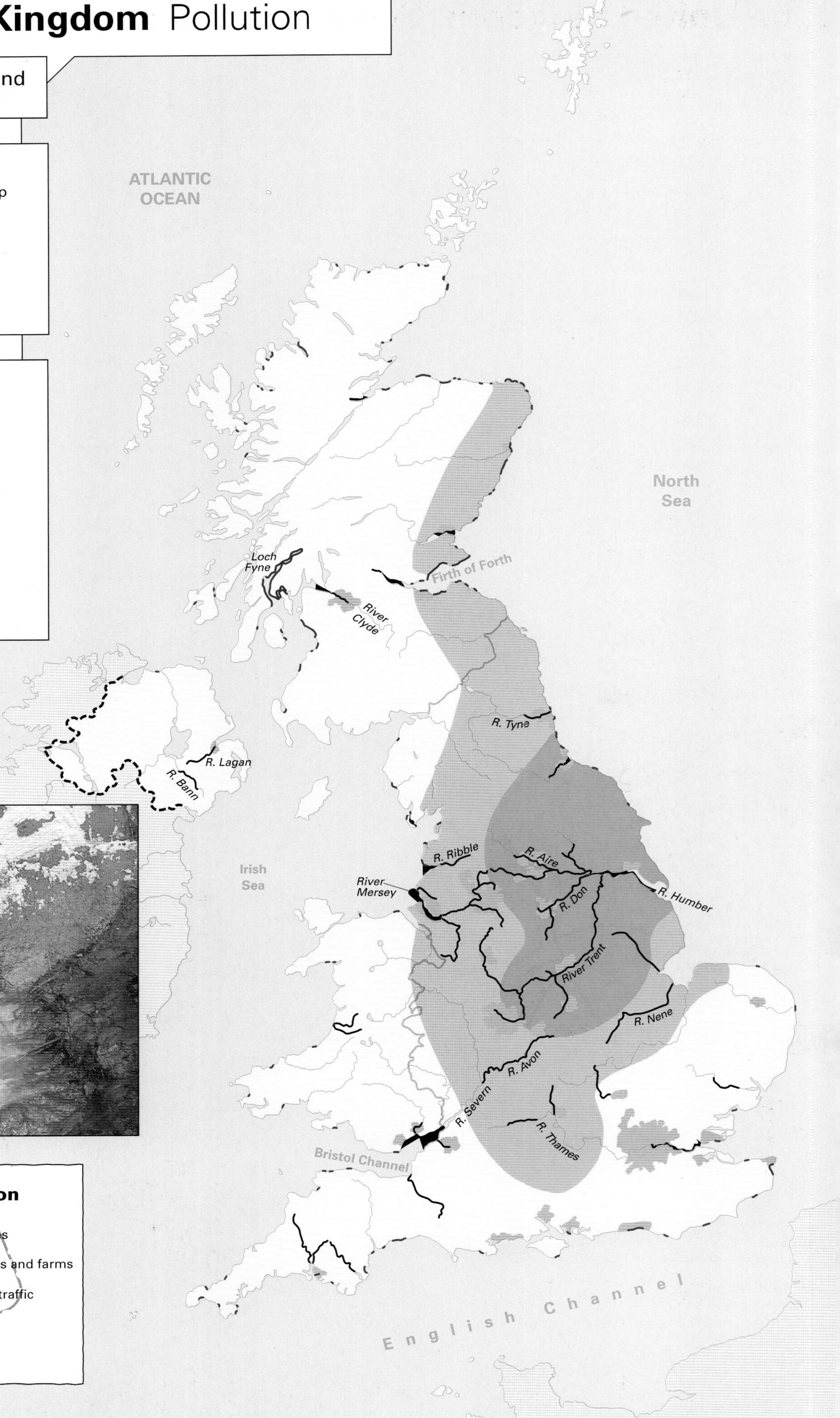

How to fight pollution

- Poisonous gases from cars and factories
- Poisonous waste in rivers from factories and farms
- Loud noise from aircraft, factories and traffic
- Dumping raw sewage in the sea
- Leaving litter

Tranverse Mercator Projection

The United Kingdom Conservation

Protecting nature, resources, and buildings is called conservation.

Scale

45 km

One centimetre on the map measures 45 kilometres on the ground.

1 cm

0 45 90 135 180 km

Key

- National Parks
- areas of outstanding scenery and beauty
- protected coast
- ★ World Heritage Sites
- major built-up areas

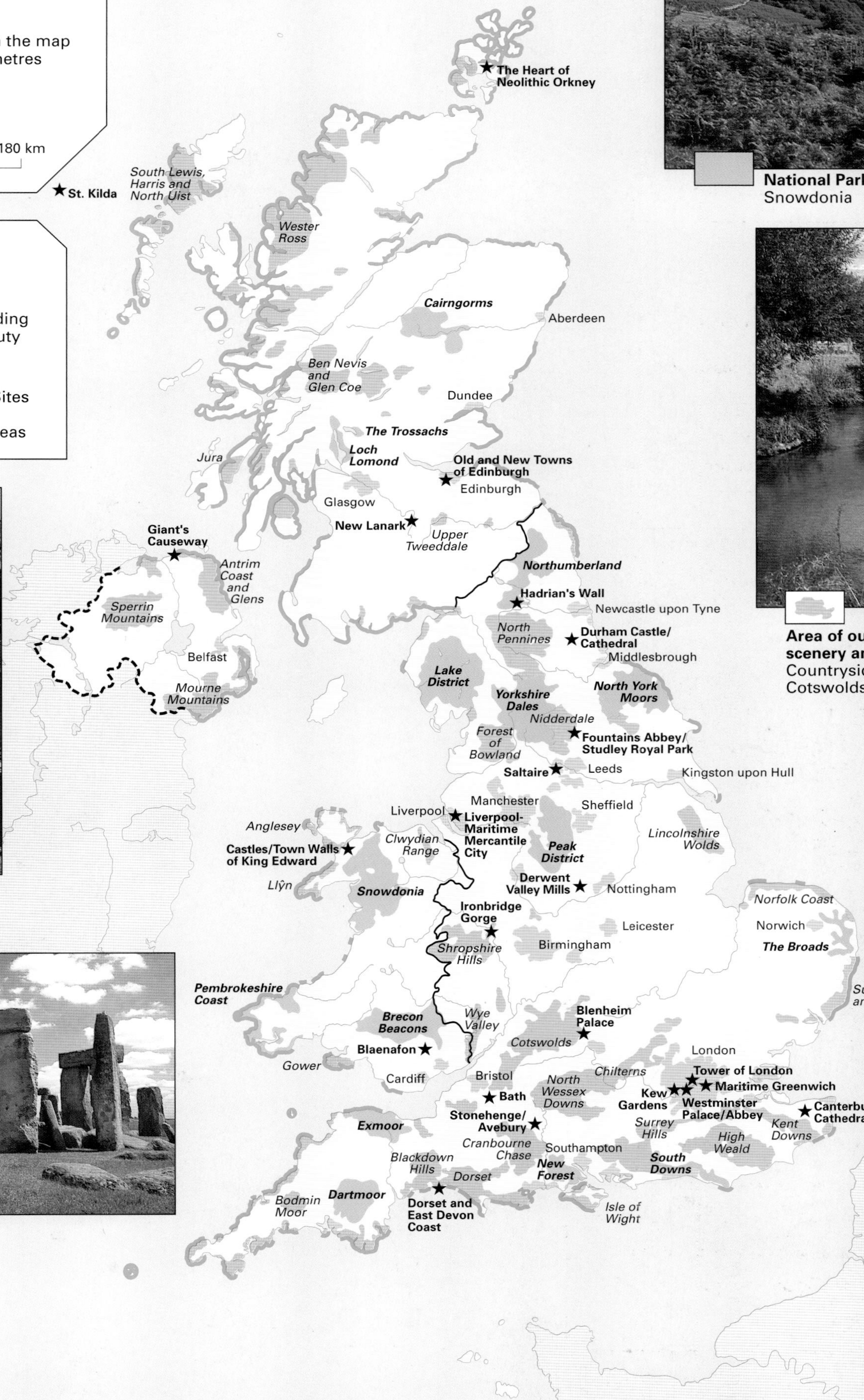

National Park
Snowdonia

Area of outstanding scenery and beauty
Countryside in the Cotswolds

Protected coast
Pembrokeshire Coast

World Heritage Site
Stonehenge, Wiltshire

Transverse Mercator Projection

Europe Countries

Europe is the smallest continent but is the most crowded.

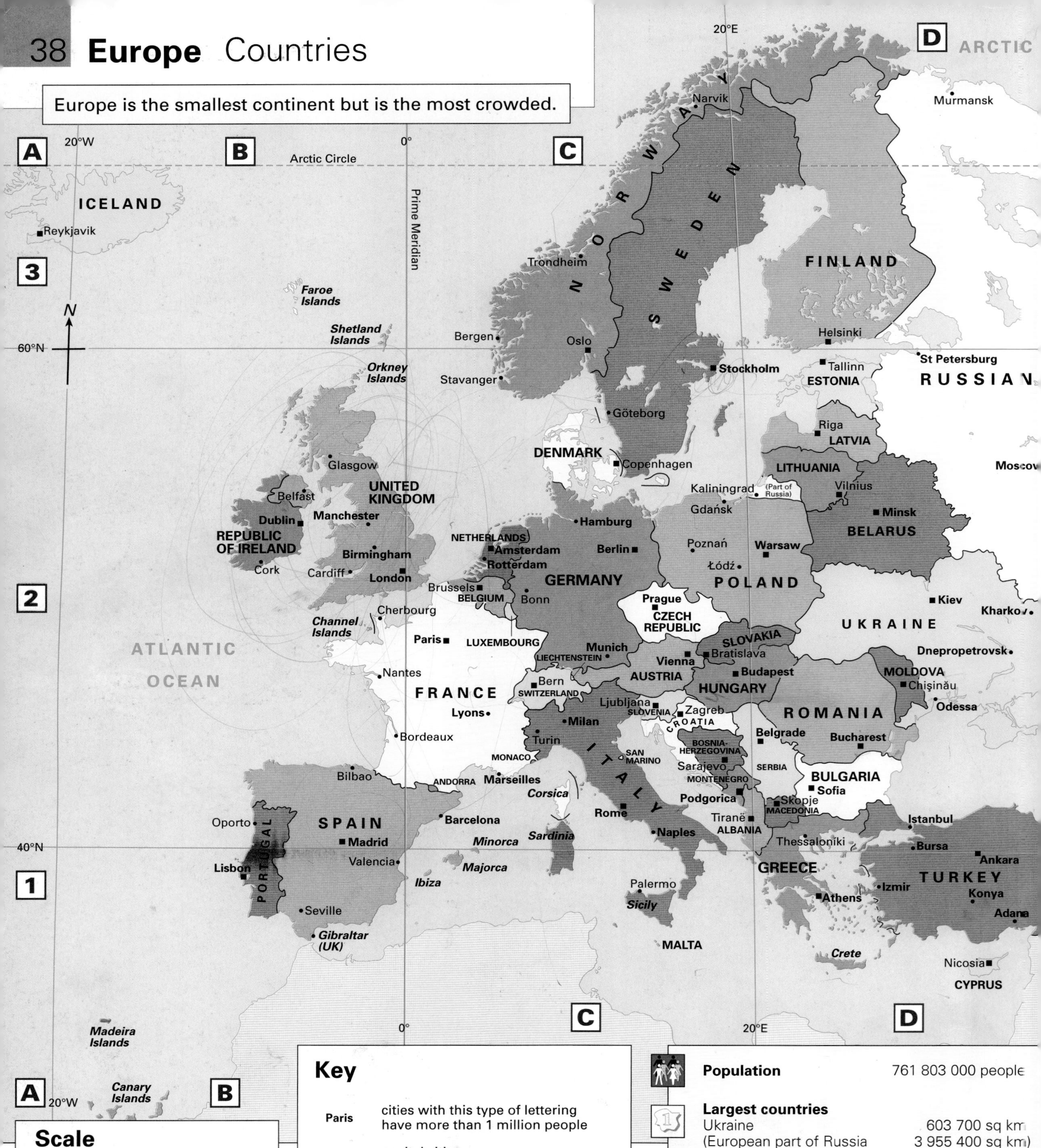

Scale

300 km — One centimetre on the map measures 300 kilometres on the ground at the Equator.

1 cm

0 — 300 — 600 — 900 — 1200 km

Key

Paris	cities with this type of lettering have more than 1 million people
■	capital cities
•	other cities
ITALY	the names of countries are shown in this type of lettering
~	country boundary

Population	761 803 000 people
Largest countries	
Ukraine	603 700 sq km
(European part of Russia)	3 955 400 sq km)
Countries with the most people	
Germany	82 690 000 people
(European part of Russia	106 603 000 people)
Largest cities	
Moscow (Russia)	13 550 000 people
London (UK)	11 950 000 people
Istanbul (Turkey)	11 100 000 people

Modified Gall Projection

The European Union

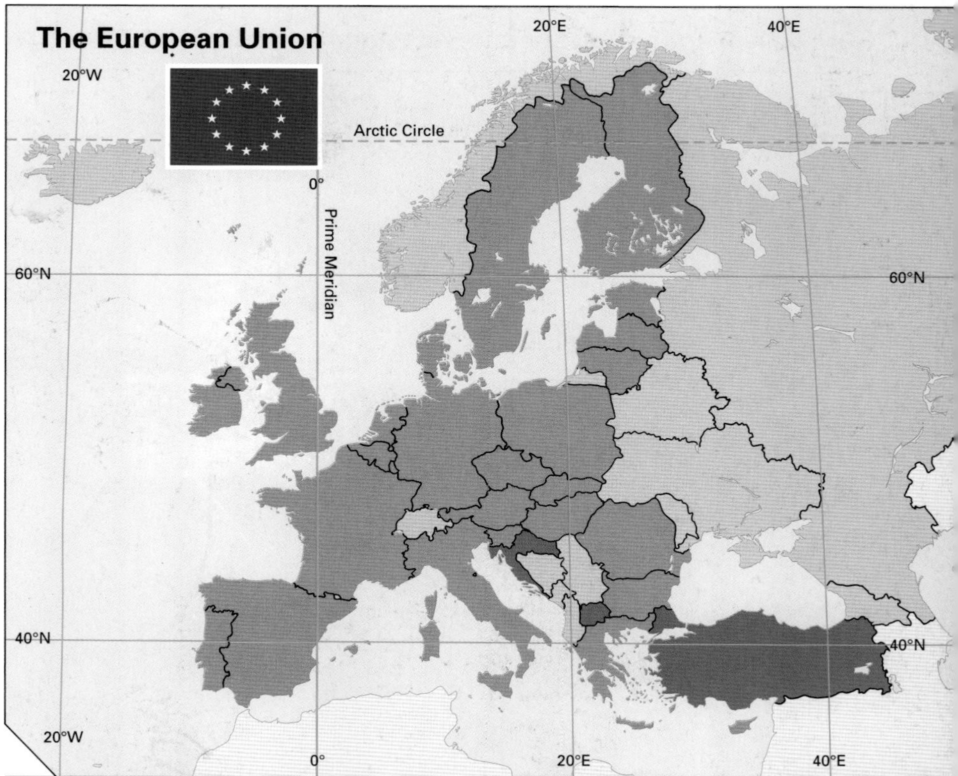

The European Union

The European Union is a group of countries which have agreed to work together and share the same plans for industry, agriculture, transport, and trade.

Key

- country boundary
- countries which are members of the European Union
- countries which have applied to be members of the European Union
- other European countries

Scale for both small maps

650 km / 1 cm

One centimetre on the map measures 650 kilometres on the ground at the Equator.

0 650 1300 1950 2600 km

How big is Europe?

See how long journeys within Europe take, by air and by rail

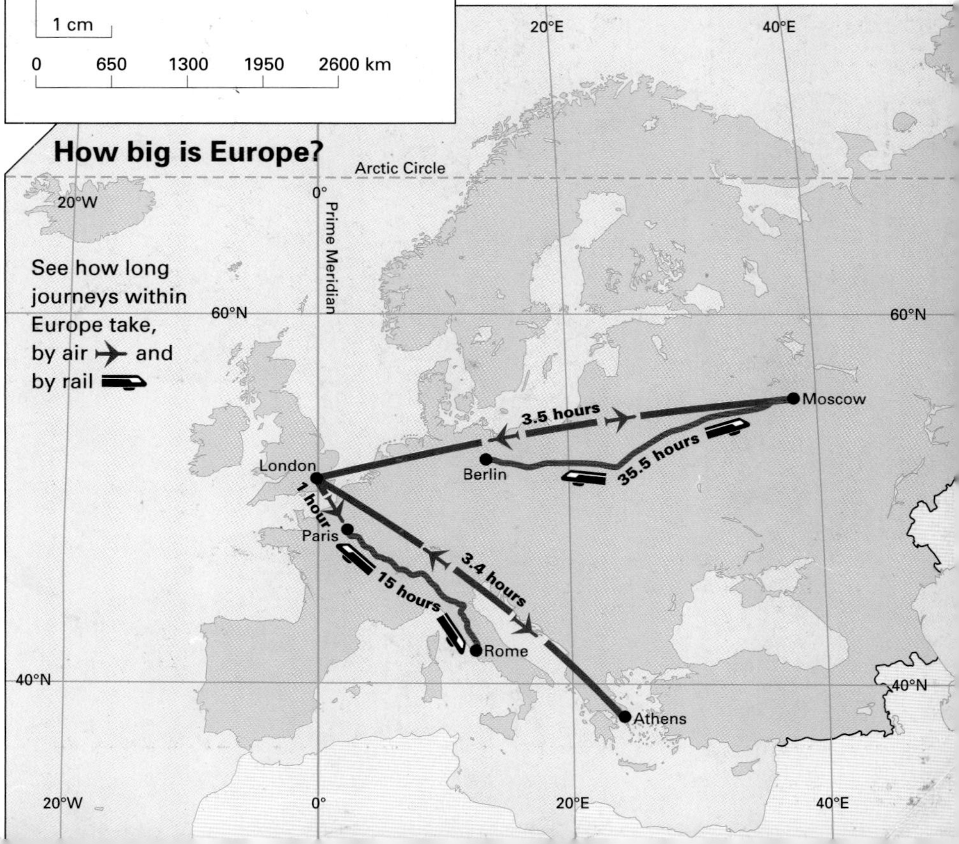

Modified Gall Projection

Europe Land height and rivers

Europe is a continent of peninsulas and islands.

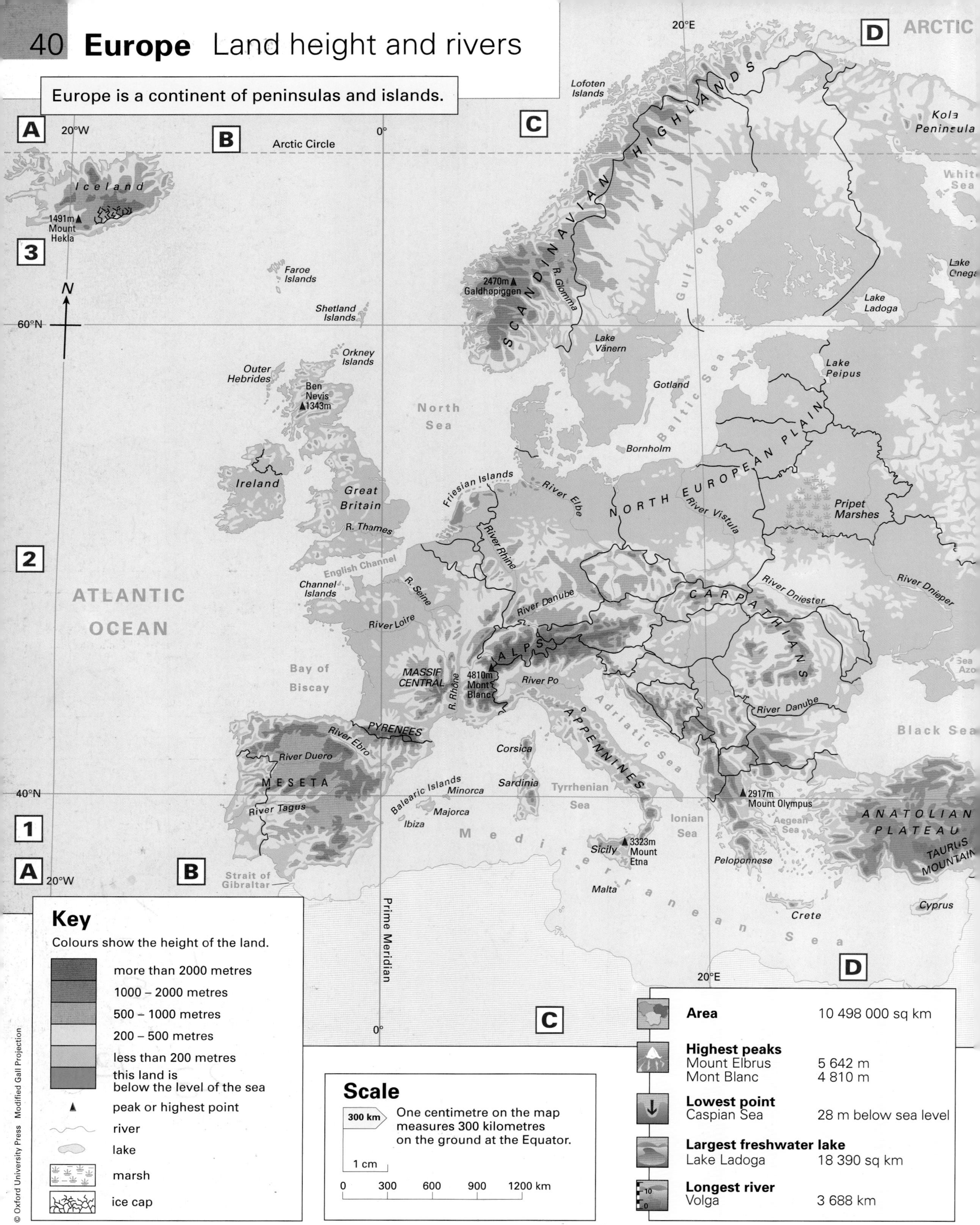

Key

Colours show the height of the land.

- more than 2000 metres
- 1000 – 2000 metres
- 500 – 1000 metres
- 200 – 500 metres
- less than 200 metres
- this land is below the level of the sea
- ▲ peak or highest point
- river
- lake
- marsh
- ice cap

Scale

300 km

One centimetre on the map measures 300 kilometres on the ground at the Equator.

1 cm

0 300 600 900 1200 km

Area	10 498 000 sq km
Highest peaks	
Mount Elbrus	5 642 m
Mont Blanc	4 810 m
Lowest point	
Caspian Sea	28 m below sea level
Largest freshwater lake	
Lake Ladoga	18 390 sq km
Longest river	
Volga	3 688 km

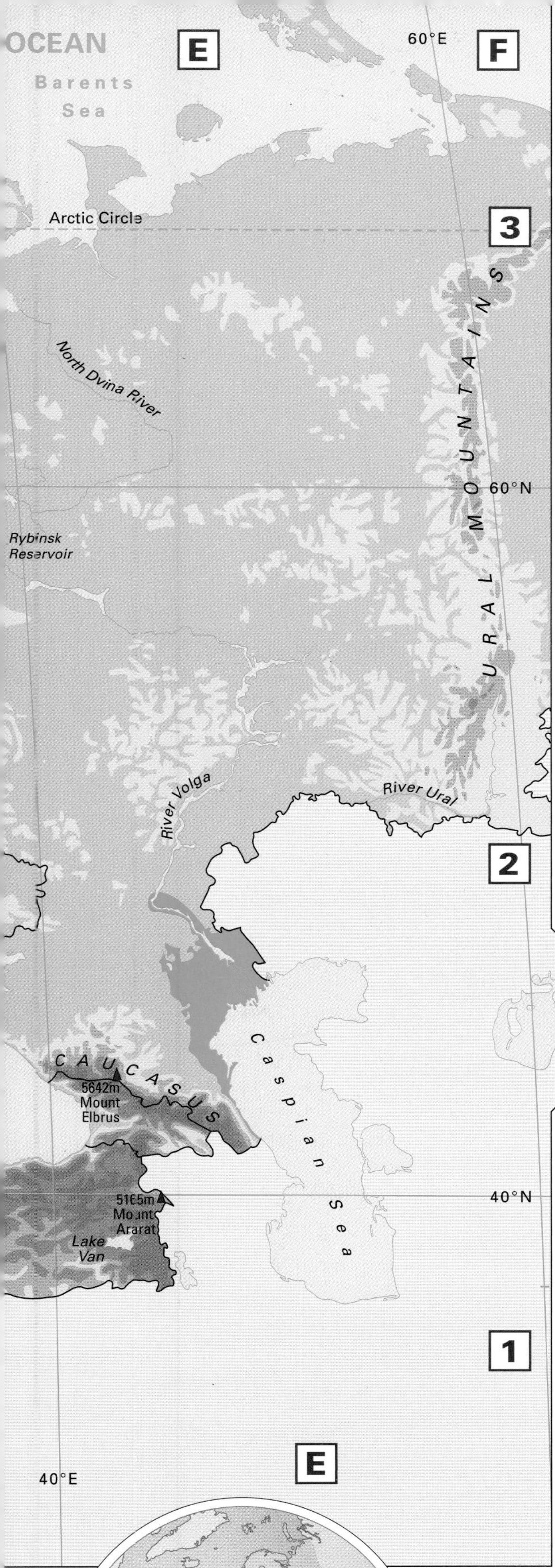

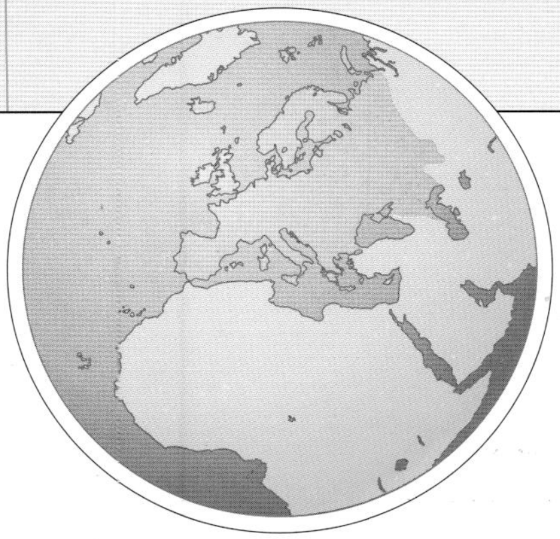

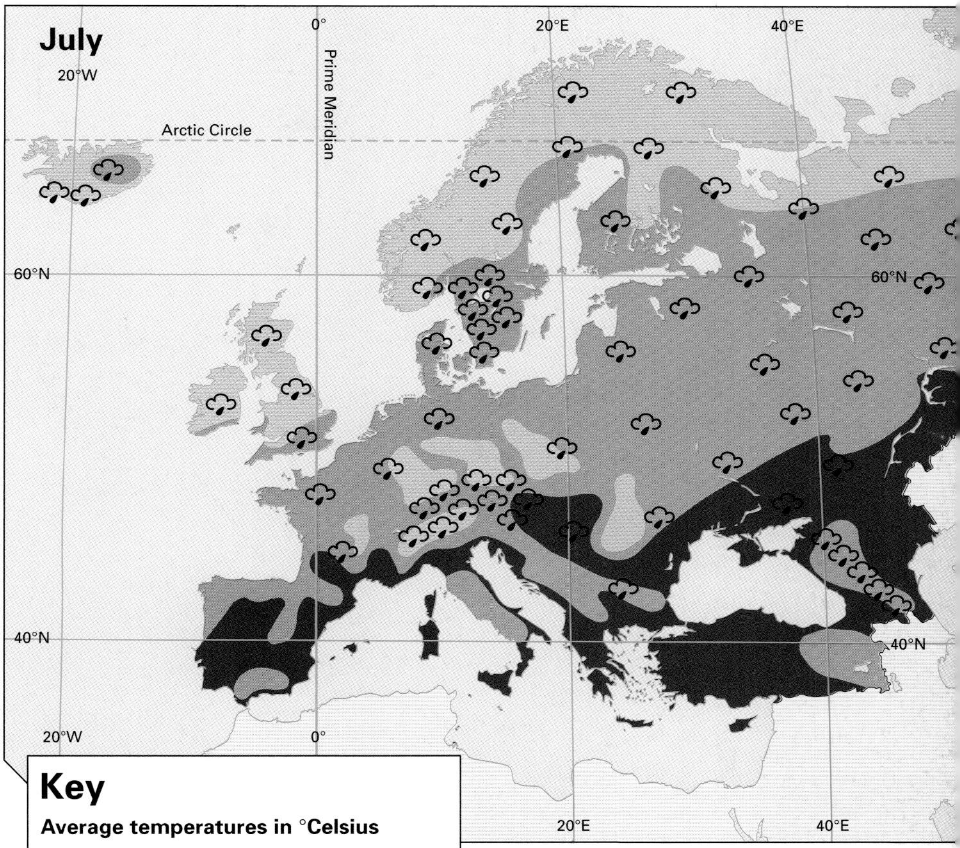

Key

Average temperatures in °Celsius

[black]	above 20	hot
[dark grey]	15 - 20	warm
[light grey]	5 - 15	cool
[grey]	0 - 5	cold
[dark grey]	below 0	very cold

Average monthly rainfall in millimetres

[three rain clouds]	over 100	very wet
[one rain cloud]	50 - 100	wet
[blank]	less than 50	dry

Scale

650 km — One centimetre on the map measures 650 kilometres on the ground.

1 cm

0 650 1300 1950 2600 km

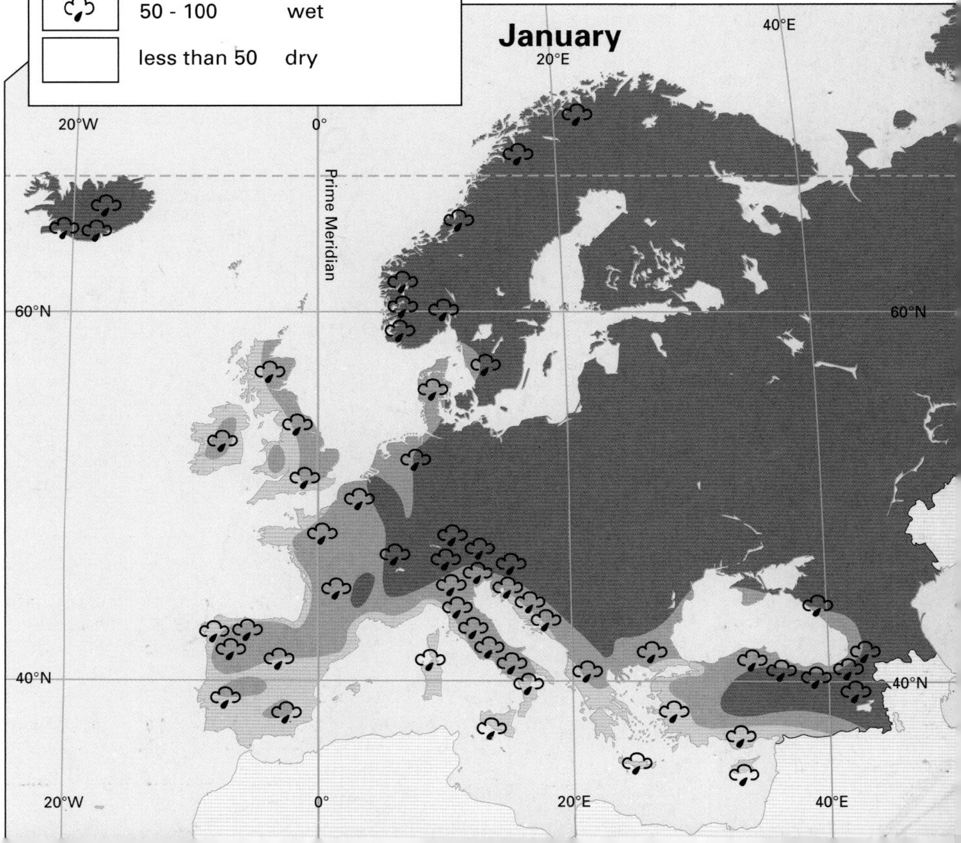

 Modified Gall Projection

Of all the continents, Asia has the greatest variety of landscapes and people.

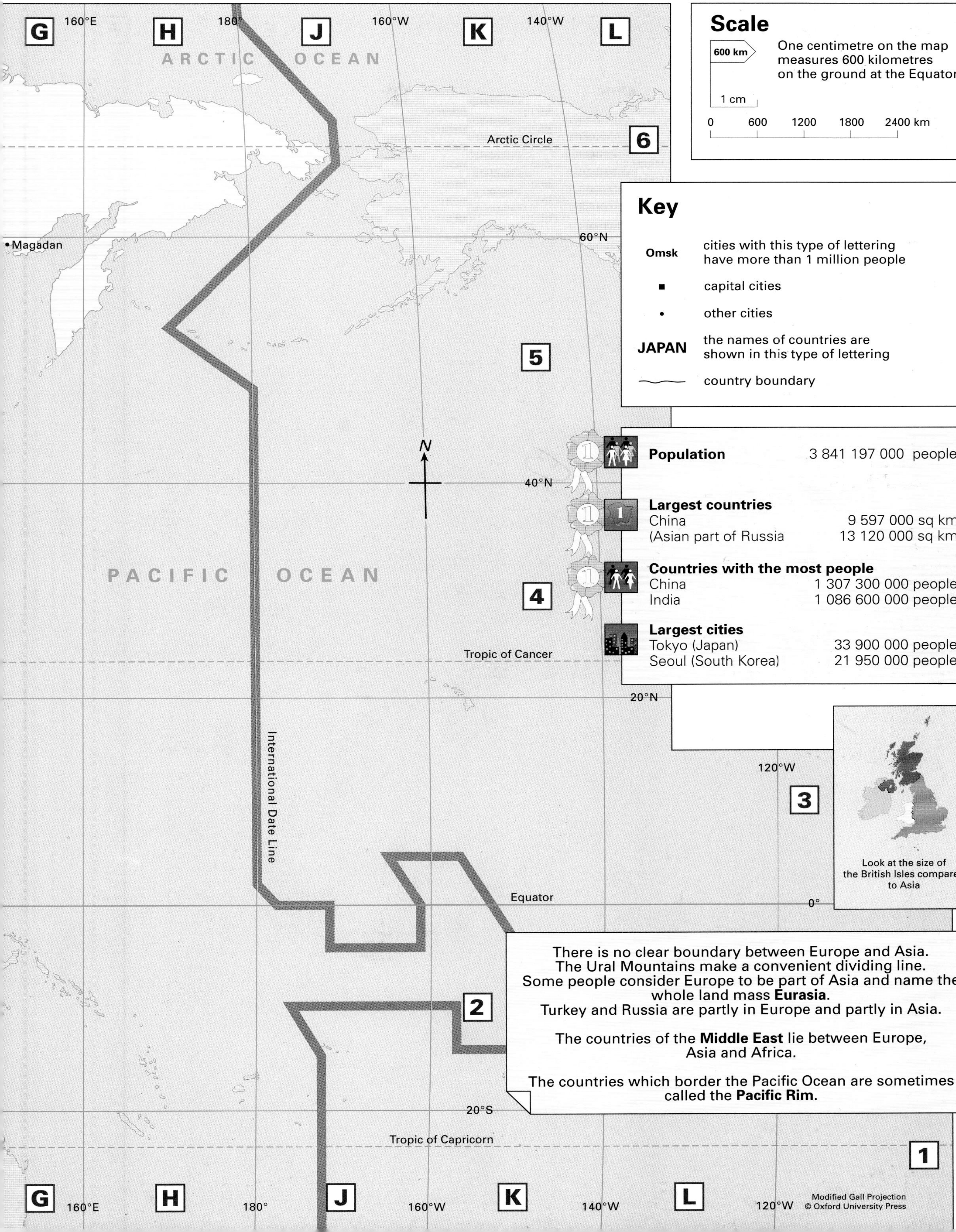

Scale

600 km — 1 cm

One centimetre on the map measures 600 kilometres on the ground at the Equator.

0 | 600 | 1200 | 1800 | 2400 km

Key

Omsk	cities with this type of lettering have more than 1 million people
■	capital cities
•	other cities
JAPAN	the names of countries are shown in this type of lettering
~~	country boundary

Population	3 841 197 000 people
Largest countries	
China	9 597 000 sq km
(Asian part of Russia	13 120 000 sq km)
Countries with the most people	
China	1 307 300 000 people
India	1 086 600 000 people
Largest cities	
Tokyo (Japan)	33 900 000 people
Seoul (South Korea)	21 950 000 people

Look at the size of the British Isles compared to Asia

There is no clear boundary between Europe and Asia. The Ural Mountains make a convenient dividing line. Some people consider Europe to be part of Asia and name the whole land mass **Eurasia**. Turkey and Russia are partly in Europe and partly in Asia.

The countries of the **Middle East** lie between Europe, Asia and Africa.

The countries which border the Pacific Ocean are sometimes called the **Pacific Rim**.

Modified Gall Projection

Asia covers one third of the land surface of the Earth.
A
B
C
D
E
F
1
2
3
4
5
6
20°E
40°E
60°E
80°E
100°E
120°E
140°E
60°N
40°N
20°N
0°
Equator
20°S
Arctic Circle
Tropic of Cancer
Tropic of Capricorn
Barents Sea
URAL MOUNTAINS
SIBERIAN LOWLAND
River Ob
Yenisei River
CENTRAL SIBERIAN PLATEAU
River Lena
Angara River
Lake Baykal
Sea of Okhots
Lake Onega
Lake Ladoga
River Volga
River Irtysh
Lake Balkhash
ALTAI MOUNTAINS
River Amur
Gobi Desert
Black Sea
CAUCASUS
5642m Mount Elbrus
5165m Mount Ararat
Caspian Sea
Aral Sea
Mount Demavend 5671m
7495m Communism Peak
KUNLUN SHAN
HINDU KUSH
8611m K2
TIBETAN PLATEAU
Hwang-Ho River
Hokkaido
Sea of Japan
Korean Peninsula
Honshu
Mount Fuji 3776m
Yellow Sea
Shikoku
Kyushu
R. Tigris
R. Euphrates
ZAGROS MOUNTAINS
River Indus
Arabian Peninsula
Dead Sea 395m below sea level
The Gulf
Red Sea
Thar Desert
HIMALAYAS
Mount Everest 8848m
River Ganges
Brahmaputra R.
Red Basin
Yangtze River
East China Sea
Ryukyu Islands
Irrawaddy River
Salween River
Mekong River
Mouths of the Ganges
Arabian Sea
DECCAN
WESTERN GHATS
Bay of Bengal
Mount Nabi Shu'ayb 3760m
Socotra
Andaman Islands
South China Sea
Luzon
Mindoro
Gulf of Thailand
Andaman Sea
Nicobar Islands
Mount Kinabalu 4101m
Mindanao
Maldive Archipelago
Malay Peninsula
Sumatra
Borneo
Sulawesi
5030m Jaya Peak
New Guinea
Java Sea
Java
Bali
Arafura Sea
Timor Sea
INDIAN OCEAN
Modified Gall Projection
© Oxford University Press

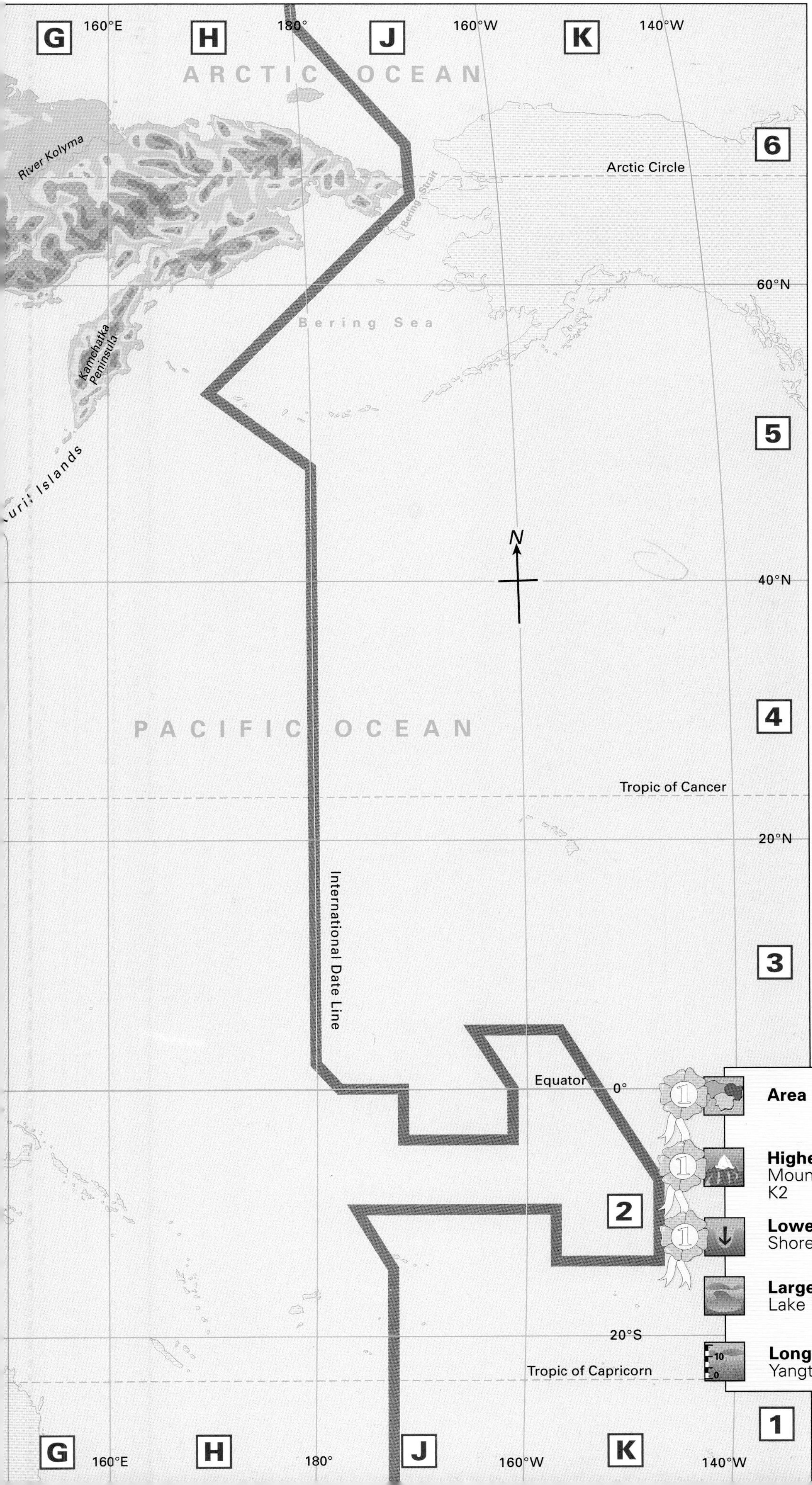

Scale

600 km

1 cm

One centimetre on the map measures 600 kilometres on the ground at the Equator.

0 600 1200 1800 2400 km

Key

Colours show the height of the land.

- more than 5000 metres
- 2000 – 5000 metres
- 1000 – 2000 metres
- 500 – 1000 metres
- 200 – 500 metres
- less than 200 metres
- this land is below the level of the sea
- peak or highest point
- river
- lake
- marsh
- desert
- ice cap

Area	44 387 000 sq km
Highest peaks	
Mount Everest	8 848 m
K2	8 611 m
Lowest point	
Shores of the Dead Sea	395 m below sea level
Largest freshwater lake	
Lake Baykal	30 500 sq km
Longest river	
Yangtze	6 380 km

Modified Gall Projection

Africa Countries

Many countries in Africa have no sea coast.

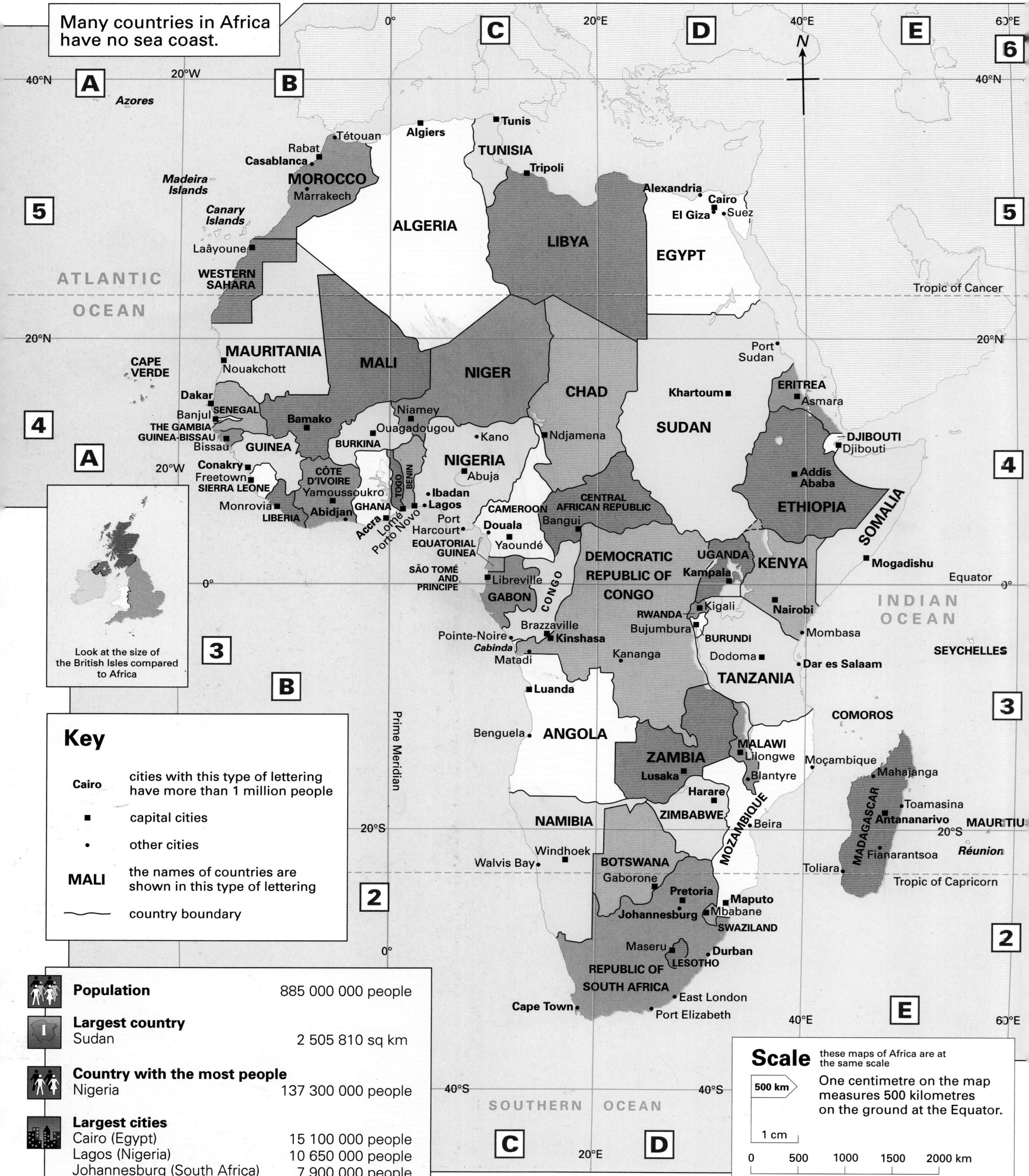

Look at the size of the British Isles compared to Africa

Key

Cairo	cities with this type of lettering have more than 1 million people
■	capital cities
•	other cities
MALI	the names of countries are shown in this type of lettering
~	country boundary

Population	885 000 000 people
Largest country Sudan	2 505 810 sq km
Country with the most people Nigeria	137 300 000 people
Largest cities Cairo (Egypt) Lagos (Nigeria) Johannesburg (South Africa)	 15 100 000 people 10 650 000 people 7 900 000 people

Scale these maps of Africa are at the same scale

500 km — One centimetre on the map measures 500 kilometres on the ground at the Equator.

1 cm

0 500 1000 1500 2000 km

Modified Gall Projection

Almost all of Africa is warm or hot.

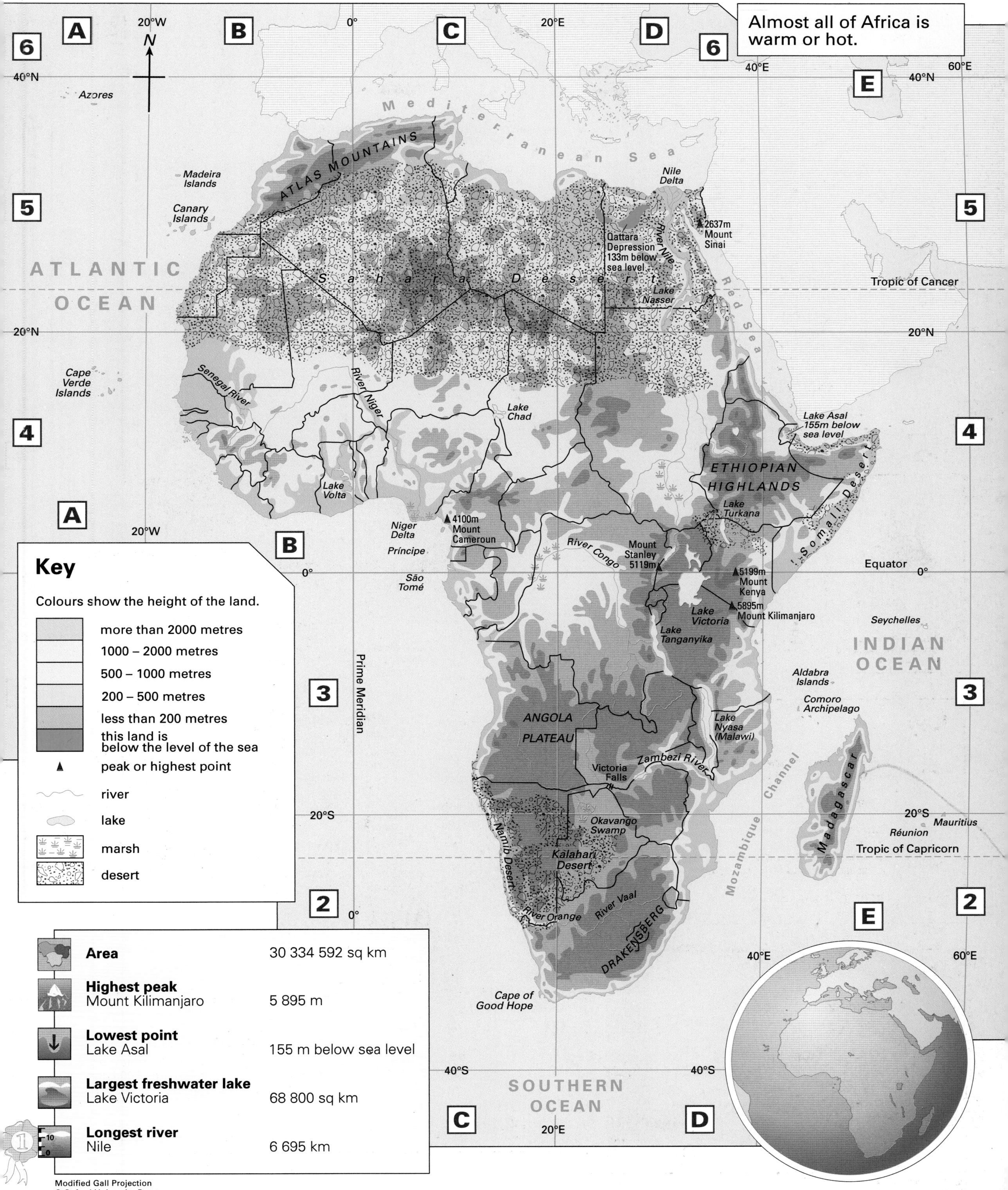

Key

Colours show the height of the land.

- more than 2000 metres
- 1000 – 2000 metres
- 500 – 1000 metres
- 200 – 500 metres
- less than 200 metres
- this land is below the level of the sea
- ▲ peak or highest point
- river
- lake
- marsh
- desert

Area	30 334 592 sq km
Highest peak Mount Kilimanjaro	5 895 m
Lowest point Lake Asal	155 m below sea level
Largest freshwater lake Lake Victoria	68 800 sq km
Longest river Nile	6 695 km

Modified Gall Projection

Oceania is sometimes called Australasia.

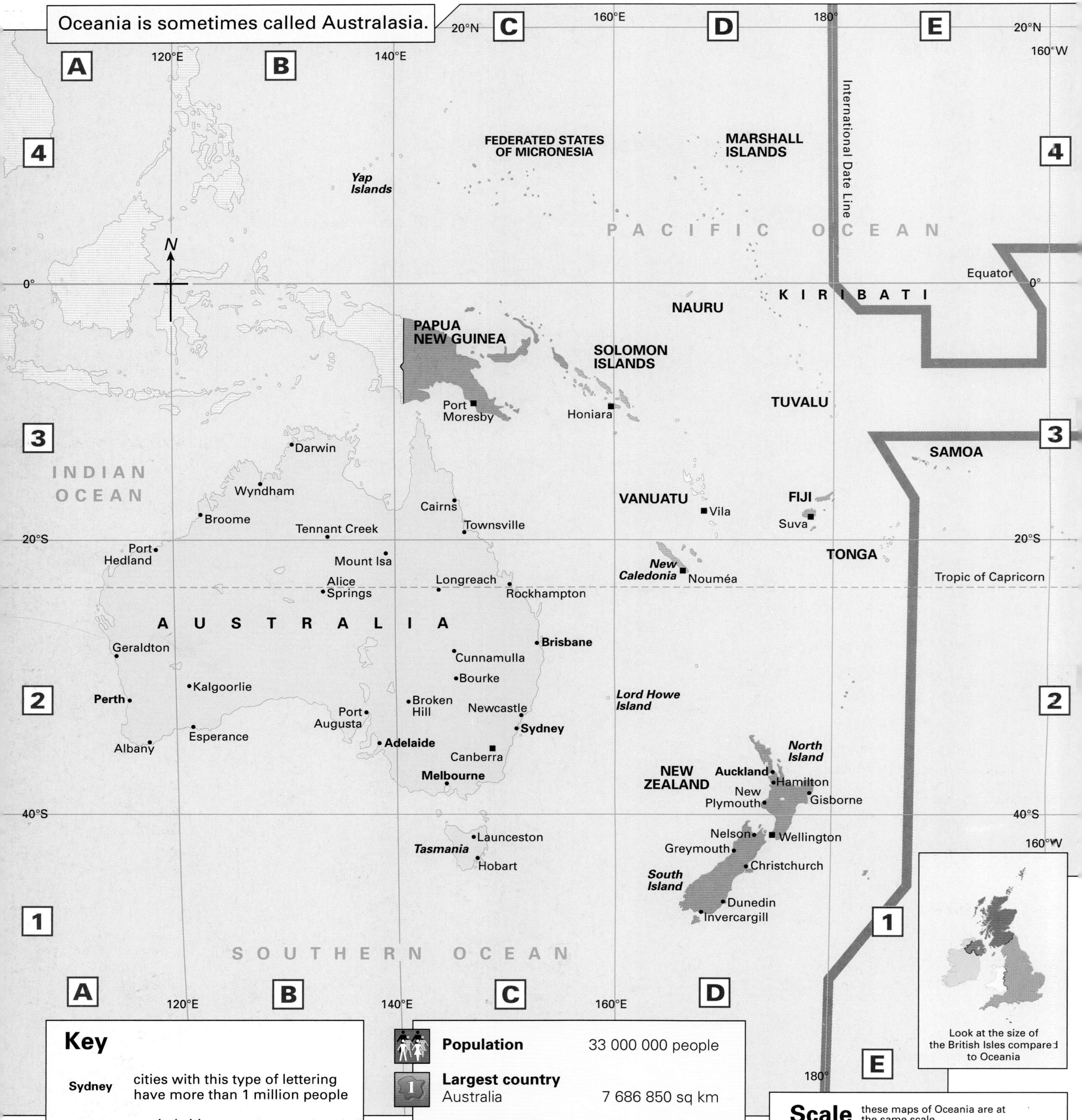

Key

Sydney	cities with this type of lettering have more than 1 million people
■	capital cities
•	other cities
FIJI	the names of countries are shown in this type of lettering
~	country boundary

Population	33 000 000 people
Largest country Australia	7 686 850 sq km
Country with the most people Australia	20 100 000 people
Largest cities Sydney	4 250 000 people
Melbourne	3 600 000 people
(both these cities are in Australia)	

Scale these maps of Oceania are at the same scale

500 km — 1 cm

One centimetre on the map measures 500 kilometres on the ground at the Equator.

0 500 1000 1500 2000 km

Modified Gall Projection

There are about ten thousand islands spread over a vast area of the central and southern Pacific Ocean.

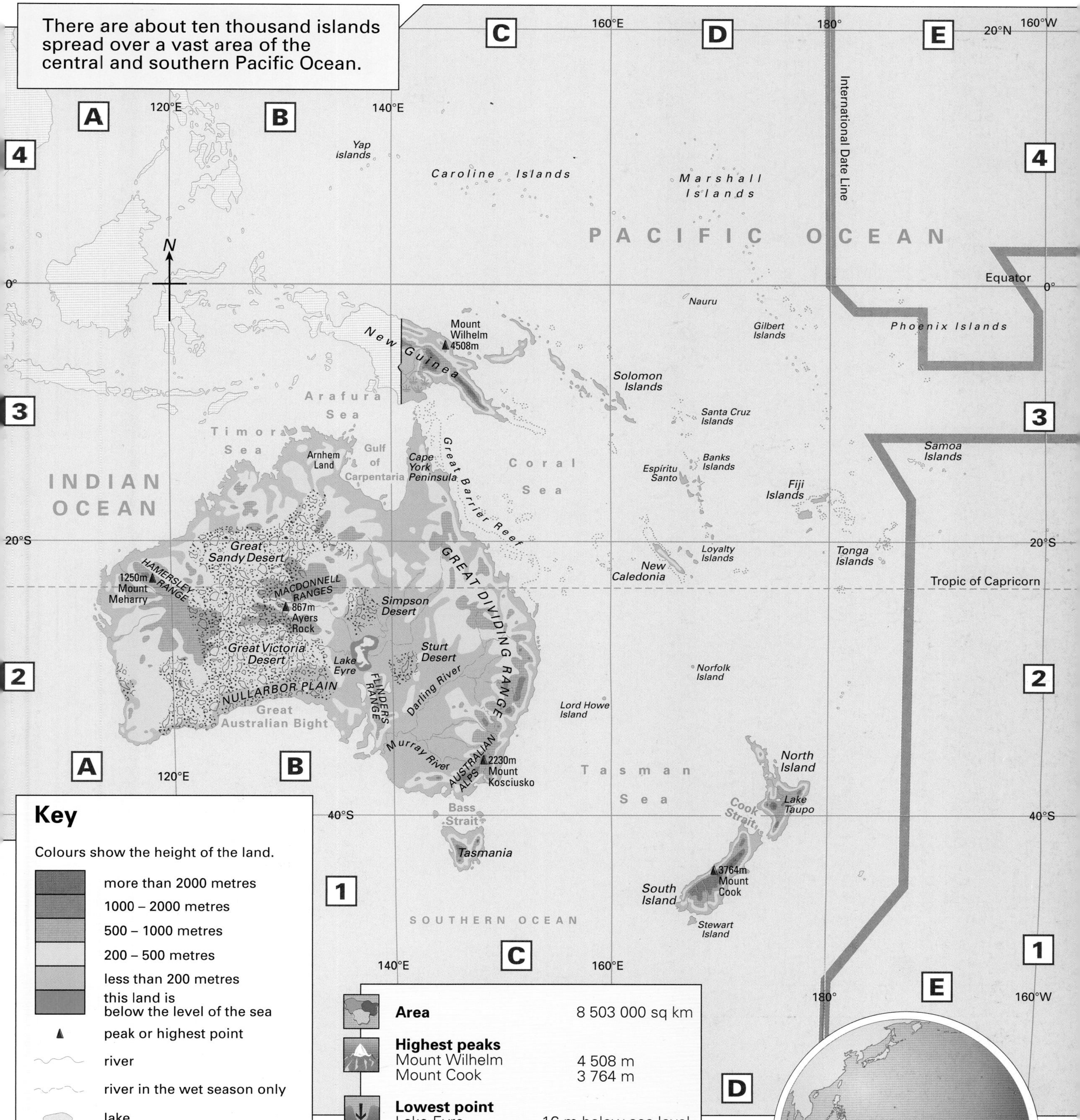

Key

Colours show the height of the land.

- more than 2000 metres
- 1000 – 2000 metres
- 500 – 1000 metres
- 200 – 500 metres
- less than 200 metres
- this land is below the level of the sea
- peak or highest point
- river
- river in the wet season only
- lake
- lake in the wet season only
- marsh
- desert
- coral reef

Area	8 503 000 sq km
Highest peaks	
Mount Wilhelm	4 508 m
Mount Cook	3 764 m
Lowest point	
Lake Eyre	16 m below sea level
Largest lake	
Lake Eyre	9 583 sq km
Longest river	
Murray-Darling	3 750 km

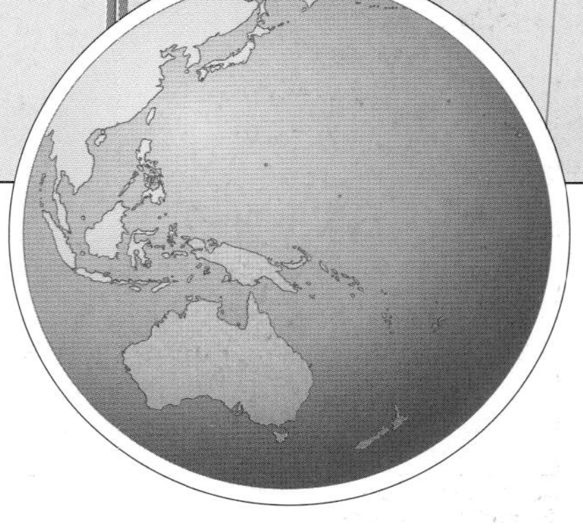

Modified Gall Projection

North America Countries

North America is dominated by the huge countries of the United States and Canada.

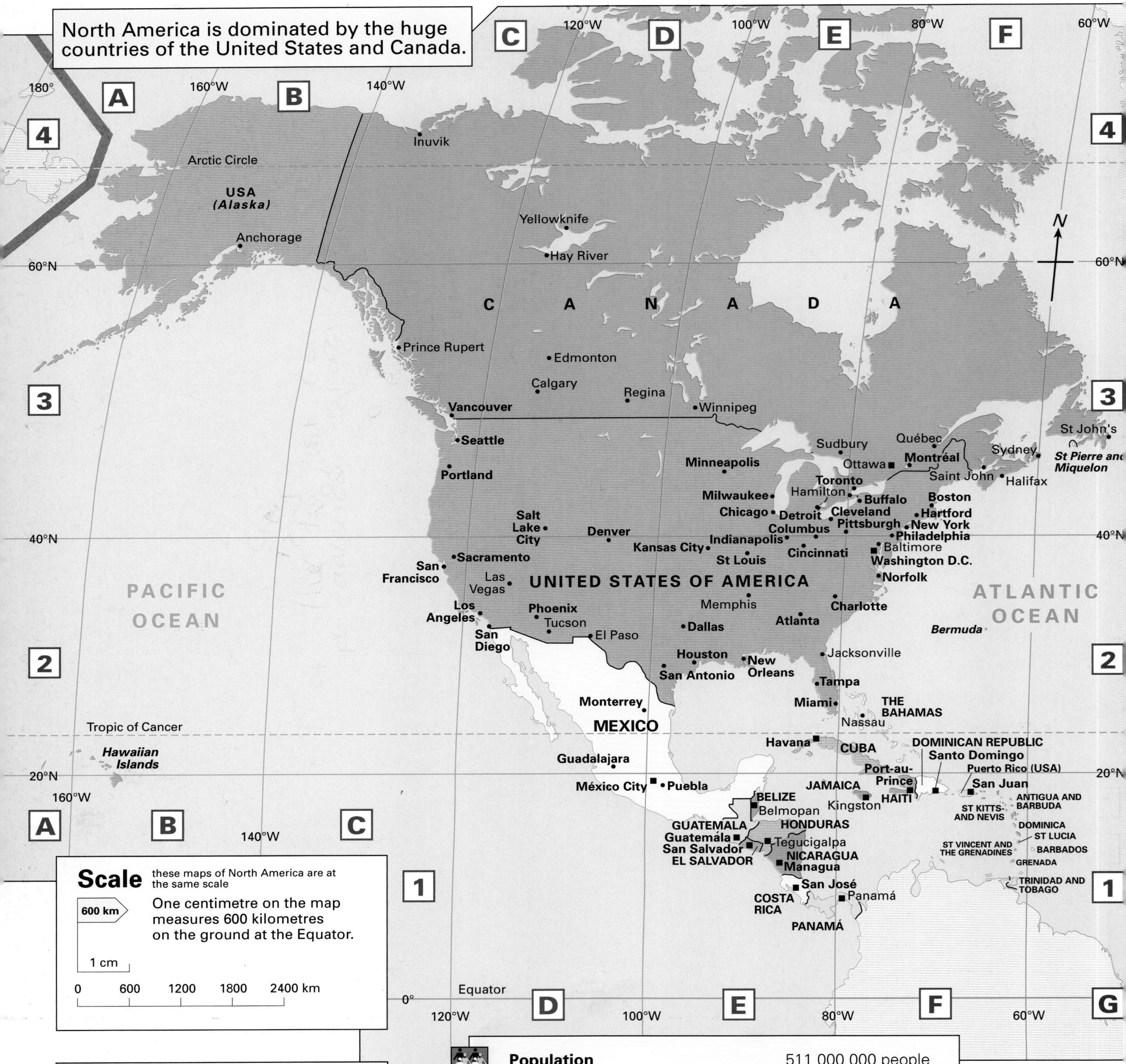

Scale these maps of North America are at the same scale

One centimetre on the map measures 600 kilometres on the ground at the Equator.

600 km

1 cm

0 600 1200 1800 2400 km

Key

Miami	cities with this type of lettering have more than 1 million people
■	capital cities
•	other cities
CUBA	the names of countries are shown in this type of lettering
⁓	country boundary

Population	511 000 000 people
Largest countries	
Canada	9 976 140 sq km
United States of America (USA)	9 629 091 sq km
(The world's longest border is between the United States and Canada.)	
Country with the most people	
United States of America	293 600 000 people
Largest cities	
México City (Mexico)	22 150 000 people
New York (USA)	21 750 000 people

Look at the size of the British Isles compared to North America

Modified Gall Projection

The huge Rocky Mountain range forms the backbone of North America.

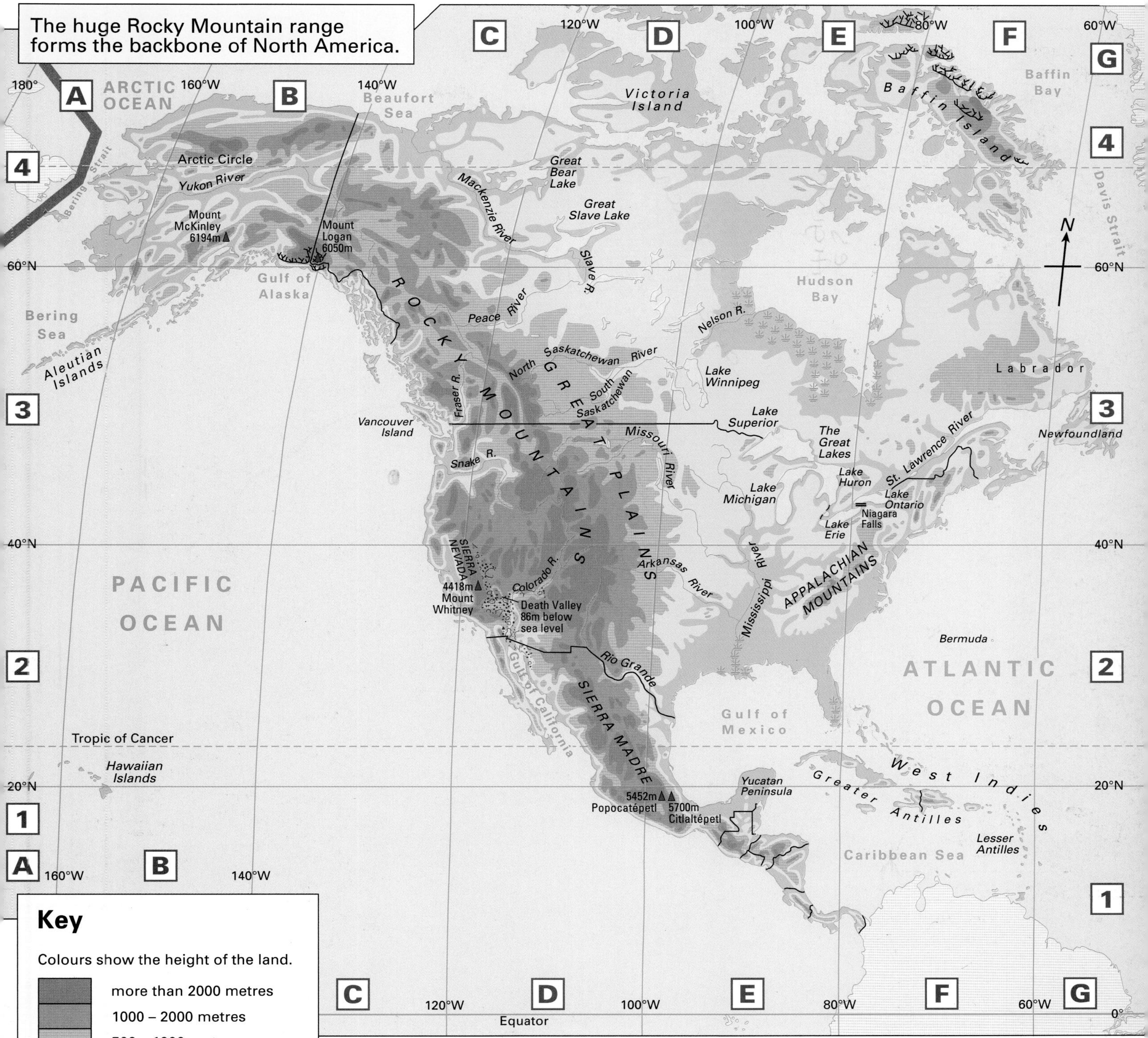

Key

Colours show the height of the land.

- more than 2000 metres
- 1000 – 2000 metres
- 500 – 1000 metres
- 200 – 500 metres
- less than 200 metres
- this land is below the level of the sea
- peak or highest point
- river
- lake
- marsh
- desert
- ice cap

Area	22 656 212 sq km
Highest peak Mount McKinley	6 194 m
Lowest point Death Valley	86 m below sea level
Largest freshwater lake Lake Superior	83 270 sq km
Longest river Mississippi-Missouri	5 969 km

Modified Gall Projection

Brazilians speak Portuguese. Most other South Americans speak Spanish.

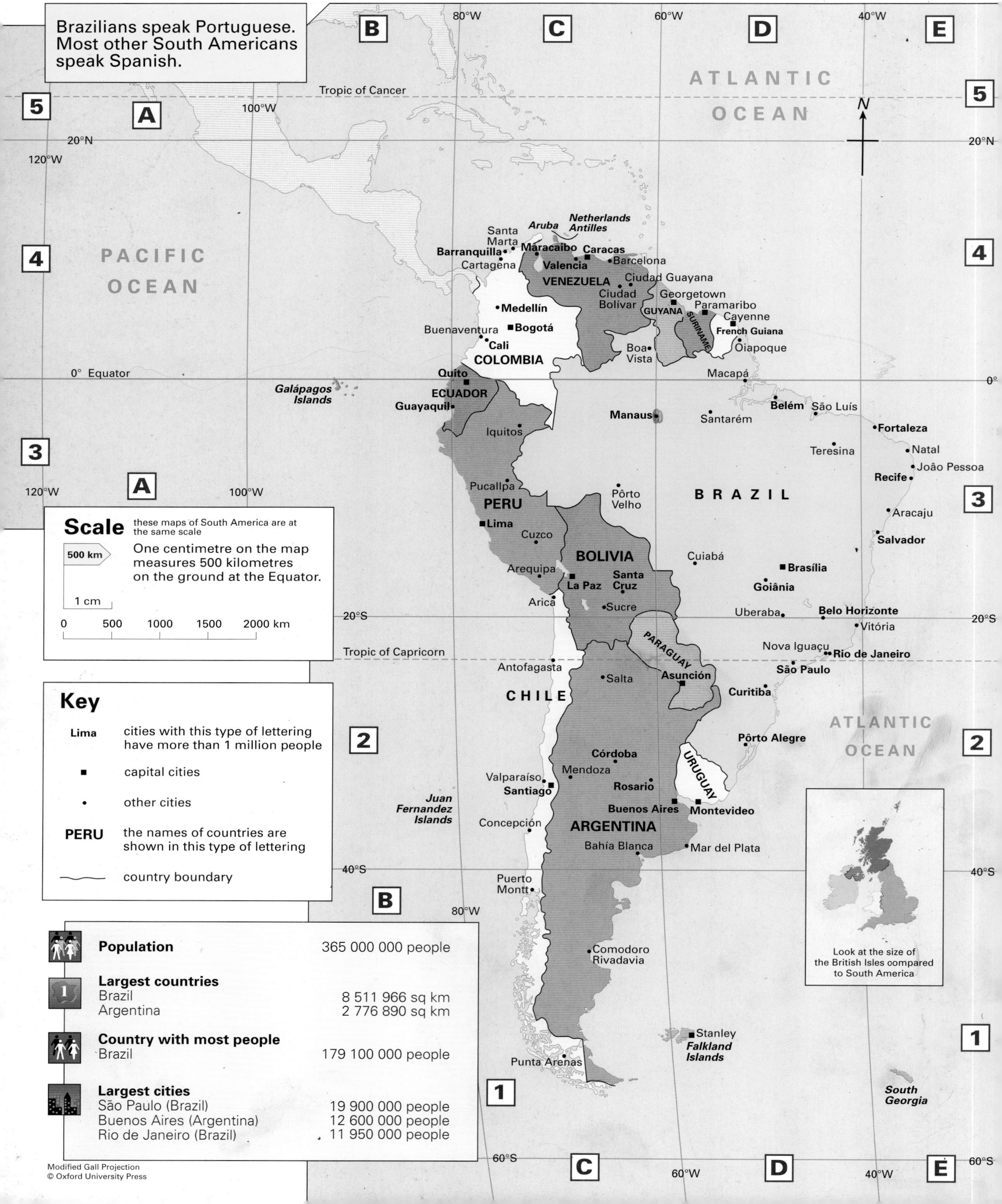

Scale

these maps of South America are at the same scale

500 km — 1 cm

One centimetre on the map measures 500 kilometres on the ground at the Equator.

0 500 1000 1500 2000 km

Key

Lima	cities with this type of lettering have more than 1 million people
■	capital cities
•	other cities
PERU	the names of countries are shown in this type of lettering
～	country boundary

Population	365 000 000 people
Largest countries	
Brazil	8 511 966 sq km
Argentina	2 776 890 sq km
Country with most people	
Brazil	179 100 000 people
Largest cities	
São Paulo (Brazil)	19 900 000 people
Buenos Aires (Argentina)	12 600 000 people
Rio de Janeiro (Brazil)	11 950 000 people

Look at the size of the British Isles compared to South America

Modified Gall Projection

The Amazon rainforest contains half of all known plants and animals in the world.

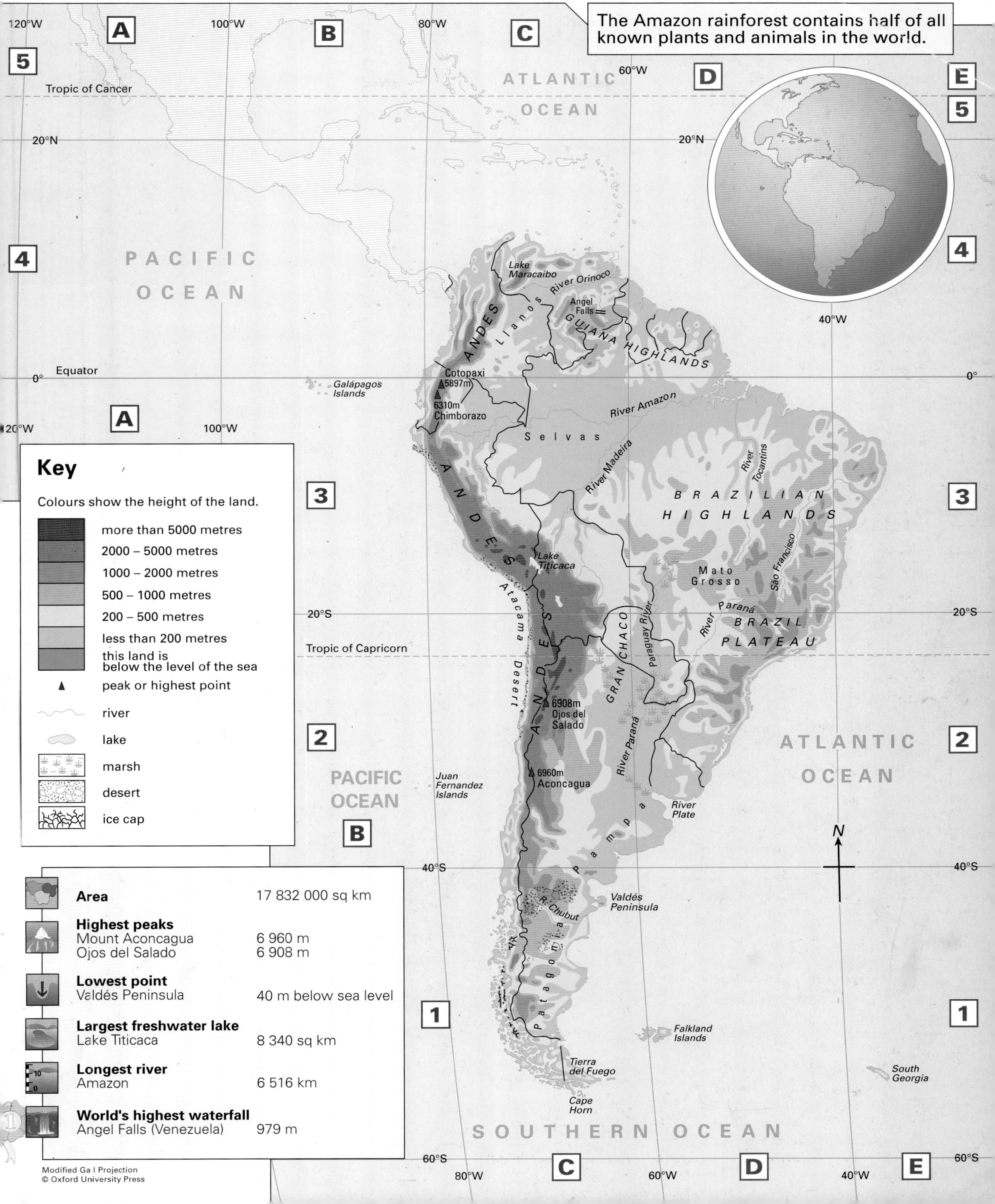

Key

Colours show the height of the land.

- more than 5000 metres
- 2000 – 5000 metres
- 1000 – 2000 metres
- 500 – 1000 metres
- 200 – 500 metres
- less than 200 metres
- this land is below the level of the sea
- ▲ peak or highest point
- river
- lake
- marsh
- desert
- ice cap

Area	17 832 000 sq km
Highest peaks	
Mount Aconcagua	6 960 m
Ojos del Salado	6 908 m
Lowest point	
Valdés Peninsula	40 m below sea level
Largest freshwater lake	
Lake Titicaca	8 340 sq km
Longest river	
Amazon	6 516 km
World's highest waterfall	
Angel Falls (Venezuela)	979 m

Modified Gall Projection

Antarctica

Antarctica has 90% of all of the ice in the world.

the South Pole

Scale

340 km
1 cm

One centimetre on the map measures 340 kilometres on the ground.

0 | 340 | 680 | 1020 | 1360 km

Look at the size of the British Isles compared to Antarctica

Area 13 340 000 sq km

Highest point Vinson Massif 5 140 m

World's longest glacier Lambert Glacier 400 km

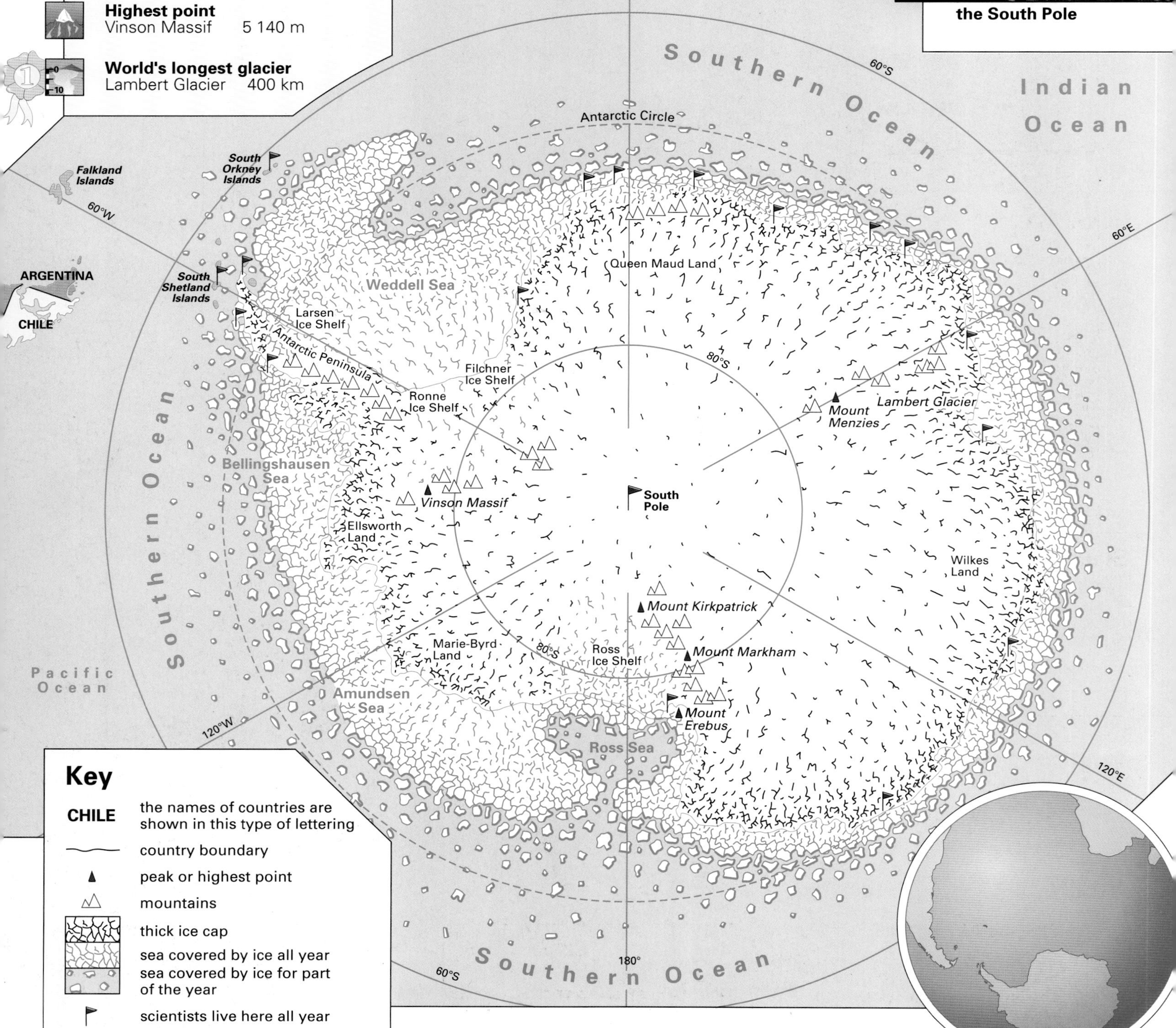

Key

CHILE the names of countries are shown in this type of lettering

country boundary

peak or highest point

mountains

thick ice cap

sea covered by ice all year

sea covered by ice for part of the year

scientists live here all year

Zenithal Equidistant Projection

The Arctic Ocean

Most of the Arctic is a huge frozen ocean.

the North Pole

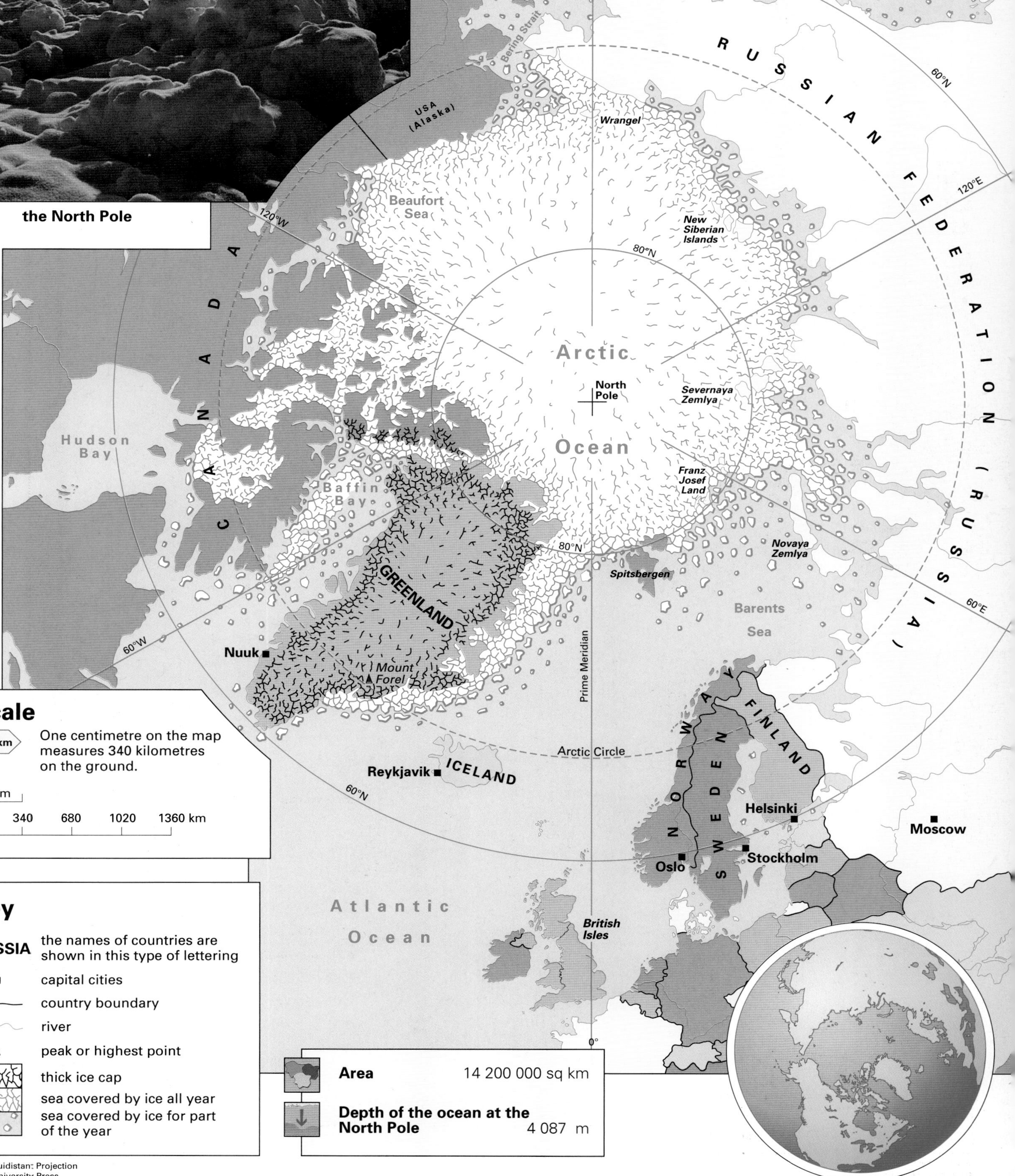

Scale

340 km — One centimetre on the map measures 340 kilometres on the ground.

1 cm

0 | 340 | 680 | 1020 | 1360 km

Key

RUSSIA — the names of countries are shown in this type of lettering

■ capital cities

country boundary

river

▲ peak or highest point

thick ice cap

sea covered by ice all year

sea covered by ice for part of the year

Area	14 200 000 sq km
Depth of the ocean at the North Pole	4 087 m

Zenithal Equidistant Projection

World Land height and rivers

Two-thirds of the surface of the earth is covered with water. The rest is land.

Scale

1050 km

One centimetre on the map measures 1050 kilometres on the ground at the Equator.

1 cm

0 1050 2100 3150 4200 km

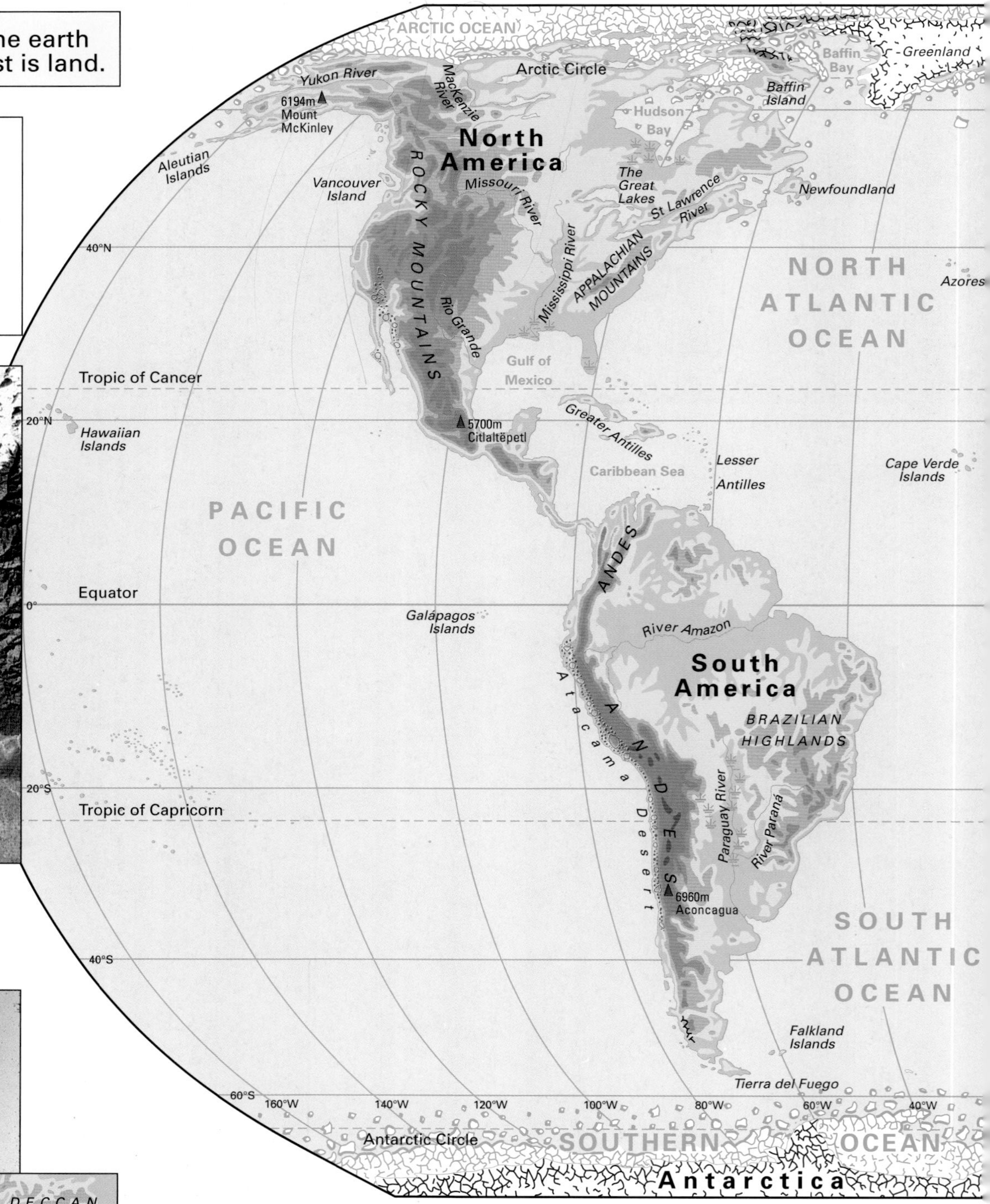

high mountains
The Himalayas seen from space

high hills and plateaux
Deccan, India

Key

Colours show the height of the land

high mountains
- more than 5000 metres

high hills and plateaux
- 2000 – 5000 metres
- 1000 – 2000 metres
- 500 – 1000 metres

plains
- 200 – 500 metres
- less than 200 metres
- this land is below the level of the sea

- ▲ peak or highest point
- river
- lake
- marsh
- desert
- ice on land
- ice on sea

Eckert IV Projection

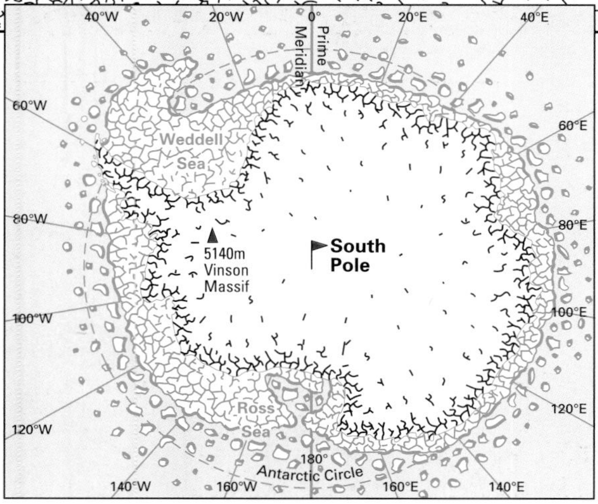

plains
The basin of the River Amazon, Brazil

Eckert IV Projection

Patterns of temperature and rainfall throughout the year make types of climate.

Scale

1050 km — 1 cm

One centimetre on the map measures 1050 kilometres on the ground at the Equator.

0 1050 2100 3150 4200 km

Key

- polar climate
- continental climate
- coastal climate
- Mediterranean climate
- desert climate
- tropical climate
- equatorial climate
- high mountain climate
- * places with record breaking climates

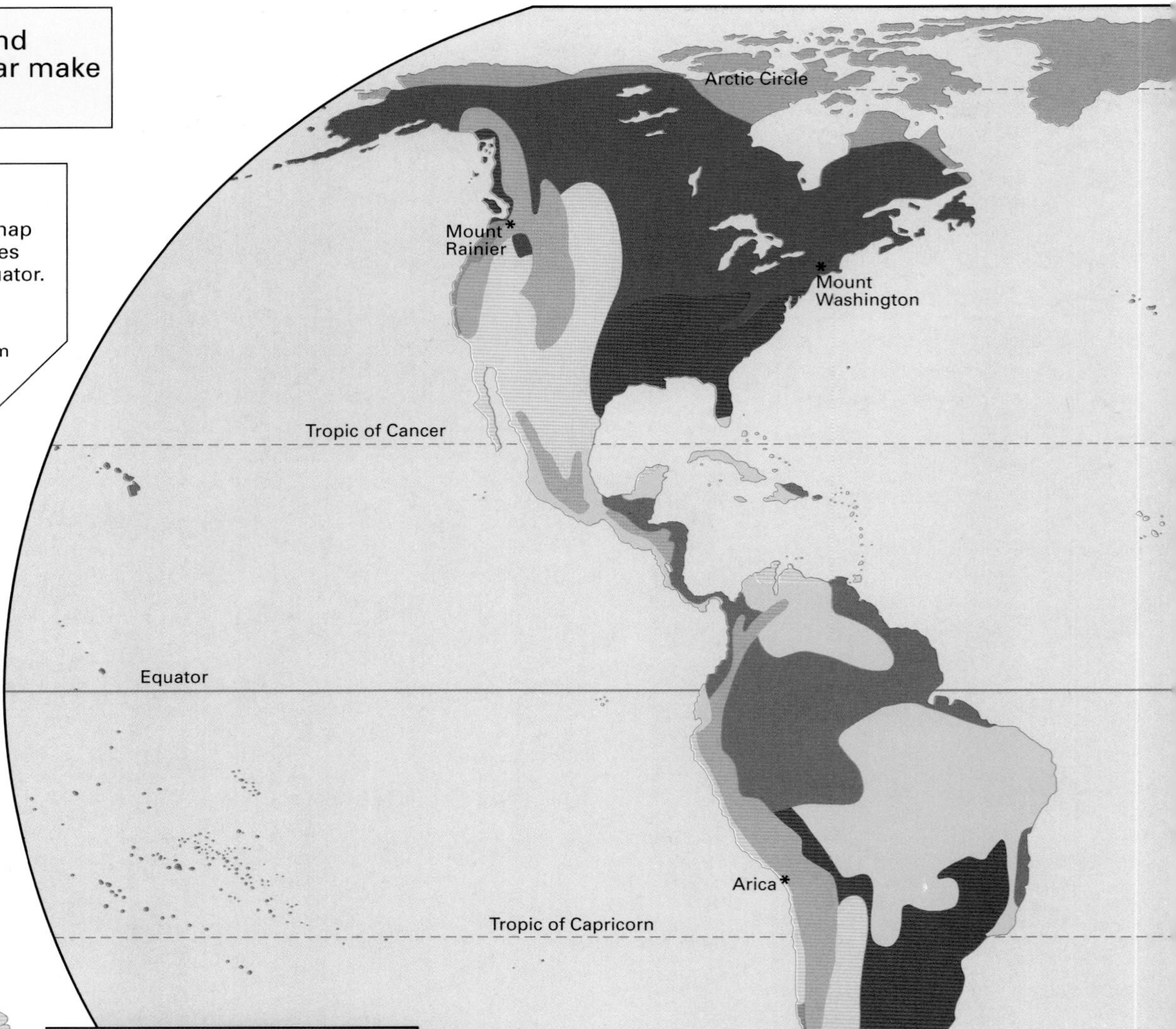
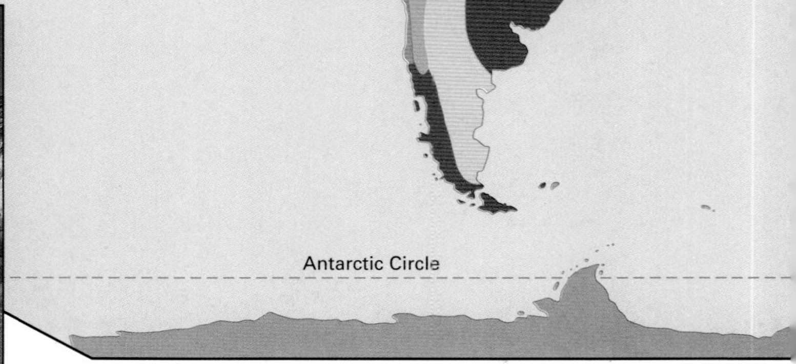

Eckert IV Projection © Oxford University Press

Hottest place
Al' Aziziyah (Libya)

Coldest place
Vostok (Antarctica)

Driest place
Arica, Atacama Desert (Chile)

Wettest place
Mawsynram (India)

Windiest place
Mount Washington (USA)

Snowiest place
Mount Rainier (USA)

polar climate
very cold all year

continental climate
very cold winters, warmer summers

coastal climate
warm summers, mild winters, rain all year

Mediterranean climate
hot dry summers, warm wet winters

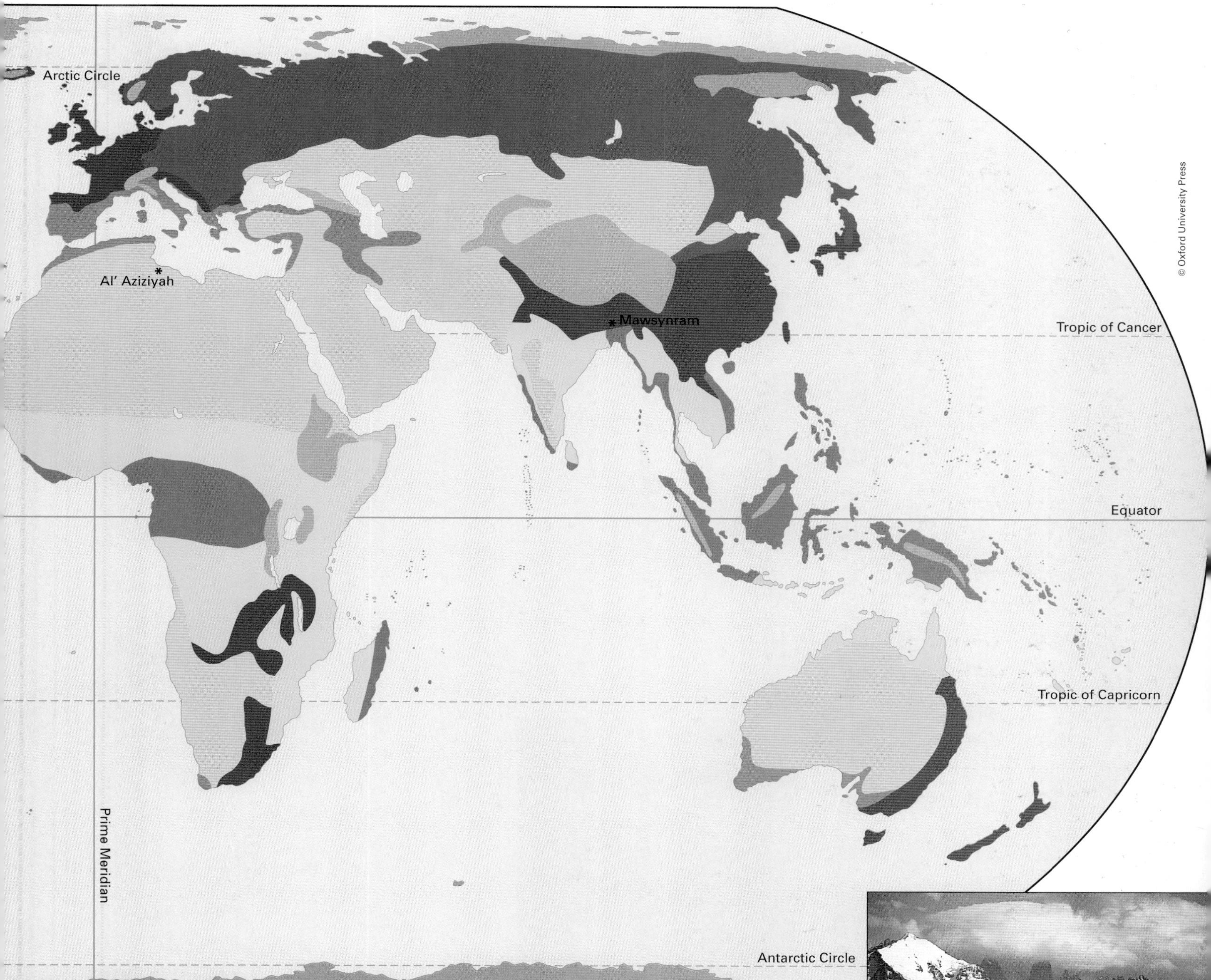

tropical climate
very hot all year with a wet season and a dry season

equatorial climate
very hot and wet all year

high mountain climate
becomes colder with height

desert climate
very dry all year

Environments are our natural and human surroundings.

Scale

1050 km

One centimetre on the map measures 1050 kilometres on the ground at the Equator.

1 cm

0 1050 2100 3150 4200 km

Key

- high mountains
- cold forest
- savannah
- hot forest
- desert
- marsh
- ice on land
- ice on the sea
- very large built up areas
- country boundary

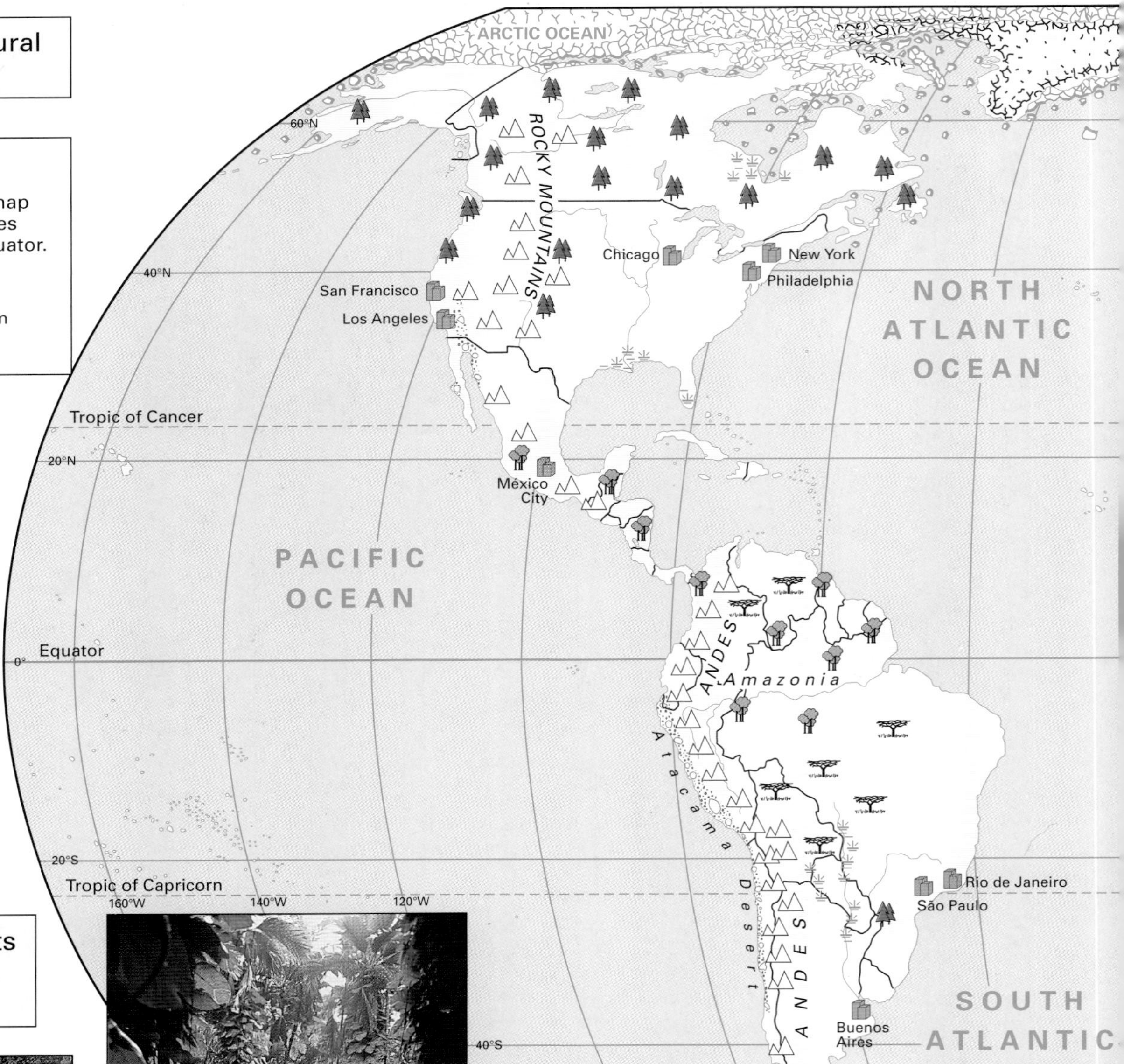

Most natural environments have been influenced by people.

very large built up area

hot forest

savannah

desert

cold forest

marsh

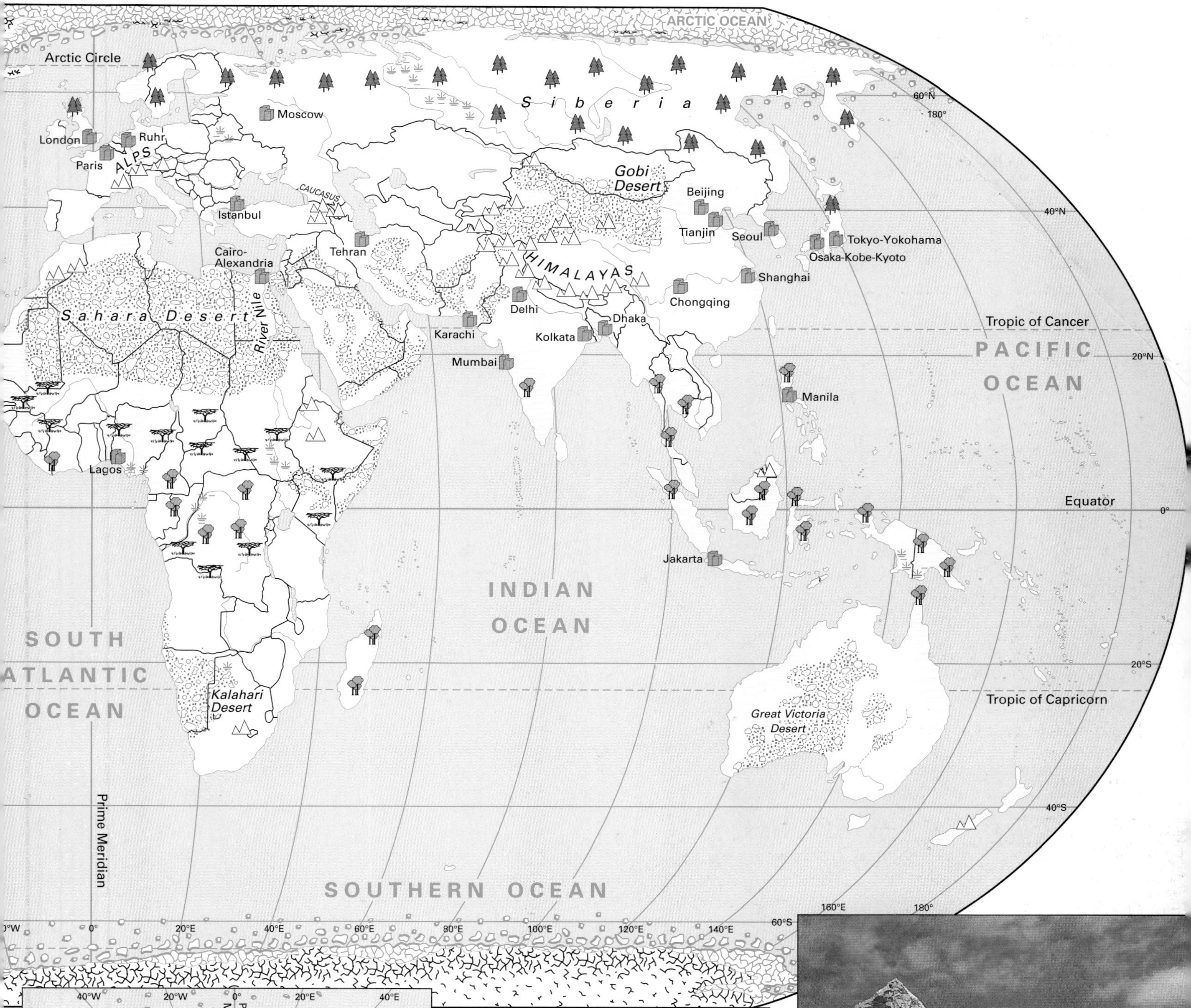

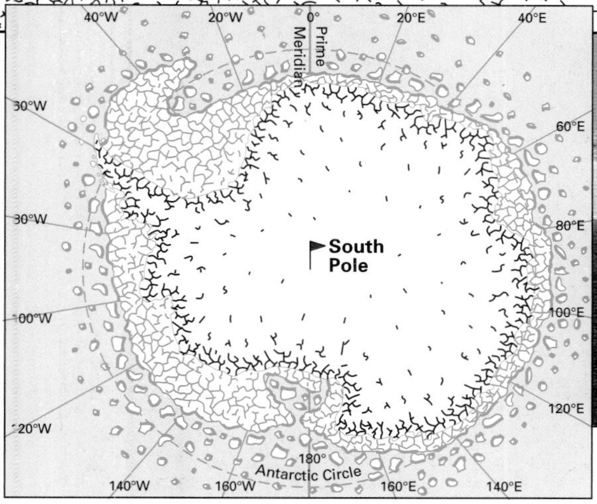

ice

high mountains

People have damaged the natural environment in many parts of the world.

Scale

One centimetre on the map measures 1050 kilometres on the ground at the Equator.

1050 km — 1 cm

0 | 1050 | 2100 | 3150 | 4200 km

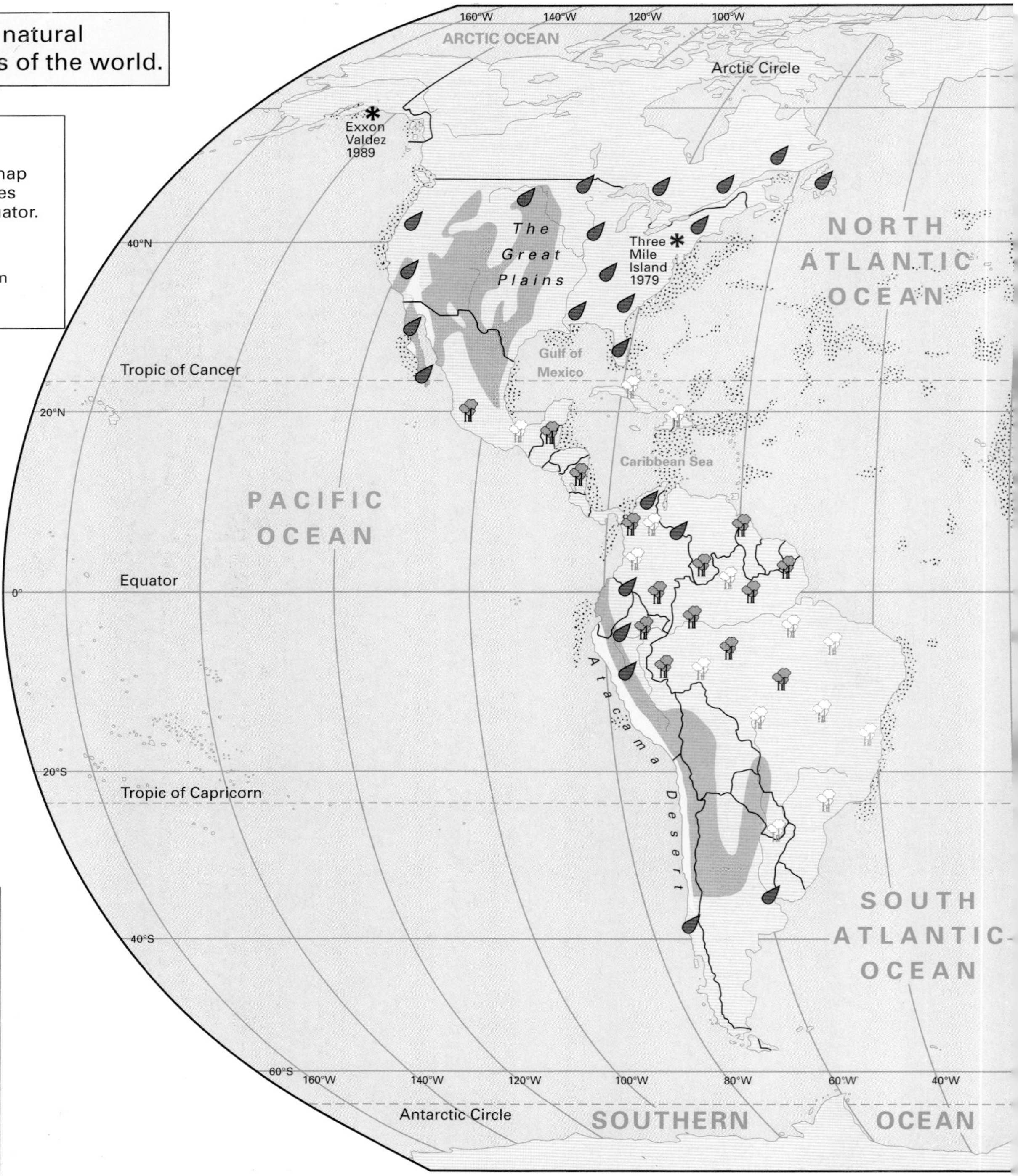

acid rain
Jelenia Gora, Poland

nuclear accident
Chernobyl, Ukraine

forest loss
Trans-Amazonian Highway, Brazil

Key

- tropical rain forest
- worst areas of forest loss
- desert
- spreading edges of desert
- areas most affected by acid rain
- sea areas most likely to be affected by major oil pollution
- recent major oil spill
- recent major nuclear or chemical accident
- country boundary

Eckert IV Projection

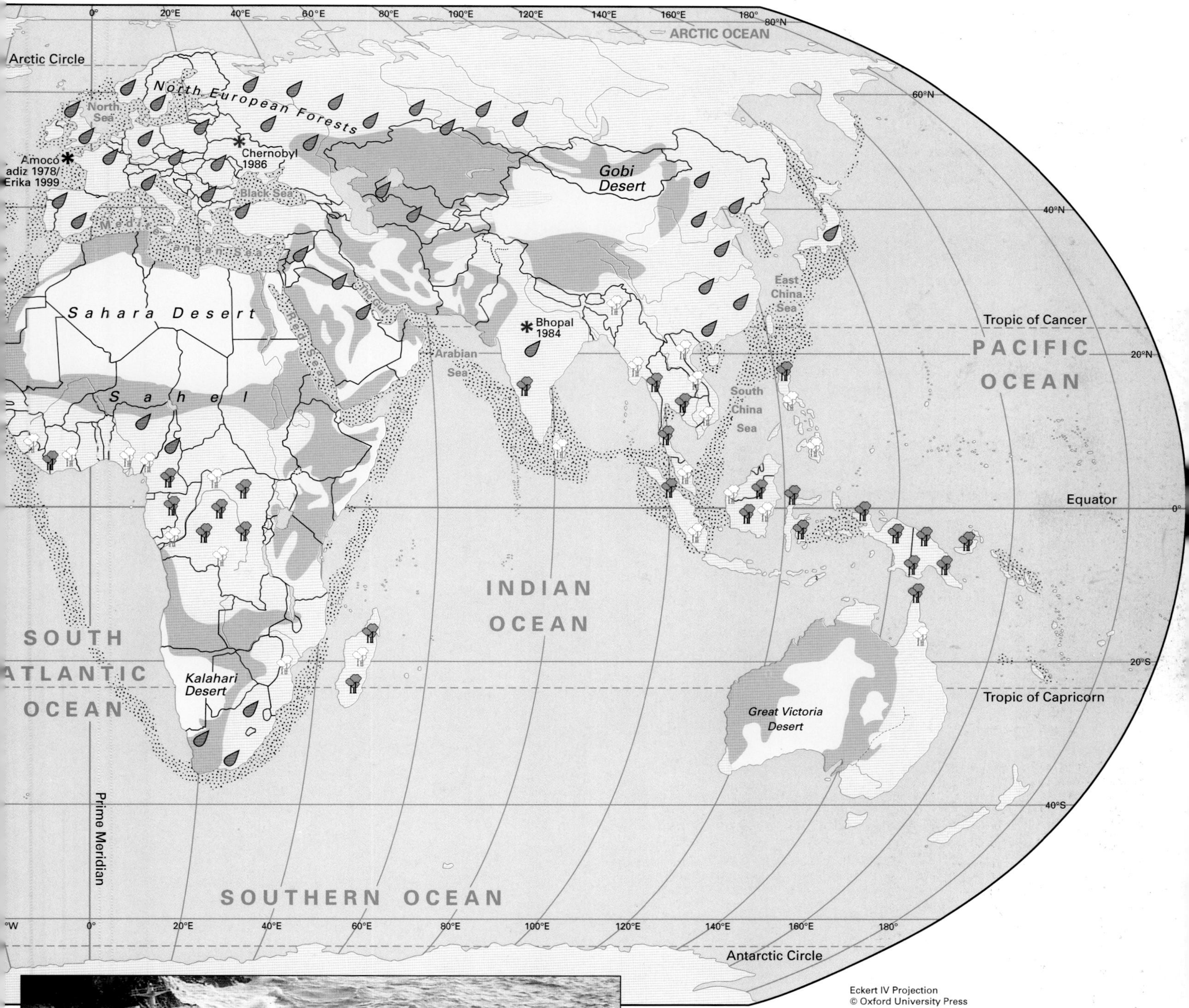

oil pollution
Shetland Islands, Scotland

spreading desert
The Sahel, Burkina

World People and cities

Some parts of the world are crowded, others have very few people.

Scale

1050 km — 1 cm

One centimetre on the map measures 1050 kilometres on the ground at the equator.

0 1050 2100 3150 4200 km

Key

one million (1 000 000) people live near each dot

very many people

many people

few people

the world's largest cities – each has more than 6 million people

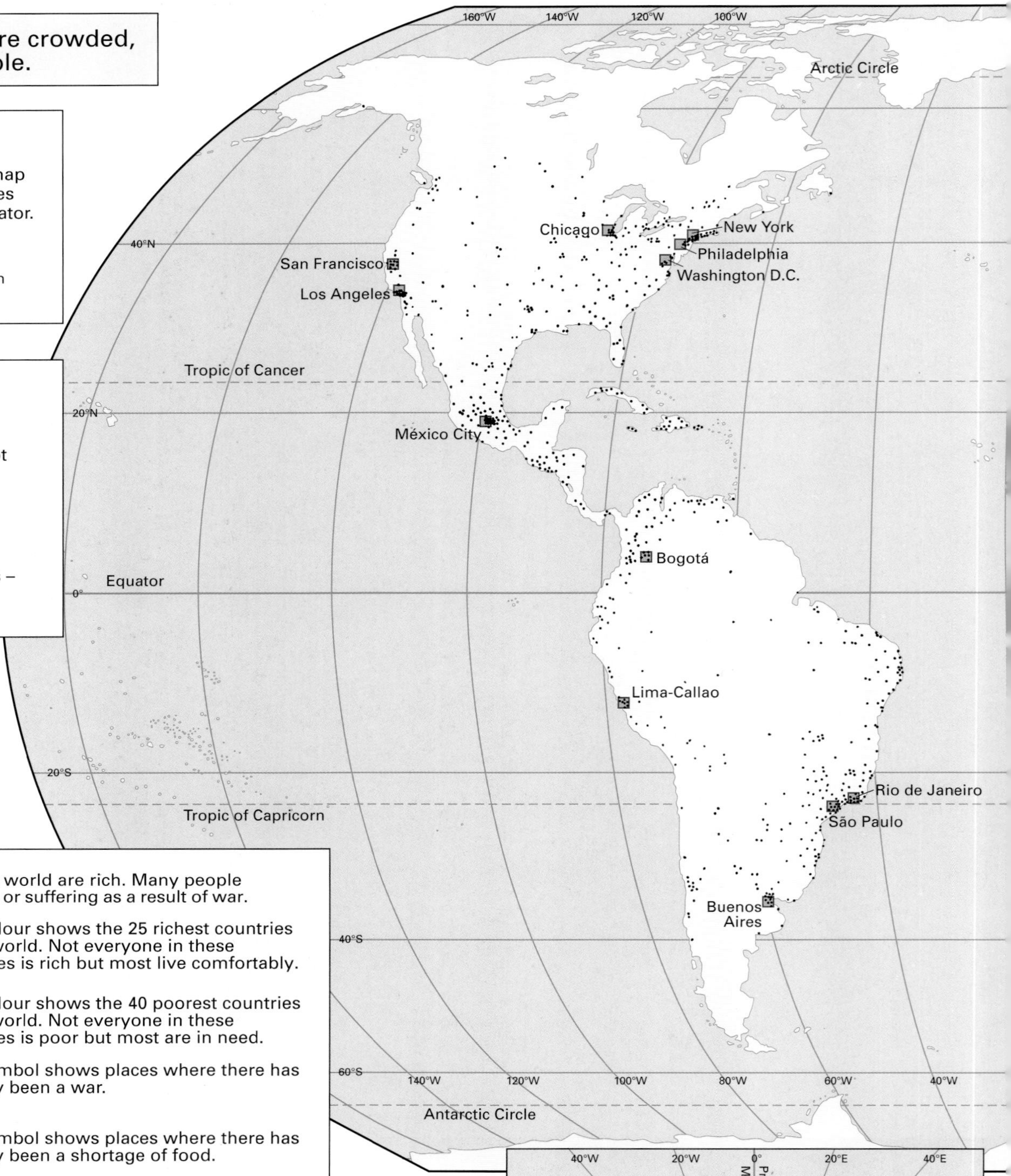

Welfare

Some people in the world are rich. Many people are poor, or hungry, or suffering as a result of war.

rich countries	This colour shows the 25 richest countries in the world. Not everyone in these countries is rich but most live comfortably.
poor countries	This colour shows the 40 poorest countries in the world. Not everyone in these countries is poor but most are in need.
war	This symbol shows places where there has recently been a war.
famine	This symbol shows places where there has recently been a shortage of food.

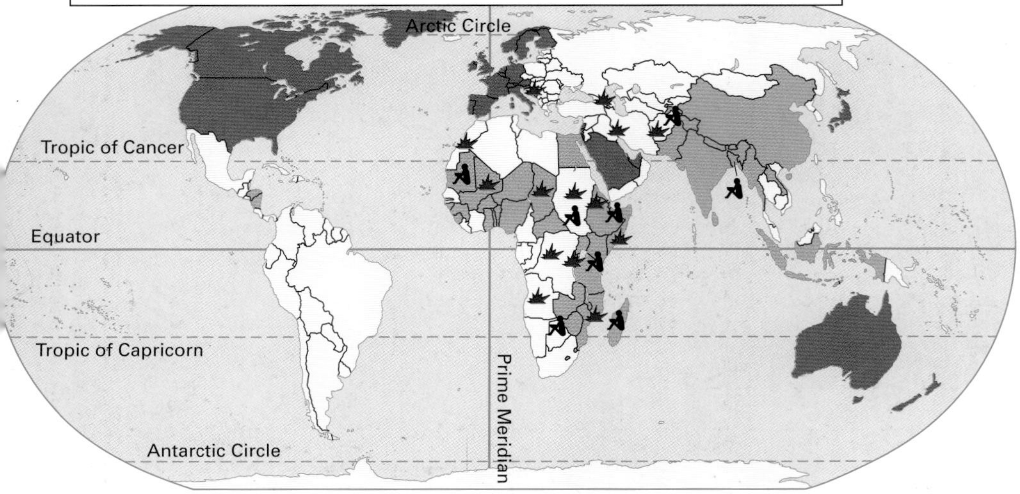

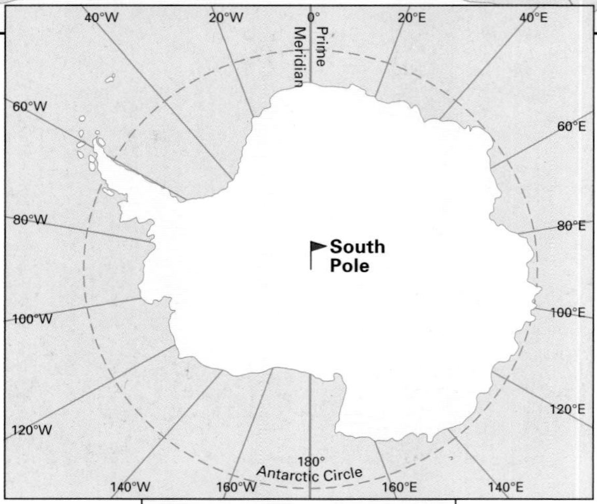

There are no permanent settlements in Antarctica.

Eckert IV Projection

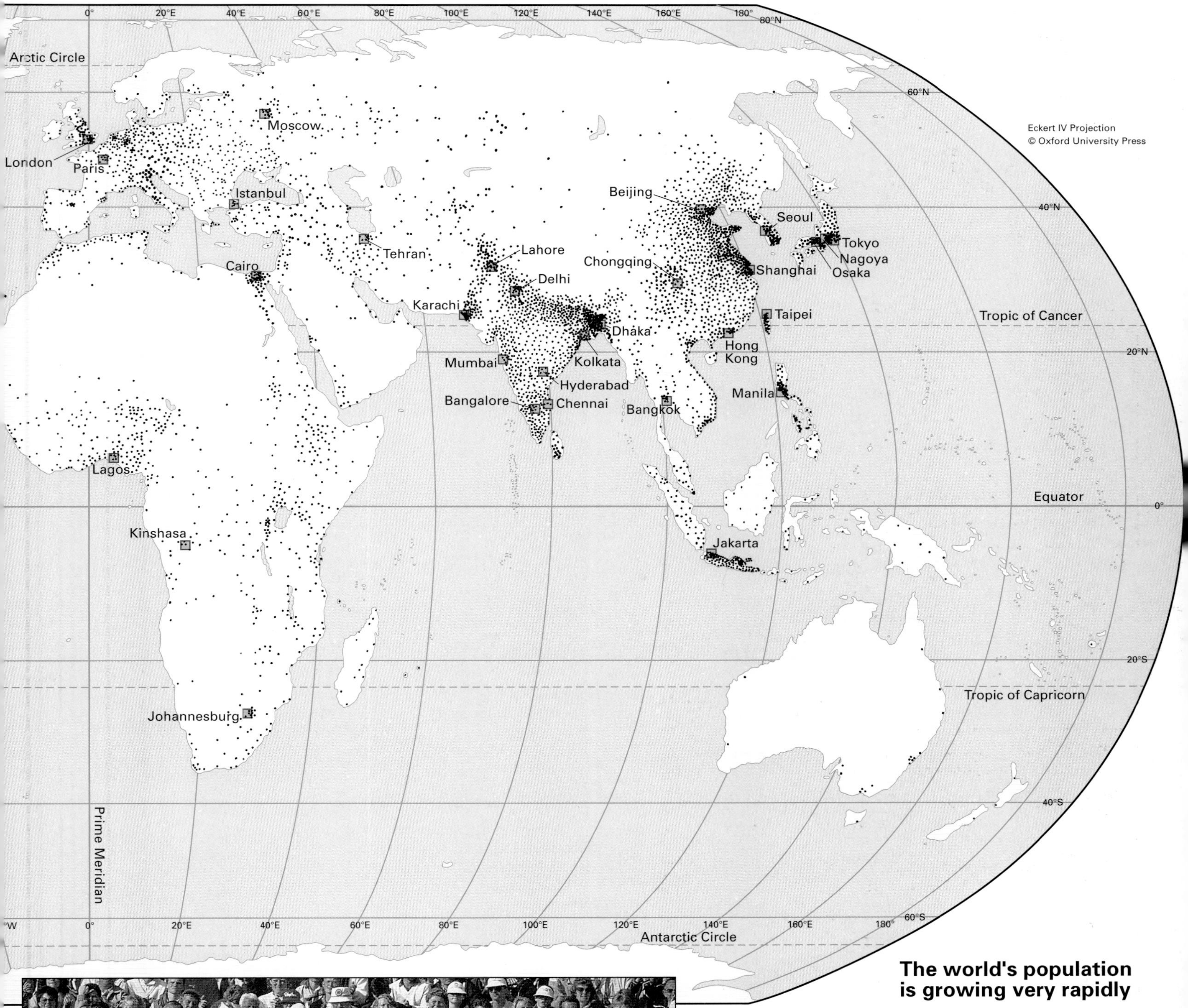

The world's population is growing very rapidly

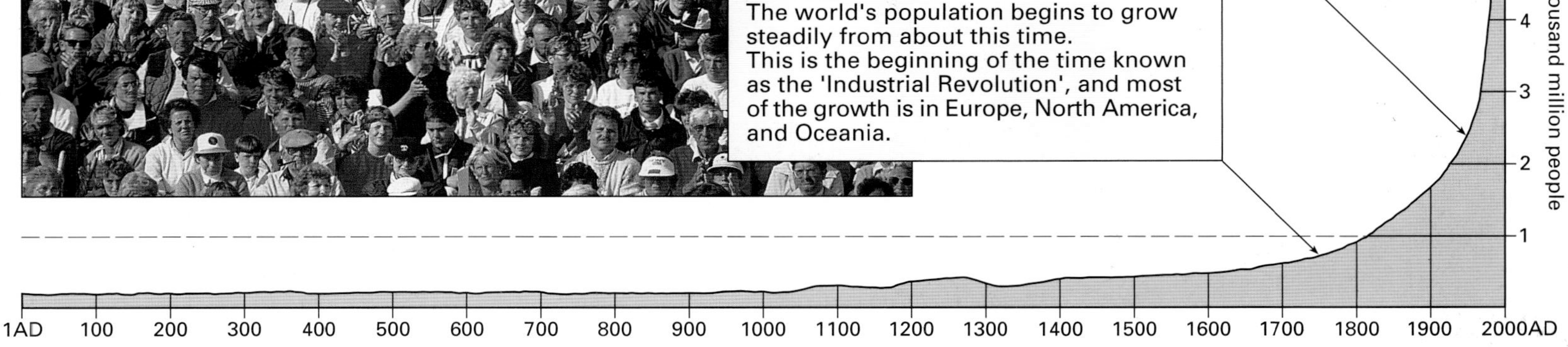

Ships and aeroplanes carry goods and passengers around the world.

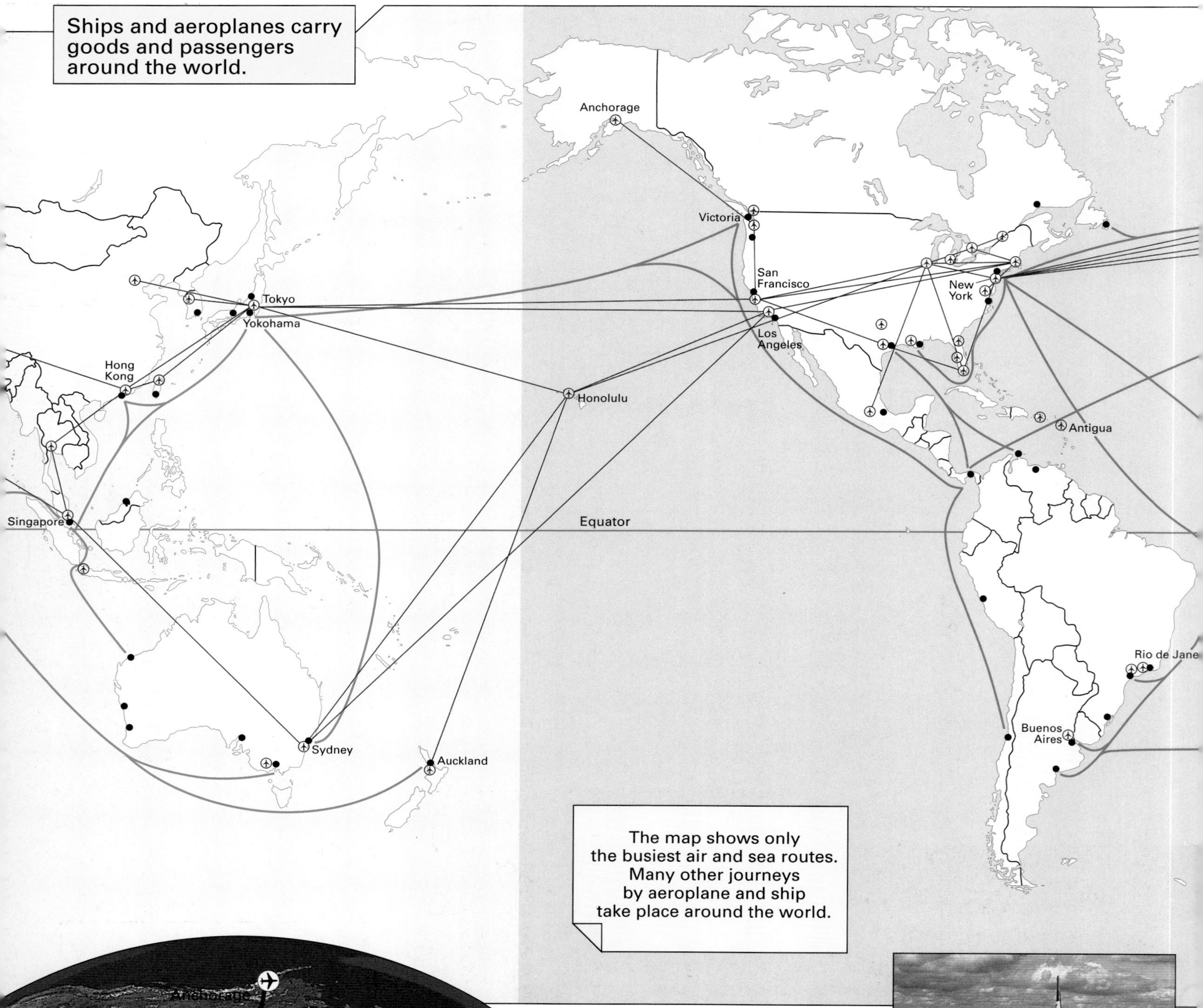

The map shows only the busiest air and sea routes. Many other journeys by aeroplane and ship take place around the world.

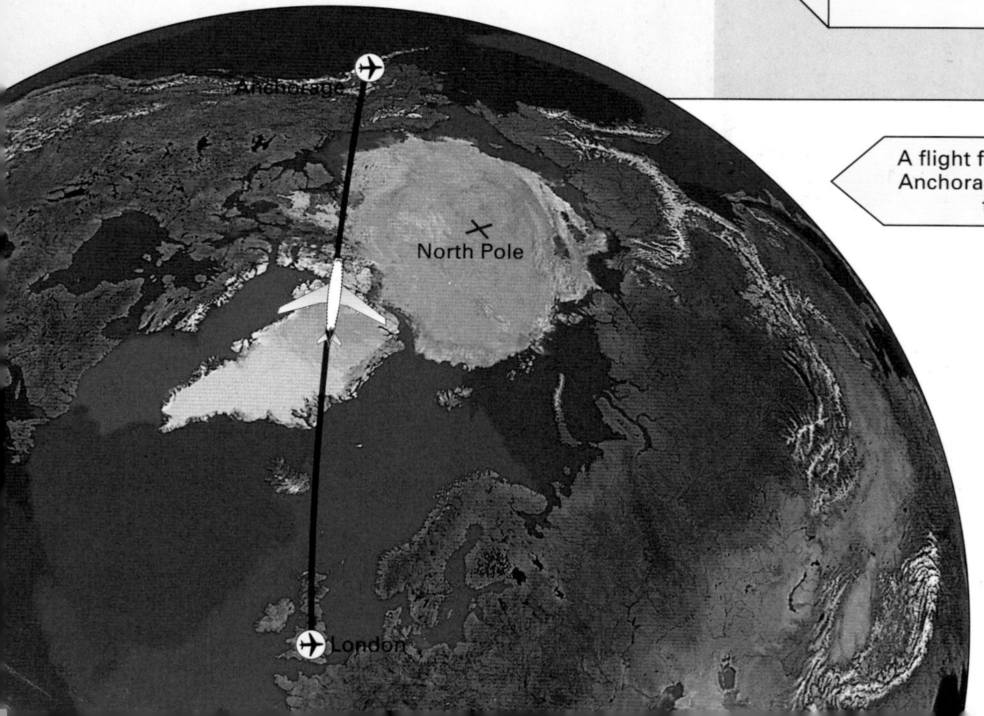

A flight from London to Anchorage passes near the North Pole.

This Boeing 747 takes 10.5 hours to fly from London Heathrow to Antigua.

Gall Projection

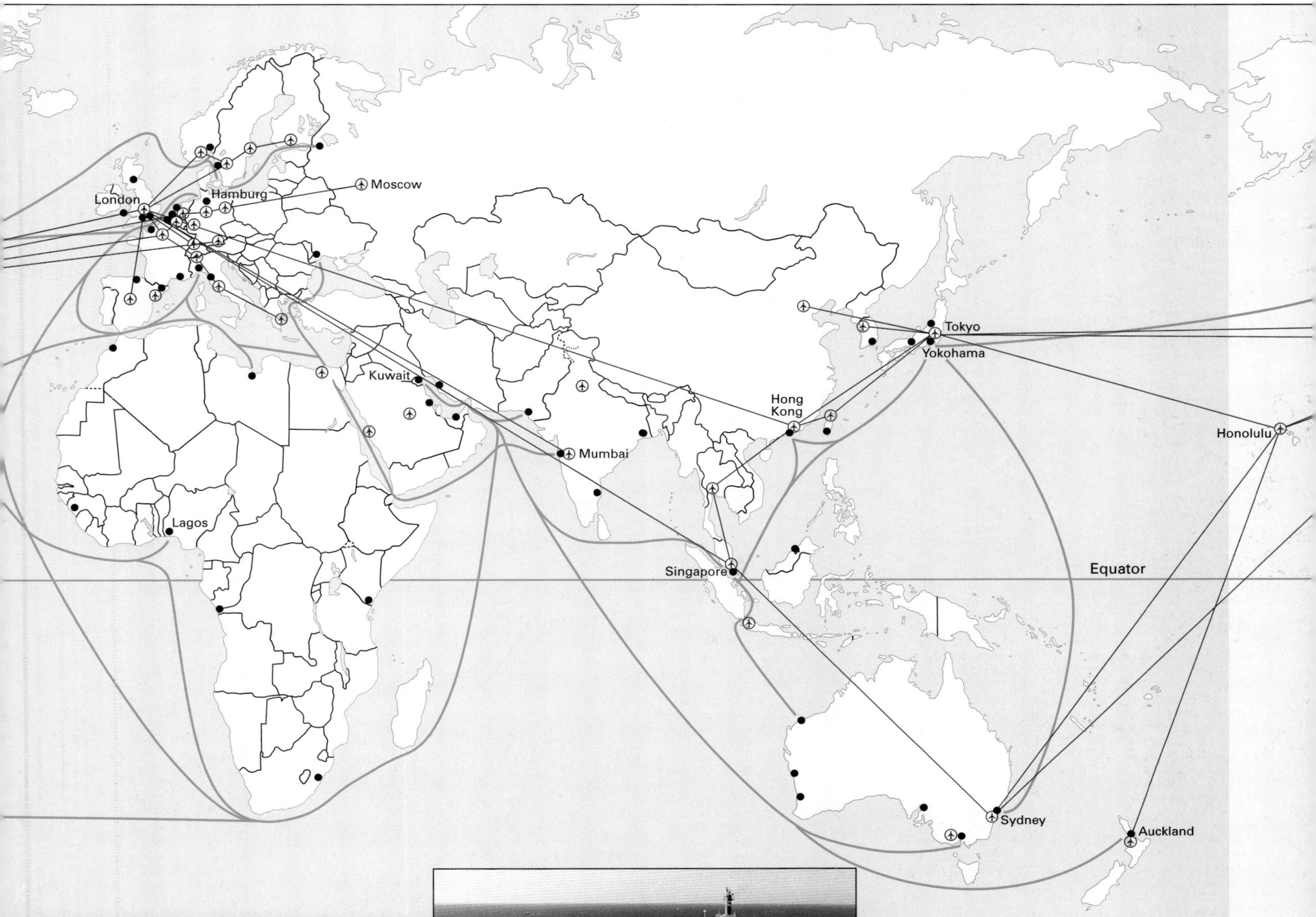

his container ship takes 25 days to sail
om Hamburg to Buenos Aires.

This oil tanker takes 18 days to sail from Kuwait to the United Kingdom.

Scale

1200 km

1 cm

One centimetre on the map measures 1200 kilometres on the ground at the Equator.

0 1200 2400 3600 4800 km

Key

- international boundary
- main shipping lanes
- major port
- main air routes
- major airport

It is about 40 000 kilometres (25 000 miles) around the world.

Gall Projection

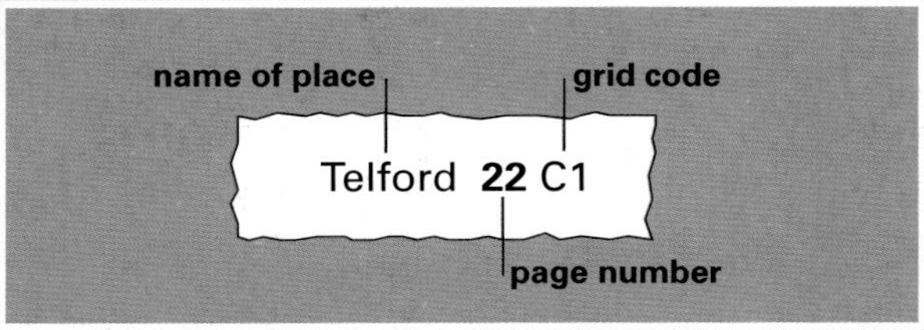

A

Aberaeron **24** C2
Aberchirder **19** G2
Aberdare **24** D1
Aberdeen **19** G2
Aberdeen City *unitary authority* **19** G2
Aberdeenshire *unitary authority* **19** F1/H2
Aberfeldy **19** F1
Abergavenny **24** D1
Abertillery **24** D1
Aberystwyth **24** C2
Abidjan **46** B4
Abingdon **25** F1
Aboyne **19** G2
Abu Dhabi **42** B4
Abuja **46** C4
Accra **46** B4
Aconcagua *peak* **53** C2
Adana **38** D1
Addis Ababa **46** D4
Adelaide **48** B2
Adriatic Sea **40** C2
Aegean Sea **40** D1
Afghanistan **42** C4
Ahmadabad **42** C4
Ailsa Craig *island* **20** D3
Airdrie **21** F3
Aire, River **22** C2
Alaska, Gulf of **51** B3
Albania **38** C2/D2
Albany **48** A2
Aldabra Islands **47** E3
Aldeburgh **27** F3
Alderney *island* **29** E2
Aldershot **26** D2
Aleppo **42** A4
Aleutian Islands **51** A3
Alexandria Egypt **46** D5
Alexandria UK **21** E3
Algeria **46** B5/C5
Algiers **46** C5
Alice Springs *town* **48** B2
Alloa **21** F4
Almaty **42** C5
Aln, River **21** H3
Alnwick **21** H3
Alps *mountains* **40** C2
Altai Mountains **44** D5
Alton **29** G4
Alyth **19** F1
Amazon, River **53** C3/D3
Amble **21** H3
Ambleside **21** G2
Amesbury **29** F4
Amman **42** A4
Amsterdam **38** C2
Amundsen Sea **54**
Amur, River **44** F5
Anatolian Plateau **40** D1/D2
Anchorage **50** B4
Andaman Islands **44** D3
Andaman Sea **44** D3
Andes *mountains* **53** C2/C4
Andorra **38** C2
Andover **29** F4
Angara River **44** D5
Angel Falls **53** C4
Angola **46** C3/D3
Angola Plateau **47** C3/D3
Angus *unitary authority* **19** F1/G1
Ankara **38** D1
Annan **21** F2
Annan, River **21** F3
Anshan **42** F5
Anstruther **21** G4
Antananarivo **21** E3
Antarctic Peninsula **54**
Antigua and Barbuda **50** F1
Antofagasta **52** C2
Antrim **20** C2
Antrim *district* **20** C2
Antrim Mountains **20** C3/D2
Appalachian Mountains **51** E2/F3
Appennines *mountains* **40** C2
Appleby-in-Westmorland **21** G2
Arabian Peninsula **44** B4
Arabian Sea **44** C3
Aracaju **52** E3
Arafura Sea **49** B3
Aral Sea **44** B5/C5
Ararat, Mount **44** B4
Arbroath **19** G1
Arctic Ocean **55**
Ardbeg **20** C3
Ardminish **20** D3
Ardres **27** F1
Ards *district* **20** D2
Ards Peninsula **20** D2
Arequipa **52** C3
Argentina **52** C1/D2
Argyll and Bute *unitary authority* **20/21** C3/E1
Arica **52** C3
Arisaig **18** D1
Arisaig, Sound of **18** D1
Arkansas River **51** D2/E2
Arklow **24** A2
Armagh **20** C2
Armagh *district* **20** C2
Armenia **42** B4/B5
Armentières **27** G1
Arnhem Land **49** B3
Arnold **23** D1
Arran *island* **20** D3
Aruba *island* **52** C4
Arundel **26** D1
Arun, River **26** D2
Asal, Lake **47** E4
Ashbourne **22** D2
Ashford **27** E2
Ashington **21** H3
Ashgabat **42** B4
Asmara **46** D4
Astana **46** C5
Asunción **52** D2
Atacama Desert **53** C2/C3
Athens **38** D1
Atlanta **50** E2
Atlantic Ocean **56/57**
Altas Mountains **47** B5/C5
Auchterarder **21** F4
Auchterrmuchty **19** F1
Auckland **48** D2
Auderville **29** F2
Australia **48** A2/C3
Australian Alps **49** C2
Austria **38** C2
Aviemore **19** F2
Avon, River Warwickshire **25** F2
Avon, River Wiltshire **29** E4
Axminster **29** E3
Ayers Rock *peak* **49** B2
Aylesbury **26** D2
Ayr **21** E3
Ayr, River **21** E3
Azerbaijan **42** B4/B5
Azores *islands* **47** A5

B

Baffin Bay **55**
Baffin Island **51** E4/F4
Baghdad **42** B4
Bahía Blanca **52** C2
Bahamas, The **50** F2
Bahrain **42** B4
Baie de la Seine *bay* **29** G2
Bakewell **22** D2
Baku **42** B5
Bala **24** D2
Bala Lake **24** D2
Balearic Islands **40** C1
Bali *island* **44** E2
Balkhash, Lake **44** C5
Ballantrae **20** D3
Ballater **19** F2
Ballybofey **20** B2
Ballycastle **20** C3
Ballymena **20** C2
Ballymena *district* **20** C2
Ballymoney **20** C3
Ballymoney *district* **20** C3
Ballyshannon **20** A2
Baltic Sea **40** C2/D2
Baltimore **50** F2
Bamako **46** B4
Bamburgh **21** H3
Banbridge **20** C2
Banbridge *district* **20** C2
Banbury **25** F2
Banchory **19** G2
Bandar Seri Begawan **42** E3
Bandung **42** E2
Banff **19** G2
Bangalore **42** C3
Bangkok **42** E3
Bangladesh **42** D4
Bangor Northern Ireland **20** D2
Bangor Wales **24** C3
Bangui **46** C4
Banjul **46** B4
Banks Islands **49** D3
Bann, River **20** C2
Barbados **50** G1
Barcelona Spain **38** C2
Barcelona Venezuela **52** C4
Barents Sea **55**
Barfleur **29** F2
Barking **27** E2
Barmouth **24** C2
Barnard Castle **21** H2
Barnet **26** D2
Barnoldswick **22** C2
Barnsley **23** D2
Barnstaple **28** C4
Barra *island* **18** B1/B2
Barranquilla **52** C4
Barrow-in-Furness **21** F2
Barry **24** D1
Barton-upon-Humber **23** E2
Basildon **27** E2
Basingstoke **26** C2
Basra **42** B4
Bass Strait **49** C1/C2
Bath **29** E4
Bath and North East Somerset *unitary authority* **26** B2
Bathgate **21** F3
Baykal, Lake **44** E5
Beachy Head **27** E1
Bearsden **21** E3
Beaufort Sea **55**
Beauly, River **19** E2
Beccles **27** F3
Bedford **26** D3
Bedfordshire *county* **26** D2/D3
Bedworth **25** F2
Beijing **42** E4
Beinn Dearg *peak* **19** E2
Beira **46** D3
Beirut **42** A4
Belarus **38** D2
Belém **52** D3
Belfast **20** D2
Belfast *district* **20** C2/D2
Belfast Lough **20** D2
Belgium **38** C2
Belgrade **38** D2
Belize **50** E1
Bellingshausen Sea **54**
Belmopan **50** E1
Belo Horizonte **52** D3
Ben Alder *peak* **19** E1
Benbecula *island* **18** B2
Ben Cruachan *peak* **18** D1
Bengal, Bay of **44** D3
Benguela **46** C3
Ben Hope *peak* **19** E3
Benin **46** C4
Ben Klibreck *peak* **19** E3
Ben Lawers *peak* **19** E1
Ben Lomond *peak* **21** E4
Ben More *peak* **18** C1
Ben More *peak* **19** E1
Ben More Assynt *peak* **19** E3
Ben Nevis *peak* **19** D1
Ben Wyvis *peak* **19** E2
Bergen **38** C3
Bering Sea **55**
Bering Strait **55**
Berlin **38** C2
Bermuda *island* **51** F2
Bern **38** C2
Berneray *island* **18** B2
Berwick-upon-Tweed **21** G3
Bethesda **24** C3
Béthune **27** G1
Beverley **23** E2
Bewdley **25** E2
Bexley **27** E2
Bhutan **42** D4
Bicester **25** F1
Bideford **28** C4
Bideford Bay **28** C4
Bigbury Bay **28** D3
Biggar **21** F3
Biggleswade **26** D3
Bilbao **38** B2
Birkenhead **22** B2
Birmingham **25** F2
Biscay, Bay of **40** B2
Bishkek **42** C5
Bishop Auckland **21** H2
Bishop's Stortford **27** E2
Bissau **46** B4
Blackburn **22** C2
Blackburn and Darwen *unitary authority* **22** C2
Black Mountains **24** D1
Blackpool **22** B2
Blackpool *unitary authority* **22** B2
Black Sea **40/41** D2
Blackwater Reservoir **19** E1
Blackwater, River **20** C2
Blaenau Ffestiniog **24** D2
Blaenau Gwent *unitary authority* **24** D1
Blairgowrie **19** F1
Blandford Forum **29** E3
Blantyre **46** D3
Blyth, River **22** D4
Boa Vista **52** C4
Bodmin **28** C3
Bodmin Moor **28** C3
Bognor Regis **29** G3
Bogotá **52** C4
Bolivia **52** C2/C3
Bolton **22** C2
Bonar Bridge *town* **19** E2
Bo'ness **21** F4
Bonn **38** C2
Bootle **22** B2
Bordeaux **38** B2
Borneo *island* **44** E2/E3
Bornholm *island* **40** C2
Boscastle **28** C3
Bosnia-Herzegovina **38** C2
Boston UK **23** E1
Boston USA **50** F3
Bothnia, Gulf of **40** C3/D3
Botswana **46** D2/D3
Boulogne-sur-Mer **27** F1
Bournemouth **29** F3
Bournemouth *unitary authority* **29** F3
Bovey Tracey **28** D3
Bracknell **26** D2
Bracknell Forest *unitary authority* **26** D2
Bradford **22** D2
Braemar **19** F2
Brahmaputra River **44** D4
Braintree **27** E2
Brampton **21** G2
Branderburgh **19** F2
Brásília **52** D3
Bratislava **38** C2
Braunton **28** C4
Bray **24** A3
Brazil **52** C3/E3
Brazilian Highlands **53** D3
Brazil Plateau **53** D2
Brazzaville **46** C3
Brechin **19** G1
Brecon **24** D1
Brecon Beacons *mountains* **24** D1
Brent **26** D2
Brentwood **27** E2
Bressay *island* **17** D3
Bridgend **24** D1
Bridgend *unitary authority* **24** D1
Bridgnorth **25** E2
Bridgwater **29** E4
Bridgwater Bay **29** D4
Bridlington **23** E3
Bridport **29** E3
Brigg **23** E2
Brighouse **22** D2
Brighton **26** D1
Brighton and Hove *unitary authority* **26** D1
Brisbane **48** C2
Bristol **29** E4
Bristol *unitary authority* **26** B2
Bristol Channel **24** C1/D1
Broad Bay **18** C3
Broadford **18** D2
Broad Law *peak* **21** F3
Broadway **25** F2
Brodick **20** D3
Broken Hill *town* **48** C2
Bromley **27** E2
Bromsgrove **25** E2
Bromyard **25** E2
Broome **48** B3
Brora **19** F3
Brough **21** G2
Brough Head **17** B2
Brown Clee Hill **25** E2
Brown Willy *peak* **28** C3
Brunei **42** E3
Brussels **38** C2
Buchan Ness **19** H2
Bucharest **38** D2
Buckfastleigh **28** D3
Buckhaven **21** F4
Buckie **19** G2
Buckingham **26** D2
Buckinghamshire *county* **26** D2
Budapest **38** C2
Bude **28** C3
Bude Bay **28** C3
Buenaventura **52** C4
Buenos Aires **52** D2
Buffalo **50** F3
Builth Wells **24** D2
Bujumbura **46** D3
Bulgaria **38** D2
Buncrana **20** B3
Bure, River **27** F3
Burghead *town* **19** F2
Burkina **46** B4/C4
Burnley **22** C2
Burry Port **24** C1
Bursa **38** D2
Burton upon Trent **22** D1
Burundi **46** D3
Bury **22** C2
Bury St. Edmunds **27** E3
Bushehr **42** B4
Bush, River **20** C3
Bute *island* **20** D3
Bute, Sound of **20** D3
Butt of Lewis *cape* **18** C3
Buxton **22** D2

C

Cader Idris *peak* **24** D2
Caernarfon **24** C3
Caernarfon Bay **24** C3
Caerphilly **24** D1
Caerphilly *unitary authority* **24** D1
Cairn Gorm *peak* **19** F2
Cairngorms *mountains* **19** F2
Cairns **48** C3
Cairo **46** D5
Calais **27** F1
Calgary **50** D3
Cali **52** C4
California, Gulf of **51** D2
Callander **21** E4
Calligarry **18** D2
Calne **29** E4
Camberley **26** D2
Cambodia **42** E3
Camborne **28** B3
Cambrian Mountains **24** D2
Cambridge **27** E3
Cambridgeshire *county* **26/27** D3/E3
Camel, River **28** C3
Cameroon **46** C4
Cameroun, Mount **47** C4
Campbeltown **20** D3
Campsie Fells *hills* **21** E4
Cam, River **27** E3
Canada **50** C3/F4
Canary Islands **47** B5
Canberra **48** C2
Canisp *peak* **19** D3
Canna *island* **18** C2
Cannock **22** C1
Canterbury **27** F2
Cap de la Hague *cape* **29** F2
Cape Town **46** C2
Cape Verde **46** A4
Cape Verde Islands **47** A4
Cape York Peninsula **49** C3
Cap Gris-Nez *cape* **27** F1
Caracas **52** C4
Cardiff **24** D1
Cardiff *unitary authority* **24** D1
Cardigan **24** C2
Cardigan Bay **24** C2
Carentan **29** F2
Caribbean Sea **51** F1
Carlingford Lough *bay* **20** C2
Carlisle **21** G2
Carmarthen **24** C1
Carmarthen Bay **24** C1
Carmarthenshire *unitary authority* **24** C1/D2
Carmel Head **24** C3
Carn Eige *peak* **19** D2
Carnforth **22** C3
Carnoustie **19** G1
Caroline Islands **49** C4
Carpathians *mountains* **40** C2/D2
Carpentaria, Gulf of **49** B3/C3
Carrickfergus **20** D2
Carrickfergus *district* **20** D2
Cartagena **52** C4
Carteret **29** F2
Casablanca **46** B5
Caspian Sea **41** E1/E2
Cassel **27** G1
Castlebay **18** B1
Castleblaney **20** C2
Castle Douglas **21** F2
Castleford **23** D2
Castlereagh *district* **20** D2
Castletown **21** E2
Caucasus *mountains* **41** E2
Cavan **20** B1
Cavan *county* **20** B1/B2
Cayenne **52** D4
Cemaes Head **24** C2
Central African Republic **46** C4/D4
Central Siberian Plateau **44** E6
Ceredigion *unitary authority* **24** C2/D2
Chad **46** C4/D4
Chad, Lake **47** C4
Changchun **42** F5
Channel Islands **29** E2
Chard **29** E3
Charlestown of Aberlour **19** F2
Charlotte **50** E2
Chatham **27** E2
Cheadle **22** C2
Chelmsford **27** E2
Cheltenham **25** E1
Chelyabinsk **42** C5
Chengdu **42** E4
Chennai **42** D3
Chepstow **25** E1
Cherbourg **29** F2

Cherwell, River 25 F1
Cheshire *county* 22 C2
Cheshunt 26 D2
Chester 22 C2
Chesterfield 23 D2
Chester-le-Street 21 H2
Cheviot Hills 21 G3
Chicago 50 E3
Chichester 29 G3
Chile 52 C1/C2
Chiltern Hills 26 C2/D2
Chimborazo *peak* 53 C3
China 42 D4/F5
Chippenham 29 E4
Chipping Norton 25 F1
Chişinău 38 D2
Chittagong 42 D4
Chongqing 42 E4
Chorley 22 C2
Christchurch New Zealand 48 D1
Christchurch UK 29 F3
Cincinnati 50 E2
Cirencester 25 F1
Citlaltépetl *peak* 51 E1
City of Edinburgh *unitary authority* 21 F3
City of Kingston upon Hull *unitary authority* 23 E2
Ciudad Bolívar 52 C4
Ciudad Guayana 52 C4
Clachan 20 D3
Clackmannanshire *unitary authority* 21 F4
Clacton-on-Sea 27 F2
Claonaig 20 D3
Cleethorpes 23 E2
Clevedon 29 E4
Cleveland 50 E3
Cleveland Hills 23 D3
Clisham *peak* 18 C2
Clones 20 B2
Clwyd, River 24 D3
Clydebank 21 E3
Clyde, River 21 F3
Coalisland 20 C2
Coalville 23 D1
Coatbridge 21 E3
Cockermouth 21 F2
Colchester 27 E2
Coldstream 21 G3
Coleraine 20 C3
Coleraine *district* 20 C3
Coll *island* 18 C1
Colne, River 27 E2
Colombia 52 C4
Colombo 42 C3
Colonsay *island* 20 C4
Colorado River 51 D2
Columbus 50 E2
Colwyn Bay *town* 24 D3
Communism Peak 44 C4
Comodoro Rivadavia 52 C1
Comoro Archipelago *islands* 47 E3
Comoros 46 E3
Conakry 46 B4
Concepción 52 C2
Congo 46 C3/C4
Congo, Democratic Republic of 46 C3/D4
Congo, River 47 D4
Coniston Water *lake* 21 F2
Consett 21 H2
Conwy 24 D3
Conwy *unitary authority* 24 D3
Conwy, River 24 D3
Cook, Mount 49 D1
Cookstown 20 C2
Cookstown *district* 20 C2
Cook Strait 49 D1/D2
Copenhagen 38 C2
Coquet, River 21 H3
Coral Sea 49 C3
Córdoba 52 C2
Cork 38 B2
Cornwall *county* 28 B3/C3
Corsewall Point 20 D3
Corsica 40 C2
Costa Rica 50 E1
Côte d'Ivoire 46 B4
Cotopaxi *peak* 53 C3
Cotswold Hills 25 E1/F1
Coupar Angus 19 F1
Coutainville 29 F2
Coutances 29 F2
Coventry 25 F2
Cowes 29 F3
Craigavon 20 C2
Craigavon *district* 20 C2
Craighouse 20 D3
Craignure 18 D1
Crail 21 G4
Cramlington 21 H3
Crawley 26 D2
Crediton 28 D3
Cree, River 21 E3
Creeslough 20 B3
Crete 40 D1
Crewe 22 C2
Crewkerne 29 E3
Crianlarich 19 E1
Crieff 19 F1
Croatia 38 C2
Cromarty 19 E2
Cromarty Firth *estuary* 19 E2
Cromer 27 F3
Cross Fell *peak* 21 G2
Crossmaglen 20 C2
Croydon 26 D2
Crumlin 20 C2
Cuba 50 E2/F2
Cuiabá 52 D3
Cuillin Hills 18 C2
Cullen 19 G2
Cullompton 28 D3
Cumbernauld 21 F3
Cumbria *county* 21 F2/G2
Cumnock 21 E3
Cunnamulla 48 C2
Cupar 19 F1
Curitiba 52 D2
Cuzco 52 C3
Cwmbran 24 D1
Cyprus 38 D1
Czech Republic 38 C2

D

Daer Reservoir 21 F3
Dakar 46 B4
Dalbeattie 21 F2
Dalian 42 F4
Dallas 50 E2
Dalmally 19 E1
Dalton-in-Furness 21 F2
Damascus 42 A4
Dandong 42 F5
Danube, River 40 D2
Dar es Salaam 46 D3
Darling River 49 C2
Darlington 21 H2
Darlington *unitary authority* 21 H2
Dartford 27 E2
Dartmoor *geog. region* 28 D3
Dartmouth 28 D3
Dart, River 28 D3
Darvel 21 E3
Darwin 48 B3
Daventry 25 F2
Davis Strait 51 G4
Dawlish 28 D3
Dead Sea 44 A4
Deal 27 F2
Death Valley 51 D2
Deccan *plateau* 44 C3/D3
Dee, River Aberdeenshire 19 G2
Dee, River Dumfries and Galloway 21 E2/F2
Demavend, Mount 44 B4
Denbigh 24 D3
Denbighshire *unitary authority* 24 D3
Denmark 38 C2
Denver 50 D2
De Panne 27 G2
Derby 23 D1
Derby City *unitary authority* 22/23 D1
Derbyshire *county* 22/23 D1/D2
Derry *district* 20 B2
Derwent, River Cumbria 21 F2
Derwent, River Derbyshire 22 D2
Derwent, River Durham/Northumberland 21 G2
Derwent, River North Yorkshire 23 E2
Derwent Water *lake* 21 F2
Detroit 50 E3
Deveron, River 19 G2
Devon *county* 28/29 C3/D3
Dewsbury 22 D2
Dhaka 42 D4
Didcot 25 F1
Dingwall 19 E2
Diss 27 F3
Djibouti 46 E4
Djibouti 46 E4
Dnepropetrovsk 38 D2
Dnieper, River 40 D2
Dniester, River 40 D2
Dodoma 46 D3
Doha 42 B4
Dolgellau 24 D2
Dominica 50 F1
Dominican Republic 50 F1
Donaghadee 20 D2
Doncaster 23 D2
Donegal 20 A2
Donegal *county* 20 A2/B3
Donetsk 39 D2
Don, River 19 G2
Doon, River 21 E3
Dorchester 29 E3
Dornoch 19 E2
Dornoch Firth *estuary* 19 E2
Dorset *county* 29 E3/F3
Douala 46 C4
Douglas 21 E2
Dover 27 F2
Dove, River 22 D2
Dover, Strait of 27 F1/F2
Down *district* 20 D2
Downham Market 27 E3
Downpatrick 20 D2
Drakensberg *mountains* 47 D2
Droitwich 25 E2
Dromore 20 C2
Drummore 20 E2
Drumnadrochit 19 E2
Dublin 38 B2
Dudley 25 E2
Duero, River 40 B2
Dufftown 19 F2
Dumbarton 21 E3
Dumfries 21 F3
Dumfries and Galloway *unitary authority* 21 E2/F3
Dunbar 21 G4
Dunblane 21 F4
Duncansby Head 17 B1
Dundalk 20 C2
Dundee 19 G1
Dundee City *unitary authority* 19 F1/G1
Dunedin 48 D1
Dunfermline 21 F4
Dungannon 20 C2
Dungannon *district* 20 B2/C2
Dungeness *cape* 27 E1
Dungiven 20 C2
Dunkerque 27 G2
Dunkery Beacon *peak* 28 D4
Dún Laoghaire 24 A3
Dunnett Head 17 B1
Dunoon 20 E3
Duns 21 G3
Dunvegan 18 C2
Durban 46 D2
Durham 21 H2
Durham *county* 21 G2/H2
Dushanbe 42 C4
Dyce 19 G2
Dyfi, River 24 D2

E

Ealing 26 D2
Earn, River 19 F1
East Ayrshire *unitary authority* 21 E3
Eastbourne 27 E1
East China Sea 44 F4
East Dereham 27 E3
East Dunbartonshire *unitary authority* 21 E3
East Kilbride 21 E3
Eastleigh 29 F3
East London 46 D2
East Lothian *unitary authority* 21 G3
East Renfrewshire *unitary authority* 21 E3
East Riding of Yorkshire *unitary authority* 23 E2/E3
East Sussex *county* 27 E1/E2
East Timor 42 F2
Ebbw Vale 24 D1
Ebro, River 40 B2
Ecuador 52 C3/C4
Eday *island* 17 C2
Eddrachillis Bay 18 D3
Eden, River Cumbria 21 G2
Eden, River Kent 27 E2
Edinburgh 21 F3
Edmonton 50 D3
Egypt 46 D5
Eigg *island* 18 C1
Elbe, River 40 C2
Elbrus, Mount 41 E2
Elgin 19 F2
El Giza 46 D5
Elgol 18 C2
Ellen, River 21 F2
Ellesmere Port 22 C2
Ellon 19 G2
Ellsworth Land 54
El Paso 50 D2
El Salvador 50 E1
Ely 27 E3
Enard Bay 18 D3
Enfield 26 D2
England 12
English Channel 40 B2
Enniskillen 20 B2
Epsom 26 D2
Equatorial Guinea 46 C4
Erebus, Mount 54
Erie, Lake 51 E3
Eriskay *island* 18 B2
Eritrea 46 D4/E4
Erne, River 20 B2
Errigal Mountain 20 A3
Esfahan 42 B4
Esha Ness *cape* 17 D3
Esk, River Cumbria/Dumfries and Galloway 21 F3
Esk, River North Yorkshire 23 E3
Esperance 48 B2
Espiritu Santo *island* 49 D3
Essex *county* 27 E2
Estonia 38 D2
Ethiopia 46 D4/E4
Ethiopian Highlands 47 D4/E4
Etna, Mount 40 C1
Euphrates, River 44 B4
Everest, Mount 44 D4
Evesham 25 F2
Exe, River 28 D4
Exeter 28 D3
Exmoor *geog. region* 28 D4
Exmouth 28 D3
Eyemouth 21 G3
Eye Peninsula 18 C3
Eyre, Lake 49 B2

F

Faroe Islands 40 B3
Fair Head *cape* 20 C3
Fair Isle 17 D2
Fakenham 27 E3
Falkirk 21 F3
Falkirk *unitary authority* 21 F3/F4
Falkland Islands 52 C1/D1
Falmouth 28 B3
Fal, River 28 C3
Fareham 29 F3
Faringdon 25 F1
Farnborough 26 D2
Farnham 26 D2
Fawley 29 F3
Felixstowe 27 F2
Fermanagh *district* 20 B2
Fetlar *island* 17 E3
Fianarantsoa 46 E2
Fife *unitary authority* 21 F4/G4
Fiji 48 D3
Fiji Islands 49 D3
Filchner Ice Shelf 54
Finland 38 D3
Finn, River 20 B2
Fionnphort 18 C1
Firth of Clyde *estuary* 20 D3/E3
Firth of Forth *estuary* 21 F4/G4
Firth of Lorn *estuary* 18 D1
Firth of Tay *estuary* 19 F1
Fishguard 24 C1
Flamborough Head *cape* 23 E3
Fleetwood 22 B2
Flinders Range *mountains* 49 B2
Flint 24 D3
Flintshire *unitary authority* 24 D3
Fochabers 19 F2
Folkestone 27 F2
Forel, Mount 55
Forest of Bowland *hills* 22 C2/C3
Formby 22 B2
Forres 19 F2
Fortaleza 52 E3
Fort Augustus 19 E2
Forth, River 21 E4
Fort William 19 D1
Foula *island* 17 C3
Fowey 28 C3
Fowey, River 28 C3
Foyle, River 20 B2
France 38 B2/C2
Fraserburgh 19 G2
Fraser River 51 C3
Freetown 46 B4
French Guiana 52 D4
Friesian Islands 40 C2
Frome 29 E4
Furnace 20 D4
Fushun 42 F5

G

Gabon 46 C3/C4
Gaborone 46 D2
Gainsborough 23 E2
Gairloch *town* 18 D2
Galapagos Islands 53 B3
Galashiels 21 G3
Galdhøpiggen *peak* 40 C3
Gambia, The 46 B4
Ganges, River 44 D4
Gatehouse of Fleet 21 E2
Gateshead 21 H2
Gdańsk 38 C2
Georgetown 52 D4
Georgia 39 E1
Geraldton 48 A2
Germany 38 C2
Ghana 46 B4
Gibraltar, Strait of 40 B1
Gigha *island* 20 D3
Gilbert Islands 49 D3
Gillingham 27 E2
Girvan 20 E3
Gisborne 48 D2
Glasgow 21 E3
Glasgow City *unitary authority* 21 E3
Glastonbury 29 E4
Glenluce 21 E2
Glenrothes 21 F4
Glomma, River 40 C3
Gloucester 25 E1
Gloucestershire *county* 25 E1/F1
Goat Fell *peak* 20 D3
Gobi Desert 44 E5
Goiânia 52 D3
Good Hope, Cape of 47 C2
Goole 23 E2
Göteborg 38 C2
Gotland *island* 40 C2
Gower *peninsula* 24 C1
Grampian Mountains 19 E1/F1
Gran Chaco *geog. region* 53 C2
Grangemouth 21 F4
Grantham 23 E1
Grantown-on-Spey 19 F2
Gravesend 27 E2
Great Australian Bight *bay* 49 B2
Great Barrier Reef 49 C3
Great Bear Lake 51 C4/D4
Great Britain 40 B2/C2
Great Dividing Range *mountains* 49 C2
Great Driffield 23 E3
Greater Antilles *islands* 51 F1
Greater London *county* 26/27 D2/E2
Greater Manchester *county* 22 C2
Great Lakes, The 51 E3/F3
Great Malvern 25 E2
Great Ouse, River 27 E3
Great Plains 51 D3
Great Sandy Desert 49 B2
Great Slave Lake 51 D4
Great Stour, River 27 F2
Great Torrington 28 C3
Great Victoria Desert 49 B2
Great Whernside *peak* 21 H2
Great Yarmouth 27 F3
Greece 38 D1/D2
Greenland 55
Greenock 21 E3
Greenwich 26 E2
Grenada 50 F1
Greta, River 21 G2
Greymouth 48 D1
Greystones 24 A3
Grimsby 23 E2
Guadalajara 50 D2
Guangzhou 42 E4
Guatemala 50 E1
Guatemala 50 E1
Guayaquil 52 C2
Guernsey *island* 29 E2
Guiana Highlands 53 C4/D4
Guildford 26 D2
Guinea 46 B4
Guinea-Bissau 46 B4
Guisborough 23 D3
Gulf, The 44 B4
Gur'yev 42 B5
Guyana 52 D4
Gwynedd *unitary authority* 24 C3/D2

H

Haiti 50 F1
Halesowen 25 E2
Halifax Canada 50 F3
Halifax UK 22 D2
Halkirk 19 F3
Halton *unitary authority* 22 C2
Haltwhistle 21 G2
Hamburg 38 C2
Hamersley Range *mountains* 49 A2/B2
Hamilton Canada 50 F3
Hamilton New Zealand 48 D2
Hamilton UK 21 E3
Hampshire *county* 26 C1/D2
Hampshire Downs *hills* 26 C2
Hangzhou 42 F4
Hanoi 42 E4
Harare 46 D3
Harbin 42 F5
Harlech 24 C2
Haroldswick 17 E3
Harris *island* 18 C2
Harris, Sound of 18 B2
Harrogate 22 D2
Harrow 26 D2
Hartford 50 F3
Hartland Point 28 C4
Hartlepool 23 D3
Hartlepool *unitary authority* 23 D3
Harwich 27 F2
Haslemere 26 D2
Hastings 27 E1
Hatherleigh 28 C3
Havana 50 E2
Havant 29 G3
Haverfordwest 24 C1
Haverhill 27 E3
Havering 27 E2
Hawaiian Islands 51 B1/B2
Hawick 21 G3
Hay-on-Wye 24 D2
Hay River *town* 50 D4
Haywards Heath 26 D2
Hekla, Mount 40 B3
Helensburgh 21 E4
Helmsdale 19 F3
Helmsdale, River 19 F3
Helsinki 38 D3
Helston 28 B3
Helvellyn *peak* 21 F2

Hemel Hempstead **26** D2
Hemsworth **23** D2
Henley-on-Thames **26** D2
Hereford **25** E2
Herefordshire *unitary authority* **25** E2
Herma Ness *cape* **17** E3
Hertfordshire *county* **26** D2
Hexham **21** G2
Heysham **22** C3
Highland *unitary authority* **18/19** D1/F3
High Wycombe **26** D2
Hillingdon **26** D2
Himalayas *mountains* **44** D4
Hinckley **25** F2
Hindu Kush *mountains* **44** C4
Hitchin **26** D2
Hobart **48** C1
Ho Chi Minh **42** E3
Hokkaido *island* **44** G5
Holderness *peninsula* **23** E2
Holsworthy **28** C3
Holyhead **24** C3
Holy Island England **21** H3
Holy Island Wales **24** C3
Honduras **50** E1
Hong Kong **42** E4
Honiara **48** C3
Honiton **29** D3
Honshu *island* **44** F4/G4
Horn, Cape **53** C1
Horncastle **23** E2
Hornsea **23** E2
Horsham **26** D2
Hounslow **26** D2
Houston **50** E2
Hove **26** D1
Howth **24** A3
Hoy *island* **17** B1
Huddersfield **22** D2
Hudson Bay **51** E3/E4
Hugh Town **28** A2
Hull, River **23** E2
Humber, River **23** E2
Hungary **38** C2/D2
Hunstanton **27** E3
Huntingdon **26** D3
Huntly **19** G2
Huron, Lake **51** E3
Hwang-Ho River **44** E4
Hyderabad **42** C3

I

Ibadan **46** C4
Ibiza **40** C1
Iceland **38** A3/B3
Ilchester **29** E3
Ilfracombe **28** C4
Ilkeston **23** D1
Ilkley **22** D2
Ilminster **29** E3
Immingham **23** E2
India **42** C3/D4
Indianapolis **50** E2
Indian Ocean **57**
Indonesia **42** E2/E3
Indus, River **44** C4
Ingleborough *peak* **21** G2
Inishowen Peninsula **20** B3
Inner Hebrides *islands* **18** C1/C2
Innerleithen **21** F3
Inner Sound **18** D2
Inuvik **50** C4
Inverary **20** D4
Inverbervie **19** G1
Invercargill **48** D1
Inverclyde *unitary authority* **21** E3
Invergarry **19** E2
Invergordon **19** E2
Inverkeithing **21** F4
Invermoriston **19** E2
Inverness **19** E2
Inverurie **19** G2
Iona *island* **18** C1
Ionian Sea **40** C1
Ipswich **27** F3
Iquitos **52** C3
Iran **42** B4
Iraq **42** B4
Ireland *island* **40** B2
Irish Sea **24** B2
Irrawaddy River **44** D4
Irthing, River **21** G2
Irtysh, River **44** C5
Irvine **21** E3
Isigny-sur-Mer **29** F2
Islamabad **42** C4
Island Magee **20** D2
Isla, River **19** F1
Islay *island* **20** C3
Isle of Anglesey *unitary authority* **24** C3
Isle of Man **12**
Isle of Wight *unitary authority* **29** F3
Isles of Scilly **28** A2
Israel **42** A4
Istanbul **38** D2
Italy **38** C1/C2
Itchen, River **29** F4
Izmir **38** D1

J

Jacksonville **50** E2
Jakarta **42** E2
Jamaica **50** F1
Japan **42** F4/G5
Java *island* **44** E2
Java Sea **44** E2
Jaya Peak **44** F2
Jedburgh **21** G3
Jeddah **42** A4
Jersey *island* **29** E2
Jerusalem **42** A4
Jilin **42** F5
Jinan **42** E4
Jinzhou **42** F5
João Pessoa **52** E3
Johannesburg **46** D2
John o'Groats **19** F3
Johnstone **21** E3
Jordan **42** A4
Juan Fernández Islands **53** B2
Jura *island* **20** D3/D4
Jura, Sound of **20** D3/D4

K

Kabul **42** C4
Kalahari Desert **47** C2/D2
Kalgoorlie **48** B2
Kaliningrad **38** D2
Kamchatka Peninsula **45** G5/H5
Kampala **46** D4
Kananga **46** D3
Kano **46** C4
Kanpur **42** D4
Kansas City **50** E2
Kao-hsiung **42** F4
Karachi **42** C4
Kathmandu **42** D4
Kazakhstan **42** B5/C5
Kazan **42** B5
Keady **20** C2
Keighley **22** D2
Keith **19** G2
Kelso **21** G3
Kendal **21** G2
Kenilworth **25** F2
Kent *county* **27** E2/F2
Kenya **46** D3/D4
Kenya, Mount **47** D3
Kerrera *island* **18** D1
Keswick **21** F2
Kettering **26** D3
Keynsham **29** E4
Kharkov **38** D2
Khartoum **46** D4
Kidderminster **25** E2
Kidsgrove **22** C2
Kidwelly **24** C1
Kielder Water *reservoir* **21** G3
Kiev **38** D2
Kigali **46** D3
Kilbrannan Sound **20** D3
Kilimanjaro, Mount **47** D3
Kilkeel **20** C2
Kilmacrenan **20** B3
Kilmaluag **18** C2
Kilmarnock **21** E3
Kilmory **20** D3
Kinabalu, Mount **44** E3
Kinbrace **19** F3
Kinder Scout *peak* **22** D2
Kingsbridge **28** D3
King's Lynn **27** E3
Kingston **50** F1
Kingston upon Hull **23** E2
Kingston upon Thames **26** D2
Kingswood **29** E4
Kington **24** D2
Kingussie **19** E2
Kinloch **18** C2
Kinross **21** F4
Kinshasa **46** C3
Kintyre *peninsula* **20** D3
Kiribati **48** D3/E3
Kirkbean **21** F2
Kirkby **22** C2
Kirkby Stephen **21** G2
Kirkcaldy **21** F4
Kirkcudbright **21** E2
Kirkintilloch **21** E3
Kirk Michael **21** E2
Kirkpatrick, Mount **54**
Kirkwall **17** C1
Kirriemuir **19** F1
Kita-Kyushu **42** F4
Knaresborough **23** D3
Knighton **24** D2
Kola Peninsula **40/41** D3
Kolkata **42** D4
Kolyma, River **45** G6
Konya **38** D1
Korean Peninsula **44** F4
Kosciusko, Mount **49** C2
Kuala Lumpur **42** E3
Kunlun Shan *mountains* **44** C4/D4
Kuril Islands **45** G5
Kuwait **42** B4
Kuwait City **42** B4
Kyle of Lochalsh **18** D2
Kyrgyzstan **42** C5
Kyushu *island* **44** F4

L

Laâyoune **46** B5
Labrador **51** F3/G3
Ladoga, Lake **40** D3
Lagos **46** C4
Lahore **42** C4
Lairg **19** E3
Lake District *geog. region* **22** B4/C4
Lambert Glacier **54**
Lambourn, River **25** F1
Lammermuir Hills **21** G3
Lampeter **24** C2
Lanark **21** F3
Lancashire *county* **22** C2/C3
Lancaster **22** C3
Land's End *cape* **28** B3
Langholm **21** G3
Lanzhou **42** E4
Laos **42** E3
La Paz **52** C3
Largs **20** E3
Larne **20** D2
Larne *district* **20** D2
Larsen Ice Shelf **54**
Las Vegas **50** D2
Latvia **38** D2
Launceston Australia **48** C1
Launceston UK **28** C3
Laurencekirk **19** G1
Leader Water *river* **21** G3
Lebanon **42** A4
Ledbury **25** E2
Leeds **22** D2
Leicester **25** F2
Leicester City *unitary authority* **25** F2
Leicestershire *county* **25** F2/G2
Leighton Buzzard **26** D2
Leith Hill **26** D2
Leitrim *county* **20** A2/B2
Lena, River **44** F6
Leominster **25** E2
Lerwick **17** D3
Lesotho **46** D2
Lessay **29** F2
Lesser Antilles *islands* **51** F1/G1
Letchworth **26** D2
Le Touquet-Paris-Plage **27** F1
Letterkenny **20** B2
Lewes **26** E1
Lewis *island* **18** C3
Leyburn **21** H2
Leyland **22** C2
Liberia **46** B4
Libreville **46** C4
Libya **46** C5/D5
Lichfield **22** D1
Liddel Water *river* **21** G3
Liechtenstein **38** C2
Lillers **27** G1
Lilongwe **46** D3
Lima **52** C3
Limavady **20** C3
Limavady *district* **20** B2/C3
Lincoln **23** E2
Lincolnshire *county* **23** E1/E2
Lincoln Wolds *hills* **23** E2
Linlithgow **21** F3
Lisbon **38** B1
Lisburn **20** C2
Lisburn *district* **20** C2
Liskeard **28** C3
Lismore *island* **18** D1
Lithuania **38** D2
Littlehampton **29** G3
Little Minch *sound* **18** C2
Little Ouse, River **27** E3
Liverpool **22** C2
Livingston **21** F3
Lizard **28** B2
Lizard Point **28** B2
Ljubljana **38** C2
Llandeilo **24** C1
Llandovery **24** D1
Llandrindod Wells **24** D2
Llandudno **24** D3
Llanelli **24** C1
Llangollen **24** D2
Llanidloes **24** D2
Llanos *geog. region* **53** C4
Lleyn Peninsula **24** C2/C3
Lochaline *town* **18** D1
Loch Arkaig **18** D1
Loch Awe **18/19** D1
Lochdon *town* **18** D1
Loch Doon **21** E3
Loch Earn **19** E1
Loch Eriboll **19** E3
Loch Ericht **19** E1
Loch Etive **18/19** D1
Loch Fyne **20** D4
Lochgilphead *town* **20** D4
Loch Katrine **21** E4
Loch Ken **21** E3
Loch Leven **21** F4
Loch Linnhe **18** D1
Loch Lochy **19** E1
Loch Lomond **21** E4
Loch Long **20/21** E4
Lochmaben *town* **21** F3
Lochmaddy *town* **18** B2
Loch Maree **18** D2
Loch Mullardoch **19** E2
Lochnagar *peak* **19** F1
Loch nan Clar **19** E3
Loch Ness **19** E2
Loch Rannoch **19** E1
Lochranza *town* **20** D3
Loch Shiel **18** D1
Loch Shin **19** E3
Loch Snizort **18** C2
Loch Tay **19** E1
Loch Torridon **18** D2
Lockerbie **21** F3
Łódź **38** C2
Lofoten Islands **40** C3
Logan, Mount **51** B4
Loire, River **40** C2
Lomé **46** C4
London **26** D2
Londonderry **20** B2
Long Eaton **23** D1
Long Mynd *peak* **25** E2
Longreach **48** C2
Looe **28** C3
Lord Howe Island **49** C2
Los Angeles **50** D2
Lossiemouth **19** F2
Lostwithiel **28** C3
Lough Allen **20** A2
Lough Beg **20** C2
Loughborough **23** D1
Lough Derg **20** B2
Lough Foyle *estuary* **20** B3
Lough Macnean Lower **20** B2
Lough Macnean Upper **20** B2
Lough Melvin **20** A2
Lough Neagh **20** C2
Lough Oughter **20** B2
Lough Swilly *estuary* **20** B3
Louth **23** F2
Lower Lough Erne **20** B2
Lowestoft **27** F3
Lowther Hills **21** F3
Loyalty Islands **49** D2
Luanda **46** C3
Luce Bay **22** A3
Ludlow **25** E2
Lundy *island* **28** C4
Lune, River **21** G2
Lurgan **20** C2
Lusaka **46** D3
Luton **26** D2
Luton *unitary authority* **26** D2
Luxembourg **38** C2
Luzon *island* **44** F3
Lybster **19** F3
Lyme Bay **29** E3
Lyme Regis **29** E3
Lymington **29** F3
Lynton **28** D4
Lyons **38** C2
Lys, River **27** G1
Lytham St. Anne's **22** B2

M

Mablethorpe **23** F2
Macapá **52** D4
Macclesfield **22** C2
Macdonnell Ranges *mountains* **49** B2
Macduff **19** G2
Macedonia (Former Yugoslav Republic of) **38** D2
Machynlleth **24** D2
Mackenzie River **51** C4
Madagascar **46** E2/E3
Madagascar *island* **47** E2/E3
Madeira Islands **47** B5
Madeira, River **53** C3
Madrid **38** B2
Magadan **43** G5
Maghera **20** C2
Magherafelt **20** C2
Magherafelt *district* **20** C2
Mahajanga **46** E3
Maidenhead **26** D2
Maidstone **27** E2
Mainland Orkney Islands *island* **17** C1/B2
Mainland Shetland Islands *island* **17** D3
Main, River **20** C2
Majorca **40** C1
Malahide **24** A3
Malawi **46** D3
Malay Peninsula **44** E3
Malaysia **42** E3
Maldive Archipelago *islands* **44** C3
Maldives **42** C3
Mali **46** B4/C4
Malin Head *cape* **20** B3
Mallaig **18** D2
Malmesbury **25** E1
Malta **38** C1
Malton **23** E3
Managua **50** E1
Manaus **52** D3
Manchester **22** C2
Mangotsfield **26** B2
Manila **42** F3
Mansfield **23** D2
Maputo **46** D2
Maracaibo **52** C4
Maracaibo, Lake **53** C4
Mar del Plata **52** D2
Margate **27** F2
Marie Byrd Land **54**
Market Drayton **22** C1
Market Harborough **25** G2
Market Rasen **23** E2
Markham, Mount **54**
Marlborough **26** C2
Marlow **26** D2
Marrakech **46** B5
Marseilles **38** C2
Marshall Islands **48** D4
Marshall Islands **49** D4
Maryport **21** F2
Maseru **46** D2
Mashhad **42** B4
Massif Central *mountains* **40** C2
Matadi **46** C3
Matlock **22** D2
Mato Grosso *geog. region* **53** D3
Mauritania **46** B4/B5
Mauritius **46** E2
Mauritius *island* **47** E2
Maybole **21** E3
Mbabane **46** D2
McKinley, Mount **51** B4
Medan **42** D3
Medellín **52** C4
Mediterranean Sea **40** C1/D1
Medway *unitary authority* **27** E2
Medway, River **27** E2
Meharry, Mount **49** A2
Meig, River **19** E2
Mekong River **44** E3
Melbourne **48** C2
Melton Mowbray **23** E1
Memphis **50** E2
Mendip Hills **29** E4
Mendoza **52** C2
Menzies, Mount **54**
Meon, River **29** F3
Mere **29** E4
Mersey, River **22** C2
Merseyside *county* **22** C2
Merthyr Tydfil **24** D1
Merthyr Tydfil *unitary authority* **24** D1
Merton **26** D2
Meseta *plateau* **40** B1/B2
Mexico **50** D2/E1
México City **50** E1
Mexico, Gulf of **51** E2
Miami **50** E2
Michigan, Lake **51** E3
Mickle Fell *peak* **21** G2
Micronesia, Federated States of **48** C2
Middlesbrough **23** D3
Middlesbrough *unitary authority* **23** D3
Midlothian *unitary authority* **21** F3
Milan **38** C2
Mildenhall **27** E3
Milford Haven **24** B1
Milton Keynes **26** D3
Milton Keynes *unitary authority* **26** D3
Milton Ness *cape* **19** G1
Milwaukee **50** E3
Mindanao *island* **44** F3
Mindoro *island* **44** F3
Minehead **28** D4
Mingulay *island* **18** B1
Minneapolis **50** E3
Minorca **40** C1
Minsk **38** D2
Mississippi River **51** E2
Missouri River **51** D3/E3
Moçambique **46** E3
Moffat **21** F3
Mogadishu **46** E4
Mold **24** D3
Moldova **38** D2
Mombasa **46** D3
Monaco **38** C2
Monadhliath Mountains **19** E2
Monaghan **20** C2
Monaghan *county* **20** B2/C2
Mongolia **42** D5/E5
Monmouth **25** E1
Monmouthshire *unitary authority* **25** E1
Monrovia **46** B4

Mont Blanc *peak* 40 C2
Montenegro 38 C2
Monterrey 50 D2
Montevideo 52 D2
Montgomery 24 D2
Montréal 50 F3
Montrose 19 G1
Moray *unitary authority* 19 F2
Moray Firth *estuary* 19 E2/F2
Morecambe 22 C3
Morecambe Bay 22 C3
Moreton-in-Marsh 25 F1
Morocco 46 B5
Morven *peak* 19 F3
Moscow 38 D2
Motherwell 21 E3
Mount Isa *town* 48 B2
Mount's Bay 28 B3
Mouths of the Ganges 44 D4
Moyle *district* 20 C3
Mozambique 46 D2/D3
Mozambique Channel 47 D2/E3
Muck *island* 18 C1
Muckle Roe *island* 17 D3
Mull *island* 18 C1/D1
Mull Head *cape* 17 C2
Mullion 28 B3
Mull of Galloway *cape* 21 E2
Mull of Kintyre *cape* 20 D3
Mull of Oa *cape* 20 C3
Mull, Sound of 18 D1
Mumbai 42 C3
Munich 38 C2
Murmansk 38 D3
Murray River 49 C2
Muscat 42 B4
Musselburgh 21 F3
Myanmar 42 D3
Mynydd Eppynt *hills* 24 D2
Mynydd Preseli *hills* 24 C1

N

Nagoya 42 F4
Nairn 19 F2
Nairn, River 19 E2
Nairobi 46 D3
Namib Desert 47 C2
Namibia 46 C2/C3
Nanchang 42 E4
Nanjing 42 E4
Nantes 38 B2
Naples 38 C2
Narvik 38 C3
Nassau 50 F2
Nasser, Lake 47 D5
Natal 52 E3
Nauru 48 D3
Nauru *island* 49 D3
Ndjamena 46 C4
Neath 24 D1
Neath Port Talbot *unitary authority* 24 D1
Nelson New Zealand 48 D1
Nelson UK 22 C2
Nelson River 51 E3
Nene, River 27 E3
Nepal 42 D4
Netherlands 38 C2
Netherlands Antilles *islands* 52 C4
Newark-on-Trent 23 E2
Newburgh 19 F1
Newbury 26 C2
New Caledonia *island* 49 D2
Newcastle Australia 48 C2
Newcastle UK 20 D2
Newcastle Emlyn 24 C2
Newcastle-under-Lyme 22 C2
Newcastle upon Tyne 21 H2
New Cumnock 21 E3
New Delhi 42 C4
Newfoundland *island* 51 G3
New Galloway 21 E3
New Guinea *island* 44 F2/G2
Newmarket 27 E3
New Orleans 50 E2
New Plymouth 48 D2
Newport Isle of Wight 29 F3
Newport Shropshire 22 C1
Newport Wales 24 D1
Newport *unitary authority* 24 D1/E1
Newquay 28 B3
New Quay 24 C2
Newry 20 C2
Newry and Mourne *district* 20 C2
New Siberian Islands 55
Newton Abbot 28 D3
Newton Aycliffe 21 H2
Newtonmore 19 E2
Newton Stewart 21 E2
Newtown 24 D2
Newtownabbey 20 D2
Newtownabbey *district* 20 C2/D2
Newtownards 20 D2
Newtownhamilton 20 C2
Newtownstewart 20 B2
New York 50 F3
New Zealand 48 D1/D2
Niagara Falls 51 F3
Niamey 46 C4
Nicaragua 50 E1
Nicobar Islands 44 D3
Nicosia 38 D1
Nidd, River 22 D3
Nieuwpoort 27 G2
Niger 46 C4/C5
Niger Delta 47 C4
Nigeria 46 C4
Niger, River 47 C4
Nile Delta 47 D5
Nile, River 47 D5
Nith, River 21 F3
Nizhniy Novgorod 39 E2
Norfolk 50 F2
Norfolk *county* 27 E3/F3
Norfolk Broads 27 F3
Norfolk Island 49 D2
Northallerton 23 D3
Northampton 26 D3
Northamptonshire *county* 26 C3/D3
North Ayrshire *unitary authority* 20/21 D3/E3
North Channel 20 D2/D3
North Down *district* 20 D2
North Downs *hills* 27 E2/F2
North Dvina River 41 E3
North East Lincolnshire *unitary authority* 23 E2
Northern Ireland 12
Northern Esk, River 19 G1
North European Plain 40 C2/D2
North Foreland *cape* 27 F2
North Island 49 D2
North Korea 42 F4/F5
North Lanarkshire *unitary authority* 21 F3
North Lincolnshire *unitary authority* 23 E2
North Pole 55
North Ronaldsay *island* 17 C2
North Saskatchewan River 51 D3
North Sea 40 C2
North Shields 23 D4
North Somerset *unitary authority* 26 B2
North Uist *island* 18 B2
Northumberland *county* 21 G3/H3
Northwest Highlands 18/19 D2/E3
Northwich 22 C2
North York Moors 23 E3
North Yorkshire *county* 22/23 C3/E3
Norton 23 E3
Norway 38 C2/D3
Norwich 27 F3
Nottingham 23 D1
Nottingham City *unitary authority* 23 D1
Nottinghamshire *county* 23 D1/E2
Nouakchott 46 B4
Noumea 48 D2
Nova Iguaçu 52 D2
Novaya Zemlya *islands* 55
Novosibirsk 42 D5
Nullarbor Plain 49 B2
Nuneaton 25 F2
Nuuk 55
Nyasa, Lake (Lake Malawi) 47 D3

O

Oban 18 D1
Ob, River 44 C6
Ochil Hills 21 F4
Odessa 38 D2
Oiapoque 52 D4
Ojos del Salado *peak* 53 C2
Okavango Swamp 47 D2/D3
Okehampton 28 C3
Oldham 22 C2
Oldmeldrum 19 G2
Olympus, Mount 40 D2
Omagh 20 B2
Omagh *district* 20 B2
Oman 42 B3/B4
Omsk 42 C5
Onega, Lake 40 D3
Ontario, Lake 51 F3
Oostende 27 G2
Oporto 38 B2
Orange, River 47 C2/D2
Orford Ness *cape* 27 F3
Orinoco, River 53 C4
Orkney Islands *unitary authority* 17 B1/C2
Orne, River 29 G2
Oronsay *island* 20 C4
Osaka 42 F4
Oslo 38 C2
Oswestry 22 B1
Ottawa 50 F3
Ouagadougou 46 B4
Oundle 26 D3
Ouse, River 23 E2
Outer Hebrides *islands* 18 B1/C3
Out Skerries *islands* 17 E3
Oxford 25 F1
Oxfordshire *county* 25 F1

P

Pabbay *island* 18 B2
Pacific Ocean 56/57
Padstow 28 C3
Paisley 21 E3
Pakistan 42 C4
Palembang 42 E2
Palermo 38 C1
Pampa *geog. region* 53 C2/D2
Panama 50 E1/F1
Panamá 50 F1
Papa Stour *island* 17 D3
Papa Westray *island* 17 C2
Papua New Guinea 48 C3
Paraguay 52 C2/D2
Paraguay River 53 D2/D3
Paramaribo 52 D4
Paraná, River 53 C2/D2
Paris 38 C2
Parrett, River 29 E4
Patagonia *geog. region* 53 C1
Peace River 51 C3/D3
Peebles 21 F3
Peel 21 E2
Peel Fell *peak* 21 G3
Peipus, Lake 40 D2
Peloponnese *island* 40 D1
Pembrokshire *unitary authority* 24 B1/C1
Penicuik 21 F3
Pennines *hills* 21 G2
Penrith 21 G2
Penryn 28 B3
Pentland Firth *sound* 17 B1
Pentland Hills 21 F3
Pen-y-Ghent *summit* 21 G2
Penzance 28 B3
Perm 39 E2
Perth Australia 48 A2
Perth UK 19 F1
Perth and Kinross *unitary authority* 19 E1/F1
Peru 52 C3
Peterborough 26 D3
Peterborough *unitary authority* 26 D3
Peterhead 19 H2
Peterlee 23 D3
Petersfield 26 D2
Philadelphia 50 F3
Philippines 42 E3/F3
Phnom Penh 42 E3
Phoenix 50 D2
Phoenix Islands 49 E3
Pickering 23 E3
Pickering, Vale of 23 E3
Pitlochry 19 F1
Pittsburgh 50 E3
Plymouth 28 C3
Plymouth *unitary authority* 28 C3
Plynlimon *peak* 24 D2
Podgorica 38 C2
Pointe-Noire *town* 46 C3
Point of Fethaland 17 D3
Poland 38 C2/D2
Pontardulais 24 C1
Pontefract 23 D2
Pontypool 24 D1
Pontypridd 24 D1
Poole 29 F3
Poole *unitary authority* 29 F3
Poolewe 18 D2
Popocatepetl *volcano* 51 E1
Po, River 40 C2
Portadown 20 C2
Port Askaig 20 C3
Port Augusta 48 B2
Port-au-Prince 50 F1
Port Elizabeth 46 D2
Port Ellen 20 C3
Port Glasgow 21 E3
Port Harcourt 46 C4
Porthmadog 24 C2
Portknockie 19 G2
Portland 50 C3
Portland Bill *cape* 29 E3
Port Moresby 48 C3
Portnahaven 20 C3
Pôrto Alegre 52 D2
Port of Ness 18 C3
Porto Novo 46 C4
Pôrto Velho 52 C3
Portpatrick 20 D2
Portree 18 C2
Portrush 20 C3
Portsmouth 29 F3
Portsmouth *unitary authority* 29 F3
Portsoy 19 G2
Portstewart 20 C3
Port Sudan 46 D4
Port Talbot 24 D1
Portugal 38 B1/B2
Powys *unitary authority* 24 D1/D2
Poznań 38 C2
Prague 38 C2
Preston 22 C2
Prestwick 21 E3
Pretoria 46 D2
Prince Rupert 50 C3
Príncipe *island* 47 C4
Pripet Marshes 40 D2
Pucallpa 52 C3
Puebla 50 E1
Puerto Montt 52 C1
Puerto Rico 50 F1
Punta Arenas 52 C1
Pusan 42 F4
Pwllheli 24 C2
Pyongyang 42 F4
Pyrenees *mountains* 40 B2/C2

Q

Qatar 42 B4
Qattara Depression 47 D5
Qingdao 42 F4
Quantock Hills 29 D4
Québec 50 F3
Queen Maud Land 54
Quezon City 42 F3
Quito 52 C3

R

Raasay *island* 18 C2
Rabat 46 B5
Ramsey 21 E2
Ramsgate 27 F2
Randalstown 20 C2
Rathlin Island 20 C3
Rathlin Sound 20 C3
Rattray 19 F1
Reading 26 D2
Reading *unitary authority* 26 C2/D2
Recife 52 E3
Red Basin 44 E4
Redbridge 27 E2
Redcar 23 D3
Redcar and Cleveland *unitary authority* 23 D3/E3
Redditch 25 F2
Rede, River 21 G3
Redhill *town* 26 D2
Redruth 28 B3
Red Sea 47 D5/E4
Regina 50 D3
Reigate 26 D2
Renfrewshire *unitary authority* 21 E3
Republic of Ireland 38 B2
Republic of South Africa 46 C2/D2
Réunion *island* 47 E2
Reykjavík 38 A3
Rhayader 24 D2
Rhine, River 40 C2
Rhondda 24 D1
Rhondda Cynon Taff *unitary authority* 24 D1
Rhône, River 40 C2
Rhum *island* 18 C1/C2
Rhyl 24 D3
Ribble, River 22 C2
Richmond 21 H2
Richmond upon Thames 26 D2
Riga 38 D2
Ringwood 29 F3
Rio de Janeiro *town* 52 D2
Río Grande *river* 51 D2
Ripon 21 H2
River Plate *estuary* 53 D2
Riyadh 42 B4
Rochdale 22 C2
Rochester 27 E2
Rockhampton 48 C2
Rocky Mountains 51 C4/D2
Romania 38 D2
Rome 38 C2
Romsey 29 F3
Ronne Ice Shelf 54
Rora Head 17 B1
Rosario 52 C2
Rosehearty 19 G2
Ross Ice Shelf 54
Ross of Mull *peninsula* 20 C4/D4
Ross-on-Wye 25 E1
Ross Sea 54
Rostov-on-Don 39 D2
Rotherham 23 D2
Rothes 19 F2
Rothesay 20 D3
Rotterdam 38 C2
Rousay *island* 17 B2
Royal Leamington Spa 25 F2
Royal Tunbridge Wells 27 E2
Royston 26 D3
Rubha Hunish *cape* 18 C2
Rugby 25 F2
Rugeley 22 D1
Runcorn 22 C2
Russian Federation (Russia) 42/43 A5/J6
Rutland *unitary authority* 23 E1
Rutland Water *reservoir* 23 E1
Rwanda 46 D3
Rybinsk Reservoir 40/41 D2
Ryde 29 F3
Rye 27 E1
Ryukyu Islands 44 F4

S

Sacramento 50 C2
Saffron Walden 27 E3
Sahara Desert 47 B5/D5
St. Abb's Head *cape* 21 G3
St. Agnes 28 B3
St. Albans 26 D2
St. Albans Head *cape* 29 E3
St. Andrews 19 G1
St. Austell 28 C3
St. Bees Head 21 F2
St. Bride's Bay 24 B1
St. Catherine's Point *cape* 29 F3
St. David's 24 B1
St. David's Head 24 B1
St. George's Channel 24 B1/B2
St. Helens 22 C2
St. Helier 29 E2
St. Ives Cambridgeshire 26 D3
St. Ives Cornwall 28 B3
St. John's 50 G3
St. John's Point 20 D2
St. John's Town of Dalry 21 E3
St. Just 28 B3
St. Kitts and Nevis 50 F1
St. Lawrence River 51 F3
St.-Lô 29 F2
St. Louis 50 E2
St. Lucia 50 F1
St. Magnus Bay 17 D3
St. Mary's *island* 28 A2
St. Mary's Loch 21 F3
St. Neots 26 D3
St.-Omer 27 G1
St. Peter Port 29 E2
St. Petersburg 38 D2
Saint-Pierre and Miquelon *islands* 50 G3
St. Vincent and the Grenadines 50 F1
Salcombe 28 D3
Sale 22 C2
Salford 22 C2
Salisbury 29 F4
Salisbury Plain 29 F4
Salta 52 C2
Saltash 28 C3
Saltcoats 21 E3
Salt Lake City 50 D3
Salvador 52 E3
Salween River 44 D3/D4
Samara 42 B5
Samoa 48 E3
Samoa Islands 49 E3
San'a 42 B3
San Antonio 50 E2
Sanday *island* 17 C2
San Diego 50 D2
Sandown 29 F3
San Francisco 50 C2
San José 50 E1
San Juan 50 F1
San Marino 38 C2
Sanquhar 21 F3
San Salvador 50 E1
Santa Cruz 52 C3
Santa Cruz Islands 49 D3
Santa Marta 52 C4
Santarém 52 D3
Santiago 52 C2
Santo Domingo 50 F1
São Francisco *river* 53 D3
São Luís 52 D3
São Paulo 52 D2
São Tomé *island* 47 C4
São Tomé and Príncipe 46 C3/C4
Sapporo 42 G5
Sarajevo 38 C2
Sardinia 40 C1/C2
Sark *island* 29 E2
Saudi Arabia 42 B3/B4
Sawel *peak* 20 B2
Scalasaig 20 C4
Scalloway 17 D3
Scalpay *island* 18 C2/D2
Scandinavian Highlands 40 C3/D3
Scapa 17 C1
Scapa Flow *sound* 17 B1
Scarba *island* 20 D4
Scarborough 23 E3
Scarp *island* 18 B3
Scotland 12
Scottish Borders *unitary authority* 21 F3/G3
Scunthorpe 23 E2
Sea of Azov 40/41 D2
Sea of Japan 44 F4/F5
Sea of Okhotsk 44/45 G5
Seascale 21 F2
Seaton 29 D3
Seattle 50 C3
Seine, River 40 C2
Selby 23 D2
Selkirk 21 G3
Selsey Bill *cape* 29 G3
Selvas *geog. region* 53 C3
Semarang 42 E2
Senegal 46 B4
Senegal River 47 B4

Sennen **28** B3
Seoul **42** F4
Serbia **38** C2/D2
Sevenoaks **27** E2
Severnaya Zemlya *islands* **55**
Severn, River **25** E1
Seville **38** B1
Seychelles **46** E3
Seychelles *islands* **47** E3
Sgurr Mór *peak* **19** D2
Shaftesbury **29** E4
Shanghai **42** F4
Shanklin **29** F3
Shannon, River **20** B2
Shapinsay *island* **17** C2
Sheerness **27** E2
Sheffield **23** D2
Shenyang **42** F5
Shepton Mallet **29** E4
Sherborne **29** E3
Sheringham **27** F3
Shetland Islands *unitary authority* **17** D3
Shiant Islands **18** C2
Shiel, River **18** D2
Shikoku *island* **44** F4
Shrewsbury **22** C1
Shropshire *county* **24/25** D2/E2
Siberian Lowland **44** C6/D6
Sicily **40** C1
Sidlaw Hills **19** F1/G1
Sidmouth **29** D3
Sierra Leone **46** B4
Sierra Madre *mountains* **51** D2
Sierra Nevada *mountains* **51** C2/C3
Simpson Desert **49** C2
Singapore **42** E3
Skegness **23** F2
Skelmersdale **22** C2
Skiddaw *mountain* **21** F2
Skopje **38** D2
Skye *island* **18** C2/D2
Slave River **51** D3/D4
Sleaford **23** E1
Sleat, Sound of **18** D2
Slieve Donard *peak* **20** D2
Slieve Snaght *peak* **20** B3
Slough **26** D2
Slough *unitary authority* **26** D2
Slovakia **38** C2/D2
Slovenia **38** C2
Snaefell *peak* **21** E2
Snake River **51** D3
Snowdon *peak* **24** C3
Soar, River **26** C3
Soay *island* **18** C2
Socotra *island* **44** B3
Sofia **38** D2
Solihull **25** F2
Solomon Islands **48** C3/D3
Solomon Islands **49** C3/D3
Solway Firth **21** F2
Somalia **46** E4
Somerset *county* **28/29** D4/E4
Southampton **29** F3
Southampton *unitary authority* **29** F3
South Ayrshire *unitary authority* **20/21** D2/E3
South Barrule *peak* **21** E2
South Benfleet **27** E2
South China Sea **44** E3
South Downs *hills* **26** D1
Southend **20** D3
Southend *unitary authority* **27** E2
Southend-on-Sea **27** E2
Southern Ocean **56/57**
Southern Uplands *mountains* **21** E3/G3
South Esk, River **19** G1
South Georgia *island* **53** E1
South Gloucestershire *unitary authority* **26** B2
South Island **49** D1
South Korea **42** F4
South Lanarkshire *unitary authority* **21** E3/F3
South Molton **28** D4
South Orkney Islands **54**
South Pole **54**
Southport **22** B2
South Ronaldsay *island* **17** C1
South Saskatchewan River **51** D3
South Shetland Islands **54**
South Shields **23** D3
South Uist *island* **18** B2
Southwold **27** F3
South Yorkshire *county* **22/23** D2
Spain **38** B1/C2
Spennymoor *town* **21** H2
Spey, River **19** F2
Spilsby **23** F2
Spurn Head *cape* **23** F2
Sri Lanka **42** D3
Stafford **22** C1
Staffordshire *county* **22** C1/D1
Staines **26** D2
Stamford **26** D3
Stanley **52** D1
Stanley, Mount **47** D4
Start Bay **28** D3
Start Point *cape* **28** D3
Stavanger **38** C2
Stevenage **26** D2
Stewart Island **49** D1
Stinchar, River **21** E3
Stirling **21** F4
Stirling *unitary authority* **21** E4/F4
Stockbridge **29** F4
Stockholm **38** C2
Stockport **22** C2
Stockton-on-Tees **23** D3
Stockton-on-Tees *unitary authority* **23** D3
Stoke-on-Trent **22** C1
Stoke-on-Trent *unitary authority* **22** C1/C2
Stonehaven **19** G1
Stornoway **18** C3
Stourbridge **25** E2
Stourport-on-Severn **25** E2
Stour, River Dorset **29** E3
Stour, River Suffolk **27** E2
Stowmarket **27** E3
Stow-on-the-Wold **25** F1
Strabane **20** B2
Strabane *district* **20** B2
Strangford Lough **20** D2
Stranraer **20** D2
Stratford-upon-Avon **25** F2
Strathy Point **19** E3
Stromness **17** B1
Stronsay *island* **17** C2
Stronsay Firth *sound* **17** C2
Stroud **25** E1
Strumble Head **24** B2
Sturt Desert **49** C2
Sucre **52** C3
Sudan **46** D4
Sudbury Canada **50** E3
Sudbury UK **27** E3
Suez **46** D5
Suffolk *county* **27** E3/F3
Sulawesi *island* **44** E2/F2
Sumatra *island* **44** D3/E2
Sumburgh Head *cape* **17** D2
Sunderland **23** D3
Superior, Lake **51** E3
Surabaya **42** E2
Suriname **52** D4
Surrey *county* **26** D2
Sutton **26** D2
Sutton ColdÜeld **25** F2
Sutton in AshÜeld **23** D2
Suva **48** D3
Swaffham **27** E3
Swale *river* **21** H2
Swanage **29** F3
Swansea **24** D1
Swansea *unitary authority* **24** D1
Swaziland **46** D2
Sweden **38** C2/D3
Swilly, River **20** B2
Swindon **25** F1
Swindon *unitary authority* **25** F1
Switzerland **38** C2
Sydney Australia **48** C2
Sydney Canada **50** F3
Symbister **17** D3
Syria **42** A4

T

Tabriz **42** B4
Tadcaster **23** D2
Tagus, River **40** B1
Tain **19** E2
Taipei **42** F4
Taiwan **42** F4
Taiyuan **42** E4
Tajikistan **42** C4
Tallinn **38** D2
Tamar, River **28** C3
Tampa **50** E2
Tamworth **25** E2
Tanganyika, Lake **47** D3
Tanzania **46** D3
Taransay *island* **18** B2
Tarbat Ness *cape* **19** F2
Tarbert Strathclyde **20** D3
Tarbert Western Isles **18** C2
Tarbet **21** E4
Tashkent **42** C5
Tasmania *island* **49** C1
Tasman Sea **49** C2/D2
Taunton **29** D4
Taupo, Lake **49** D2
Taurus Mountains **40/41** D1
Tavistock **28** C3
Tavy, River **28** C3
Taw, River **28** D3
Tay, River **19** F1
Tbilişi **39** E2
Tees, River **21** G2
Tegucigalpa **50** E1
Tehran **42** B4
Teifi, River **24** C2
Teignmouth **28** D3
Teign, River **28** D3
Telford **22** C1
Telford and Wrekin *unitary authority* **22** C1
Teme, River **25** E2
Tenby **24** C1
Tennant Creek *town* **48** B3
Teresina **52** D3
Test, River **29** F4
Tétouan **46** B5
Teviot, River **21** G3
Tewkesbury **25** E1
Thailand **42** D3/E3
Thailand, Gulf of **44** E3
Thame, River **26** D2
Thames, River **27** E2
Thar Desert **44** C4
The Deeps *bay* **17** D3
The Fens *geog. region* **23** E1/F1
The Minch *sound* **18** D3
The Needles *rocks* **29** F3
The Solent *sound* **29** F3
The Storr *peak* **18** C2
Thessaloníki **38** D2
Thetford **27** E3
The Vale of Glamorgan *unitary authority* **24** D1
The Wash *bay* **27** E3
The Weald *geog. region* **27** E2
The Wrekin *peak* **22** C1
Thimphu **42** D4
Thirsk **23** D3
Thornaby-on-Tees **23** D3
Thornhill **21** F3
Thurrock *unitary authority* **27** E2
Thurso **19** F3
Thurso, River **19** F3
Tianjin **42** E4
Tibetan Plateau **44** D4
Tierra del Fuego *island* **53** C1
Tignabruaich **20** D3
Tigris, River **44** B4
Timor Sea **44** F2
Tiranë **38** C2
Tiree *island* **18** C1
Titicaca, Lake **53** C3
Tiverton **28** D3
Toamasina **46** E3
Tobermory **18** C1
Tocantins, River **53** D3
Togo **46** C4
Tokyo **42** F4
Toliara **46** E2
Tonbridge **27** E2
Tonga **48** E2
Tonga Islands **49** E2
Torbay **28** D3
Torbay *unitary authority* **28** D3
Torfaen *unitary authority* **24** D1
Toronto **50** F3
Torpoint *town* **28** C3
Torridge, River **28** C3
Tory Island **20** A3
Tory Sound **20** A3
Totnes **28** D3
Towcester **26** D3
Townsville **48** C3
Trent, River **23** E2
Tresco *island* **28** A2
Trevose Head *cape* **28** B3
Trinidad and Tobago **50** F1
Tripoli **46** C5
Trondheim **38** C3
Troon **21** E3
Trowbridge **29** E4
Truro **28** B3
Tucson **50** D2
Tunis **46** C5
Tunisia **46** C5
Turin **38** C2
Turkana, Lake **47** D4
Turkey **38/39** D1/E2
Turkmenistan **42** B4
Turriff **19** G2
Tuvalu **48** D3
Tweed, River **21** F3
Tyndrum **19** E1
Tyne and Wear *county* **22/23** D3/D4
Tynemouth **23** D4
Tyne, River **22** D3
Tyrrhenian Sea **40** C1/C2
Tywi, River **24** C1

U

Uberaba **52** D3
Ufa **42** B5
Uganda **46** D3/D4
Ukraine **38** D2
Ulan Bator **42** E5
Ullapool **18** D2
Ullswater *lake* **21** G2
Ulva *island* **18** C1
United Arab Emirates (UAE) **42** B4
United Kingdom (UK) **38** B2/C2
United States of America (USA) **50** C2/F3
Unst *island* **17** E3
Upper Lough Erne *lake* **20** B2
Ural Mountains **44** B5/C6
Ural, River **41** E2
Ure, River **21** H2
Uruguay **52** D2
Usk, River **24** D1
Uttoxeter **22** D1
Uzbekistan **42** B5/C4

V

Vaal, River **47** D2
Valdés Peninsula **53** C1
Valencia Spain **38** B1
Valencia Venezuela **52** C4
Valognes **29** F2
Valparaíso **52** C2
Vancouver **50** C3
Vancouver Island **51** C3
Vänern, Lake **40** C2
Van, Lake **41** E1
Vanuatu **48** D3
Venezuela **52** C4
Veurne **27** G2
Victoria Falls **47** D3
Victoria Island **51** D4
Victoria, Lake **47** D3
Vienna **38** C2
Vientiane **42** E3
Vietnam **42** E3
Vila **48** D3
Vilnius **38** D2
Vinson Massif *peak* **54**
Vire, River **29** F2
Vistula, River **40** C2/D2
Vitória **52** D2
Volga, River **41** E2
Volgograd **39** E2
Volta, Lake **47** B4/C4
Vyrnwy, Lake **24** D2
Vyrnwy, River **24** D2

W

Wadebridge **28** C3
Wakefield **23** D2
Walbury Hill **29** F4
Wales **12**
Wallasey **22** B2
Walls **17** D3
Walsall **25** E2
Waltham Forest **26** D2
Walton-on-the-Naze **27** F2
Walvis Bay *town* **46** C2
Wansbeck, River **21** H3
Wantage **25** F1
Ward Hill **17** B1
Ward's Stone *peak* **22** C3
Wareham **29** E3
Warley **25** F2
Warminster **29** E4
Warrenpoint *town* **20** C2
Warrington **22** C2
Warrington *unitary authority* **22** C2
Warsaw **38** D2
Warwick **25** F2
Warwickshire *county* **25** F2
Washington **21** H2
Washington D.C. **50** F2
Waterlooville **29** F3
Water of Luce *river* **20** E2/E3
Watford **26** D2
Waveney, River **27** F3
Wear, River **21** G2
Weddell Sea **54**
Welland, River **26** D3
Wellingborough **26** D3
Wellington New Zealand **48** D1
Wellington UK **29** D3
Wells **29** E4
Wells-next-the-Sea **27** E3
Welshpool **24** D2
Welwyn Garden City **26** D2
Wenlock Edge *hills* **25** E2
Wenzhou **42** F4
West Berkshire *unitary authority* **26** C2
West Bromwich **25** F2
Westbury **29** E4
West Dunbartonshire *unitary authority* **21** E3/E4
Western Ghats *mountains* **44** C3
Western Isles *unitary authority* **18** B1/C3
Western Sahara **46** B5
West Indies *islands* **51** F1/F2
West Lothian *unitary authority* **21** F3
West Midlands *county* **25** E2/F2
Weston-super-Mare **29** E4
Westray *island* **17** B2/C2
Westray Firth *sound* **17** B2/C2
West Sussex *county* **26** D1/D2
West Yorkshire *county* **22/23** D2
Wetherby **23** D2
Weymouth **29** E3
Whalsay *island* **17** D3/E3
Wharfe, River **22** C3
Whernside *peak* **21** G2
Whitby **23** E3
Whitchurch **22** C1
Whiteadder Water *river* **21** G3
Whitehaven **21** F2
White Sea **40** D3
Whithorn **21** E2
Whitley Bay *town* **21** H3
Whitney, Mount **51** D2
Wick **19** F3
Wicklow **24** A2
Widnes **22** C2
Wigan **22** C2
Wigston **25** F2
Wigton **21** F2
Wigtown **21** E2
Wigtown Bay **21** E1
Wilhelm, Mount **49** C3
Wilkes Land **54**
Wiltshire *county* **26** B2/C2
Wimborne Minster **29** F3
Wincanton **29** E4
Winchester **29** F4
Windermere **21** G2
Windermere *lake* **21** G2
Windhoek **46** C2
Windsor **26** D2
Windsor and Maidenhead *unitary authority* **26** D2
Winnipeg **50** E3
Winnipeg, Lake **51** E3
Winsford **22** C2
Wisbech **27** E3
Wishaw **21** F3
Witham **27** E2
Witham, River **23** E2
Witney **25** F1
Woking **26** D2
Wokingham **26** D2
Wokingham *unitary authority* **26** D2
Wolverhampton **25** E2
Woodbridge **27** F3
Wooler **21** G3
Worcester **25** E2
Worcestershire *county* **25** E2
Workington **21** F2
Worksop **23** D2
Worms Head *cape* **24** C1
Worthing **29** G3
Wrath, Cape **19** D3
Wrexham **22** C2
Wrexham *unitary authority* **24/25** D3/E3
Wuhan **42** E4
Wye, River **24** D2
Wymondham **27** F3
Wyndham **48** B3
Wyre, River **22** C2

X

Xi'an **42** E4

Y

Yakutsk **42** F6
Yamoussoukro **46** B4
Yangon **42** D3
Yangtze River **44** E4
Yaoundé **46** C4
Yap Islands **49** B4
Yarrow Water *river* **21** F3
Yekaterinburg **42** C5
Yell *island* **17** D3
Yellowknife **50** D4
Yellow Sea **44** F4
Yell Sound **17** D3
Yemen Republic **42** B3
Yenisey River **44** D6
Yeo, River **29** E4
Yeovil **29** E3
Yerevan **42** B5
Yes Tor *peak* **28** C3
Yingkou **42** F5
Yokohama **42** F4
York **23** D2
York *unitary authority* **23** D2
Yorkshire Wolds *hills* **23** E3
York, Vale of **23** D3
Ypres **27** G1
Yucatan Peninsula **51** E1/E2
Yukon River **51** B4

Z

Zagreb **38** C2
Zagros Mountains **44** B4
Zambezi River **47** D3
Zambia **46** D3
Zibo **42** E4
Zimbabwe **46** D2/D3